ENGAGEMENT
AUSTRALIA FACES THE ASIA-PACIFIC
PAUL KEATING

MACMILLAN
Pan Macmillan Australia

Hokkaido

JAPAN

NORTH KOREA
◦ P'YŎNGYANG
◦ TOKYO

◦ BEIJING
◦ SEOUL
SOUTH KOREA
Kōbe ◦ ◦ Osaka

CHINA

Nanjing ◦
◦ Shanghai

East China Sea

PACIFIC

Chang Jiang R. (Yangtse)

◦ TAIPEI
TAIWAN

◦ Hong Kong
MACAO

BURMA
HANOI ◦
LAOS
VIETNAM

South China Sea

◦ MANILA

Philippine Sea

RANGOON ◦
THAILAND

Mekong R.

PHILIPPINES

MICRONESIA

BANGKOK ◦
CAMBODIA
PHNOM ◦
PENH
◦ Ho Chi Minh
(Saigon)

PALAU

◦ BRUNEI

MALAYSIA
◦ KUALA LUMPUR
SINGAPORE
◦ SINGAPORE

Borneo

Strait of Malacca

Sumatra

INDONESIA

Celebes

◦ Ambon

Irian Jaya

PAPUA NEW GUINEA
◦ Popondetta
◦ PORT MORESBY

◦ Makassar
(Ujungpandang)

Torres Strait

◦ Bogor ◦ JAKARTA ◦ Surabaya
Java ◦ Bali
◦ Dili
Timor

Java Sea

Timor Sea

◦ Darwin

Coral S

INDIAN OCEAN

NORTHERN TERITORY

QUEENSLAND

◦ Brisb

AUSTRALIA

WESTERN AUSTRALIA

SOUTH AUSTRALIA

NEW SOUTH WALES

◦ CANBERRA

◦ Adelaide
VICTOR

◦ Perth

AUSTRALIA AND
THE ASIA-PACIFIC

UNITED STATES
OF AMERICA

Seattle
San Francisco

CEAN

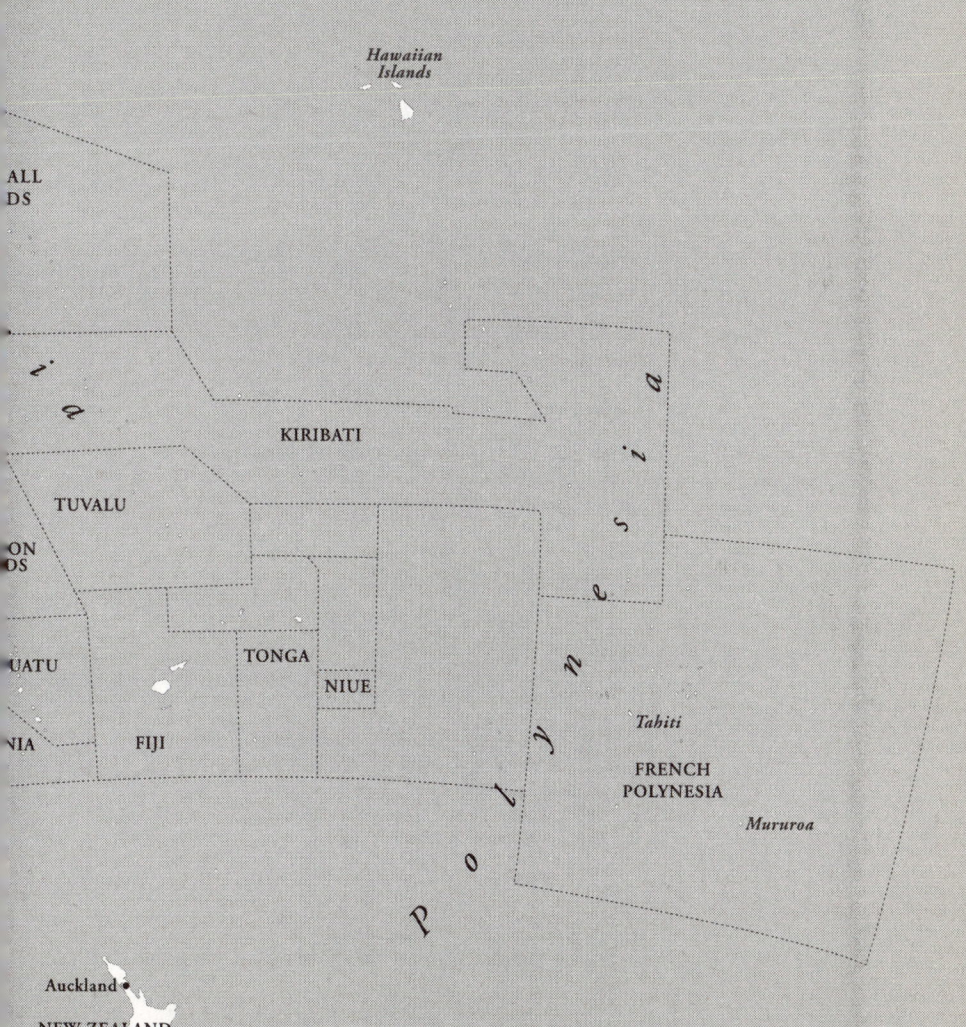

Hawaiian
Islands

ALL
DS

KIRIBATI

TUVALU

ON
DS

*UATU

TONGA
NIUE

Tahiti

FIJI

FRENCH
POLYNESIA

Mururoa

Polynesia

Auckland
NEW ZEALAND
WELLINGTON

Sea

First published 2000 in Macmillan by Pan Macmillan Australia Pty Limited
St Martins Tower, 31 Market Street, Sydney

Copyright © Paul Keating 2000

All rights reserved. No part of this book may be reproduced or transmitted in any form or by any means, electronic or mechanical, including photocopying, recording or by any information storage and retrieval system, without prior permission in writing from the publisher.

National Library of Australia
Cataloguing-in-Publication data:

Keating, Paul, 1944– .
Engagement : Australia faces the Asia-Pacific.

ISBN 0 7329 1019 6.

1. Asia Pacific Economic Cooperation (Organization).
2. Nationalism – Australia. 3. Australia – Relations – Asia.
4. Australia – Relations – Oceania. 5. Australia – Social conditions – 20th century. 6. Asia – Relations – Australia.
7. Oceania – Relations – Australia. I. Title.

327.94

Typeset in Janson Text by Midland Typesetters
Printed in Australia by McPherson's Printing Group

CONTENTS

ACKNOWLEDGEMENTS		vii
PREFACE		ix
CHAPTER 1	1991	1
CHAPTER 2	The Biggest Dog on the Block	24
CHAPTER 3	The Northern Tribes	46
CHAPTER 4	Building an Asia-Pacific Community	76
CHAPTER 5	Bogor and Beyond	98
CHAPTER 6	Our Largest, Nearest Neighbour	123
CHAPTER 7	The Arc Around Us	159
CHAPTER 8	The Other Pacific	195
CHAPTER 9	Nuclear Clouds	221
CHAPTER 10	Our Place in the World	241
CHAPTER 11	Into the New Millennium	275
INDEX		301

ACKNOWLEDGEMENTS

Although I play a large part in the narrative that follows, the external policies developed by the Government I led, and the actions we took, involved the ideas and the work of many people. I was lucky – and Australia was lucky – to have had during the period of my prime ministership the support of one of the strongest-ever ministerial teams working on our external policies. Gareth Evans's intelligence, creativity and political courage made him, I believe, this country's finest foreign minister. And he was matched by the strengths of John Kerin, Peter Cook, and Bob McMullan working on the Uruguay Round, APEC, and bilateral trade; by Robert Ray, building on Kim Beazley's inheritance in Defence to cement a fundamental repositioning of our defence policies; and by Gordon Bilney, who helped push through major reforms in the Pacific and in aid policy. This book is as much their story as mine.

They, like me, were greatly assisted by hard-working personal staff and by the much-undervalued Australian public service, a group of men and women as creative and efficient as any of their counterparts in the world.

The Government and I received outstanding support from Australian officials. They cannot all be named; indeed, there are many I did not know. But I am grateful to them all. In particular, I want to thank Michael Costello, the Secretary of the Department of Foreign Affairs and Trade during this period, and his senior officers, the staff of our overseas missions, who work frequently in conditions of great difficulty and pressure, and the staff of AusAID. On so many fronts Dr Michael Keating and the officers of the Department of the Prime Minister and Cabinet gave me outstanding support, and none more than the hard-working team in International Division, headed through much of this period by Michael Thawley. I am grateful, too, to senior members of the Australian Defence Force such as General Peter Gration, Admiral Alan Beaumont and, later, General John Baker, and the officers of the Defence Department, including Tony Ayers and Hugh White.

Of my own staff, Don Russell, Don Watson, John Bowan, John Edwards, Ric Simes and Geoff Walsh made important contributions to this aspect of the Labor Government's work as, naturally, did my principal international advisers, Ashton Calvert and Allan Gyngell.

Since leaving Parliament I have had an enjoyable association with the University of New South Wales as Visiting Professor in Public Policy, and some of these chapters draw on from lectures I have given there. I am grateful to Vice-Chancellor Professor John Niland, a great Australian educationalist, and his colleagues, including the Asia Australia Institute, for their hospitality.

I am grateful for the support of Pan Macmillan during the book's preparation, and especially for the editorial help of Amanda Hemmings and Julie Nekich.

This book could not have been written without Allan Gyngell's assistance. As the First Assistant Secretary in the Department of the Prime Minister and Cabinet's International Division in 1991, and after 1993 as foreign policy adviser in my office, he was directly involved in most of the issues discussed in these chapters. Since 1996 he has continued to work with me in Keating Associates and has had an important role in shaping this book.

PREFACE

The genesis of this book is my view that the way Australia comes to terms with the region around us will be fundamental to all we want to do in the future.

I believe there is some interest and some long-term value for Australia in setting out the background to a number of the decisions my colleagues and I took between 1991 and 1996, the period of my prime ministership, and the conclusions we reached about Australia's external relationships. These events lay close to the core of so much else we tried to do, and are central to the continuing job of building Australia's future in the world. I also want to set out some of the external challenges which I believe lie ahead for Australia.

This text is not a history of Australian foreign policy. It is not even a history of foreign policy during the time I was prime minister. Much of importance happened in those years – for example, in the reform of the United Nations, in the search for peace in the Middle East, or the first stirrings of regional cooperation in the Indian Ocean – which I have said little or nothing about in this book. The chapters that follow reflect my own particular interests and the issues in which I was most directly involved as prime minister. For the most part, they form part of an interlinked story of engagement with the region around us.

CHAPTER 1

1991

This book tells a small part of a long and still-unfinished story: how the people of Australia, this vast continent on the edge of the Asian landmass, are slowly coming to terms with the implications of their place in the world.

The story has been unfolding since a British colony was established at Port Jackson more than two hundred years ago, in part to preserve from French challenge Britain's access to the wealth of Asian trade. It has shaped our sense of threat and opportunity ever since. And it has been the dominant theme of our foreign policy since we came to the slow recognition that our interests and those of Britain could diverge.

What follows is partly a personal story – an account of my own involvement with Australia's external relations during the time I was prime minister – and partly some reflections, on Australia, its place in the world and the future of our region. It is not so much a record of what my colleagues and I did as why we did it.

I was elected to succeed Bob Hawke as Leader of the Parliamentary Labor Party on 19 December 1991. In politics you seldom have the luxury of choosing your timing and, as is well known, this was not mine. But I could hardly have become Prime Minister of Australia at a more interesting moment.

At the end of 1991 I believed we were living through one of

the pivotal periods of modern history. The world was entering an era that was different in form, not just in degree, from anything we had known before. The year had begun with Operation Desert Storm, the war in the Gulf. It was to end with the dissolution of the Soviet Union. The broad multinational coalition brought together in response to Saddam Hussein's invasion of Kuwait had been hailed as the beginning of a new, more cooperative approach to international relations. The divisions of the Cold War were to be replaced by a 'New World Order', based on a revitalised United Nations and cooperation between the great powers.

But even by year's end differences were emerging within the Gulf coalition, and it was clear it did not offer a sustainable model for the future. The phrase 'New World Order' had come to mean more to the world's right-wing conspiracy theorists than to those who were trying to understand what was happening to the international system. To describe the world, politicians and their speech-writers had to fall back on terms such as 'the post-Cold War world'. This only demonstrated that it was still much easier to describe our lives in terms of what had passed rather than what was to come. We were living in what seemed, in so many ways, to be a 'post' world – post-Cold War, post-modern, post-industrial ... Our language reflected our uncertainty about what was coming next.

Since the end of the Second World War we had inhabited a bipolar world. We had defined our countries and ourselves as of the East or the West, or, if we were from the newly independent Third World, we hovered somewhere along a spectrum between them.

The Cold War had been, on both sides, ideological as well as geo-strategic; that is, it had been rooted in a struggle for ideas. As Australian political history – and not least the history of the Australian Labor Party – attested, the struggle had domestic as well as international ramifications. It had been instrumental in maintaining the conservative majority in the Australian Federal Parliament for thirty long years. And in theory (at least on the Soviet side), and at various periods in practice, too, the Cold War was seen by those engaged in it as a Manichean battle which could be won only by the complete victory of one side and the annihilation of the other. Or even, as we sometimes feared in our nightmares, the annihilation of us all.

Yet for a combination of wholly unexpected reasons (expected least of all by the two main protagonists, the United States and the Soviet Union), we were blessed by an epiphany at the end of a century that had given us few reasons to expect one. Thanks to a combination of good luck and good judgement by some of the key figures involved, in a miraculous few years the Cold War ended, and the Berlin Wall was reduced to rubble. Europe was no longer divided, and the Soviet Union disappeared from the map.

Of course, powerful underlying forces like technology, economic strength and the power of ideas shaped this outcome. But the form and the manner in which the Cold War ended owed much to particular individuals: Mikhail Gorbachev, who saw that the system he had inherited had reached a dead end and who had the courage to face it; Ronald Reagan and George Bush, who both knew when to take yes for an answer; Helmut Kohl, who acted with vision and expedition to reunite Germany against the odds and all manner of cautious advice; and Boris Yeltsin, who stood on the tanks outside the Moscow White House and stared down the putschists. The world was utterly changed.

It wasn't just the structures of the preceding fifty years that were toppling in 1991. At the very core of the international system, subterranean rumblings foreshadowed more profound change. With the constraints of the Cold War gone, the foundations of the nation-state, which had formed the basis of the international system for more than 150 years, were looking much less immutable. This was not to say that the state was suddenly irrelevant, or that national governments were about to disappear, or that quite old-fashioned (indeed, prehistoric) concepts of what power rested upon – wealth, technology, and armed force, and the willingness to use it – were about to be swept away. But, like termites, the twin forces of globalisation and the information revolution were gnawing away at the struts and joists that had forever separated our national house from the world around it.

Economic globalisation had been transforming the world since the 1980s. An Australian approach to it had been one of the principal concerns of my time as Australian treasurer. International statistics measuring international trade and investment revealed just how comprehensively and quickly the transformation was taking place. Globally, direct investment abroad rose from around $US50 billion in 1983 to $US150 billion in 1992. Between 1965 and 1990 the percentage of world output going to exports doubled.

One result was that the share of world trade in the global economy rose three times as fast between 1985 and 1994 as in the preceding ten years. And more than one-third of that trade was conducted by firms trading with themselves. In fact, the bulk of all goods traded internationally were parts and components for assembly by an estimated 40,000 transnational companies producing goods across national borders. The top one hundred of these companies had global assets worth approximately $US3.4 trillion.

Developing countries had been major beneficiaries of globalisation and, as a result, they were becoming much more central to global trade. By 1991 it was already clear that the negotiations that had been under way since 1986 on the future of international trade (the Uruguay Round of multilateral trade negotiations – so-called, because that was where they had been launched) could no longer be settled in quiet back-room discussions between the Americans, the Europeans and the Japanese. The developing economies were increasingly vital participants in the global economy and they had to be involved.

This was particularly important to us in Australia. The Asian economies had grasped the importance of globalisation earlier than most and had been opening up their economies to participate in it. The result had been the extraordinary surge of growth known as 'the East Asian miracle', with the economies of some of Australia's neighbours growing year by year at eight and nine per cent and higher. For the first time in our history, Australia was situated within the fastest growing region of the world.

Non-economic issues were also forcing the pace of globalisation and changing the international agenda. Environmental pollution, for example, often had causes and effects that spread well beyond national boundaries and could not be addressed, let alone fixed, by national governments.

Overlaying globalisation was the information revolution. I was sure we were at the point with the information revolution we had been at 150 years earlier with the industrial revolution. We were on the verge of changes that would not only transform our economies but our lives as well. Personal computers and telecommunications technologies were pulling distance in at a meteoric pace. In 1991 the World Wide Web had just been created, and even among the technological elite few people comprehended its eventual impact. But it was clear that for the first time in human history we were moving into a world that was information-rich, information-drenched. This had all sorts of consequences for the way our societies and economies were organised and governed, and the way countries dealt with one another.

The combined pressures of globalisation and information were coming at us like a wall of water. We could understand it and be prepared for it, or it could wash over us, leaving us at a standstill as it carried others around us to greater wealth and prosperity.

This was the world in December 1991. Some of these developments were obvious; some we had already made long preparations for; others were cloudy. But it was clear as day that in combination they were determining Australia's future. The question on my mind was how we should harness their power and ride the wave.

In the usual way we think of it, foreign policy is a remarkably recent development in Australia. The country's first real effort to mark out an international position of its own came at the 1919 Paris Peace Conference which ended the First World War. The results were decidedly mixed. Prime Minister Billy Hughes lobbied successfully to secure Australian control over New Guinea but also to preserve the White Australia Policy. (He argued against a Japanese proposal that the Covenant of the new League of Nations should include an assertion that racial equality was a condition of world peace on the grounds that such a sentiment might undermine Australia's immigration policy.)

We had no fully functioning external affairs department until 1935. Arguably, we had no status in international affairs until 1931, when the Statute of Westminster gave autonomy to the whiter parts of the British Empire – Australia, New Zealand, South Africa and Canada. But even then Australia was well behind the other dominions in carving out a place for itself in the world. The conservative Lyons administration was actually affronted by Whitehall seeking to kick us out of the nest. Our first independent representative overseas was R.G. Casey, sent to Washington as Australian Minister in 1940. We didn't ratify the Statute of Westminster until late in 1942. We were not going to be tricked into autonomy.

Australia's lack of interest in – even hostility to – the idea of an independent foreign policy was shared in different ways on the right and left of the political spectrum. For the conservative parties, it reflected a fervent wish to remain under the wing of imperial protection and a deeply ingrained fear of what would happen to us – socially and culturally, as well as economically and strategically – if we dared strike out on our own. In 1937 Robert Menzies could explain to Parliament the delay in ratifying the Statute of Westminster by saying: 'I know that quite a number of responsible people are troubled about the proposal to adopt the Statute of Westminster for the reason that they feel it may give some support to the idea of separatism from Great Britain.'

On Labor's side, the caution about Australia's role in the world stemmed more from the deep isolationism into which the party sank after the First World War. Labor saw our international involvements in Belgium, in France, and at Gallipoli as the events which snuffed out the flame of Australia's rising nationalism: the movement to Federation, the ethos of equality, the formation of unions and, in the 1890s, the creation of the Labor Party itself.

This mix of caution from both sides of politics, coupled with the malign role of White Australia, impeded our capacity to think of ourselves as ourselves and of our place in the world around us. As Kim Beazley Snr. wrote perceptively in 1966: 'The White Australia Policy never did Australia as much harm in the thinking of foreigners as it did in keeping Australia small, self-centred and without a program for Asia.' The very few far-sighted politicians, academics and officials who saw a different future for Australia were drowned out by the conservatism and jingoism that followed the First World War and the incantations that extolled the monoculture.

The Second World War was a watershed for Australia. After the fall of the British bastion of Singapore it was impossible to doubt that Australia had vital interests in the world – including our national survival – that did not always coincide with Great Britain's. The Labor Prime Minister of the time, John Curtin, turned to the United States for assistance 'free of any pangs as to our traditional links or kinship with the United Kingdom'. 'We know,' he said, '... that Australia can go and Britain can still hold on. We are therefore determined that Australia shall not go ...' Here began our first serious engagement with Asia. We were frogmarched by history to find our security in the region.

After the war, our neighbours were no longer European colonial powers but independent and assertive national governments. Now we had to deal with them directly, and not through London. The Labor Government's early support for the Indonesian revolution in 1947 set the stage for a new sort of Australian engagement with the region: our effective resignation from the Colonial Club. Labor knew that if our interests were to be protected we had to develop our own foreign policy, our own institutions, our own approaches.

In large measure, because of the war, the collective voice of those Australians who saw our future in this region became louder and more assertive. Journalists like Peter Hastings and Denis Warner, academics like W. Macmahon Ball and Heinz Arndt, and diplomats like Tom Critchley, Alf Parsons and Richard Woolcott brought Asia more forcefully to the attention of the Australian Government and its people.

So in 1991, Australian foreign policy, formally at least, was less than fifty years old. As it was so critical to what we could become, the question in my head was how might a prime minister shape it and give it force and direction. The Prime Minister of Australia has no job description. The Constitution doesn't even mention the position. The job can be performed in ways as different as the people who occupy it. That is especially true of the position's external dimensions. Apart from turning up to shake hands with visitors and attending a couple of more-or-less compulsory international meetings, there is nothing the prime minister must do in the area of foreign policy. Some have done little more.

No prime minister's day is long enough to accommodate all the things that others are urging to fill it. Choices about how much time to spend on one issue or another, whether to see one visitor rather than another, to attend one function and not another are among the most important decisions any prime minister has to take. And the choices have to be taken deliberately. Otherwise the agenda for the whole government ends up being shaped by accident, or the relentless burden of precedent, not by design.

To some extent, like any job, it responds to the events of the time. James Scullin had to deal with the Depression, John Curtin with the Second World War. Responding to crises – handling what lands on your plate – is an important responsibility of any prime minister. But so, too, is setting the agenda: knowing why you want the job, knowing what to do with it. Above all, it is imagining something better and fashioning the policies to get there.

The international 'system' – the way governments and other international entities react with each other and shape the way the world operates – is almost incomprehensibly complex. Any system that depends on national interests and human psychology has to be. As a result, international events rarely lend themselves to careful pre-planning. Decisions frequently have to be taken at short notice and with incomplete data.

As prime minister, the information you are working with is almost always thinnest at the beginning of any crisis than later, but it is the initial responses which often determine the outcome. That is why it is so singularly important for any prime minister to bring to the job a framework or view of the world within which to provide context to often seemingly random developments. Without such a framework, foreign policy becomes a series of ad hoc reactions to external events, an approach that leaves the country hostage to luck or misadventure.

With external policy, all of my predecessors had done the

job in individual ways. Many had been very successful. Gough Whitlam, in particular, had given new hope and international standing to Australian foreign policy. His intelligence and energy contrasted with the 'All the way with LBJ' banalities of Harold Holt and the national torpor induced by Billy McMahon and Menzies before him. With recognition of China and his emphasis on Australia's role in our region, he also bequeathed the country a new bipartisanship in foreign policy which had existed with odd fluctuations ever since.

Malcolm Fraser and Bob Hawke each had a continuing and creative interest in foreign affairs. Notwithstanding Bob's interest in Australia's engagement with Asia, especially China, and his proposal for establishing the economic and trade body APEC, each of them had spent a large amount of their time on global issues, particularly on Southern Africa, where they worked through the Commonwealth on both Zimbabwe's independence and the end of apartheid in South Africa. Bob had a long-standing and deep personal interest in the Middle East as well.

As prime minister, I was not interested in being, as both Gough Whitlam and Malcolm Fraser had in essence been, my own foreign minister. Nor did I have any interest in the ceremonial or symbolic aspects of the job. I could not have cared less if I never attended a diplomatic banquet or walked to a fanfare of trumpets down a red carpet or inspected an honour guard. I certainly did not want to spend my time engaged in exchanges of views with other leaders for which officials had carefully worked out the talking points in advance and where the responses were scripted. I was determined to focus on those things that only a prime minister could do. I often described the job of politics in Australia as being in 'the change business'. There seems to me no other reason to be in the service of the public. If the only work to be done is to preside over the status quo, bureaucrats, I am sure, would do a much better job of it.

The Australian version of the Westminster system of government sets the broad structures of government – a Cabinet drawn from the party or coalition which commands a majority in the House of Representatives, and so on. But the precise operations of each government differ according to its own internal dynamics. I thought the core dynamics for Labor when I became prime minister were the quality and experience of our ministers. They needed no prime ministerial micro-management of their portfolios. The team we had working on our external policies was particularly strong, with Gareth Evans in Foreign Affairs, Robert Ray in Defence, John Kerin, Peter Cook and Bob McMullan in Trade, and Gordon Bilney on aid and Pacific affairs.

The country was exceptionally fortunate to have in Gareth Evans an outstanding foreign minister, and I had no wish to duplicate his work or to intrude into the subtle webs he had put together. I greatly admired Gareth's commitment, courage, energy, idealism and ideas. But being different people, we approached international issues in different ways. Gareth is a lawyer, an internationalist and very much the idealist. I have a more sceptical, intuitive and power-based view of the international system. History, the dynamics of power, and an understanding of the personalities informed my view of events, while I think Gareth, very conscious of these things too, placed more weight on argumentative symmetry and the protocols by which international events and responses were calibrated and weighted.

Any differences we had were more evident at the beginning of our working relationship than at the end. By then we had grown familiar with each other and had shaped each other's views as well. Contrary, perhaps, to many views, we are particularly good listeners, especially of one another. Throughout our entire time in government, our sometimes different approaches to the world were contained within a very similar view of Australia's interests, and an identical commitment to Australia's position in the world.

The formal decision-making body for foreign policy, as for all government policy, was Cabinet. For reasons of security, the most sensitive defence, foreign policy and intelligence issues were handled through the limited-membership Security Committee. But because of the fluid and fast-moving nature of most international events (and the inevitable frequent absence overseas of the foreign minister and trade minister), informal discussions between the relevant ministers, directly, on the telephone, or through our staff, were the most important means of coordination. Communication between offices was a daily, even hourly, process, especially when Parliament was sitting.

Within my office I had a senior adviser on international relations. When I became prime minister, I asked Dr Ashton Calvert to take this job. Ashton was an outstanding diplomat and expert on Japan whose hard-headed, take-no-prisoner approach to international affairs I had admired on earlier visits to Tokyo. When Ashton went to Tokyo as our ambassador, he was succeeded in 1993 by Allan Gyngell, another former diplomat who had been heading the important International Division of the Department of the Prime Minister and Cabinet. Allan had a great sense of structure to his thinking about foreign relations and a particularly sure touch to issues-management. While somewhat different, Calvert and Gyngell shared common views with me about how Australia should set itself up in the region and how and where we should point it over the long haul.

The job of the senior adviser on international affairs in the office was a coordinating and advising one. The adviser managed the voluminous flow of paper coming into the office – foreign affairs telegrams, raw and assessed intelligence reports, Cabinet papers and submissions from the public service, official and unofficial correspondence under the weight of which any prime minister would otherwise drown. He decided what required my personal attention and what did not. He was a sounding board for me about international issues and could act as a conduit for other ministers and ministerial offices. Next to the foreign minister, the adviser's job is, I believe, the second most important in the Australian foreign policy firmament. Free of the administrative burden which the secretaryship of the Department of Foreign Affairs and Trade has, the adviser's job is principally about policy. But unlike most policy jobs, it carries with it the live conduit of power.

Like all ministers, my office and I drew on, and were supported by, the great resource of the Australian public service. In the area of external policy this meant the Department of Foreign Affairs and Trade, the senior defence force and civilian officers in the Department of Defence, and the Prime Minister's department, especially its International Division.

In addition to the policy advice and briefing coming from their government departments, the prime minister and his colleagues also have access to raw and assessed intelligence from the Australian intelligence agencies. The Australian Secret Intelligence Service collected human intelligence – what most people think of as 'spying' – and the Defence Signals Directorate collected signals and electronic intelligence, largely by technical means. This raw intelligence was then assessed, along with diplomatic reports coming in from our overseas posts and news reports, by the Office of National Assessments (ONA), Australia's main analytical intelligence organisation. ONA's assessments were often of a high quality, and as the subsequent inadvertent publication of some views of South-Pacific developments showed, they were written in a decidedly non-bureaucratic manner.

Intelligence is more abundant in the information age. The days are long gone when the inner workings of the Kremlin were a state secret and our knowledge of any scrap of information could add hugely to our ability to make accurate judgements about the behaviour of such countries. Governments still have secrets, of course, but the relative size of the closed world – and its relative importance – is shrinking by the day, part of a fundamental change in the role of government in a global age.

In the area of defence, intelligence is an essential force-multiplier for a country as small as Australia. But I was less convinced of the value of political and economic intelligence. Sometimes intelligence could confirm an approach or point in new directions, but on too many issues it could be characterised as no more than modestly useful. It is almost always, and perhaps inevitably, weakest on the subject of the intentions of others.

I was always more interested in ideas than in data. It is always ideas that are in shortest supply. For that reason, I was a more sceptical and disinterested consumer of secret intelligence than some other prime ministers have been. Very sceptical, in fact. It is easy to be seduced by documents stamped with code-words and handled through special channels, and easy to forget to ask, 'Yes, but does it matter?' For this reason, I did not usually see, or want to see, unassessed intelligence but preferred it properly analysed and placed in the context of what we knew from all sources.

However professional our intelligence agencies, official advisers and diplomats may be, they can never do the whole job for a country. I knew from long experience that political leaders could do things which no official, however skilled and imaginative, could do. Politicians shape the world. They have to be open to the views of their officials and academics and business interests, and must be aware of the other ideas flowing around in the community. But in the end they alone carry the authority of the democratic contest, the authority that gives them the opportunity and the responsibility to change the way the country functions and to determine for it a place in the world.

I brought with me to the prime ministership three particular convictions about Australia's place in the world, and these informed my actions in the following years. The first was that Australia's economic success at home was heavily dependent upon what we did, and how we related externally; the second, that our future lay comprehensively in Asia; and the third, that the times gave Australia an unprecedented opportunity and responsibility to help shape the world and the region around us.

My first conviction had been reinforced by my eight years' experience as treasurer. The daily business of contending with the countless international influences on the Australian economy – a middle-sized industrial economy – brought home to me just how powerful were the forces at work in a globalised world and how futile it was for a country of Australia's size to pretend we could hold the pressures of a more integrated world at bay. I believed that openness to the world was the only way that Australia could optimise its creative potential and give our people the growth, jobs, and the satisfying lives they deserved.

We had tried the other, completely opposite approach through most of the century and it did not work. The old trade-off, brought to its apogee by the Country Party under John McEwan, involved relying on our efficient mining and agricultural sectors to prop up and subsidise a manufacturing sector which, because of protection from competition by high tariffs, became lethargic and lacked serious ambitions beyond our shores. The policy depended on the national good fortune of our inheritance of an abundant continent. But by the mid-1980s, the terms of trade – that is, the prices we broadly received for the things we produced, compared with the prices we paid for the things we bought – had turned well against us, as indeed they did against all commodity suppliers. In just two years, from March 1985 to March 1987, the terms of trade fell by 14 per cent. As the full implications of the globalised economy made themselves felt, the old ways had become unsustainable. My references at that time to Australia being at risk of becoming a banana republic reflected my deep concern and foreboding about this inexorable trend.

Australia had a rich legacy of innovation and pure scientific research on which to draw, and services that could compete with any in the world. But I always believed that our industry, including our services industry, would only develop the skills it needed to survive in tough international competition if it also faced competition at home.

Labor's national ambition for Australia was a world-competitive economy underpinning an egalitarian and inclusive society. So from 1983 onwards, the Labor Government began the painful but necessary task of opening up the Australian economy. We let the Australian dollar find its true competitive level by floating it. We removed exchange controls, freed the domestic financial sector and opened up the financial sector to international competition; we deregulated our aviation and telecommunications industries, established a more efficient national competition policy, privatised the Commonwealth Bank and Qantas and embarked on the huge task of breaking down the tariff wall.

I was sure in 1991 that we had to maintain this direction. Not to do so would have eroded the prosperity, and eventually the security, of future generations of Australians. I am just as sure of it now.

My experience as treasurer had given me a strong sense of the central role of economics in foreign policy, a role I believed would grow dramatically now the shackles of the Cold War had been removed. One of the most significant administrative changes made by the Labor Government had been the amalgamation in 1987 of the competing bureaucratic empires of Foreign Affairs and Trade into one new department. This had strengthened the link between our political and economic interests and made our diplomats much more attuned to economic and commercial interests, but I thought still more should be done.

I could also see that almost every issue Australia would have to contend with in coming years now had an international dimension. Wherever you looked, this was evident. Employment growth and the sorts of industries we created, social policy and pensions, the future of culture and popular entertainment, our relations with indigenous Australians, even the future of the sports we played and watched were all increasingly tied up with and shaped by – and in some cases determined by – what happened abroad. Foreign policy had become a sinew of domestic policy rather than the outrider it had mostly been in Australia.

My second conviction was that Asia was where Australia's future substantially lay and that we needed to engage with it at a level and with an intensity we had never come close to doing in the past. This was not because we had not been interested in Asia before. But what was different in 1991 was that never before had *all* our national interests – political, economic, strategic, and cultural – coalesced so strongly in the one place as they did now.

Once the Opposition abandoned the line that I had no interest in Asia and decided instead that I was obsessed with it, they regularly accused me of claiming to have invented Australia's relationship with Asia. That arrogant Paul Keating again. Of course, I did no such thing. I made it clear in almost every major speech I gave that Australia's relationship with Asia was long and, in large measure, honourable.

From Hodogaya in Tokyo to Kranji in Singapore, the war cemeteries of the region alone are moving testament to that. In the baking heat of the Kanchanaburi cemetery near Hellfire Pass in Thailand I found the graves of three young Australian soldiers killed on the day I was born: 18 January 1944. Those fields of white crosses throughout Asia and the Pacific are a reminder of the role Australian forces played during the Second World War in turning back the tide of Japanese imperialism.

Since then we have had a long record of involvement. Our contribution to Indonesia's independence struggle, the Korean War, the creation of the Colombo Plan, our early support for ASEAN, and our great partnership in the economic development of Japan and Korea were all things in which earlier generations of political leaders had been involved, some of them passionately, and of which we could be proud.

It was not the whole story, however, and another, equally valid, history of Australia's relationship with the region around us would refer to the tenacious hold which fear of Asia held over the imagination of Australians.

Australia's first view of Asia was heavily tied up with a sense of threat. The strategic threat was largely seen as coming from European colonial powers – the French first, then the Russians, and after the First World War, the Germans. Australia was an outpost of Europe and the threats to our security were the same as the threats to Britain. Canberra itself was established at its present location in part because it was out of the range of Russian gunboats. But reinforcing the strategic fear was the economic and cultural fear of the teeming hordes of Asians waiting just beyond our shores for the opportunity to undercut our wages, flood into our cities and countryside, and destroy our culture.

This fear had its most obvious manifestation in the White Australia Policy, which was an affront to those who were excluded by it as it was to morality and to commonsense. It was a policy in which my party, the ALP, had been more culpable than any, although the ALP was more willing than any to finally abandon it.

Following the very real threat from Japan during the Second World War and the subsequent transformations brought about by rising nationalism and decolonisation in Asia, a new set of fears emerged. Robert Menzies expressed them in 1946 when speaking about the departure of the European colonial powers: 'When we have, in this absurd frenzy, cleared our powerful friends out of the places that are vital to us, we in Australia will know all about isolation. I hope that day will never come.'

Menzies was voicing the fear that we would one day wake up and find ourselves on our own without a great and powerful friend to preserve us from the yellow peril, or the red arrows thrusting downwards, or the simple terror of abandonment. Australia's struggle was never to avoid the 'foreign entanglements' the early American revolutionaries feared. On the contrary, we set about searching them out, roping them in, dragging them down, and clutching them tight.

Throughout the 1950s and '60s the fear of Asia, or of something from Asia, remained the dominant undercurrent in Australian policy towards the region. Fear of a resurgent Japan, fear of an expansionary China, fear of a united Sino-Soviet challenge to our way of life, fear that unless we did our bit to support US policy in Vietnam we would be left alone. That was not all there was to Australian policy by any means, but it set the tone.

Both strands of thought about Asia – positive and creative, negative and defensive – were at work in Australian policy and politics. But by 1991 we faced a new issue. For a decade East Asia had been the fastest-growing region on earth, with economic growth at twice the global average. What was happening in East Asia represented the greatest increment to economic growth in human history. Greater than the growth that came from the industrial revolution in Europe. Greater than the great surge of development that transformed the United States in the middle of the nineteenth century. As the US economist David Hale noted, it took Britain and the United States fifty to sixty years to double per capita income in the early stages of the industrial revolution, but the countries of East Asia had been doing it every ten years.

Two-thirds of Australia's exports were going there. And it was no longer just our traditional commodity exports. Between 1983 and 1993 Australian manufactured exports to Asia grew twice as fast as the traditional areas of trade, and exports of services grew even more rapidly. Frankly, it no longer mattered how effectively we had dealt with Asia in the past, but how we would deal with a new Asia – newer, at any rate, than at any time since the great decolonisation period of the late 1940s and early 1950s. And, the equally valid question for us – one we were unused to asking – was how Asia would deal with Australia. I believed we started from the best possible position, that of having no historical or fundamental conflicts of interest with any country in the region. No point of aggravation, no enmities.

A wide coalition of people, ranging from the Prime Minister of Malaysia, Dr Mahathir, to the Australian opposition parties, accused me at various times of trying to turn Australia into an Asian nation. Behind all these charges seemed to lie the belief that Australia faced only one simple choice: to be 'Asian' or to be 'European'. Of course, I never saw Australia in those terms. For all that we had done and created here, we could only be the nation we had become: the Australian nation. A unique group of people; a derivative of no other country.

In December 1993, after Dr Mahathir had claimed Australia could not be part of Asia because we were not (or more specifically, I suppose, I was not) behaving, in his view, as Asians, I said explicitly in a speech transmitted directly into Asia on Australia Television that:

> Claims that the Government is trying to turn Australia into an 'Asian country' are based on a misunderstanding of both my own approach and the direction of government policy. This is something I want to be understood very clearly because it is at the core of my view of Australia and of the

Government's approach to relations with our neighbourhood. Put simply, Australia is not, and can never be, an 'Asian nation' any more than we can – or want to be – European or North American or African. We can only be Australian and can only relate to our friends and neighbours *as* Australian.

I was to make this same point many times. 'Asia' is a very fluid term. It originated in the West. But however broadly you define it, I don't believe Australia makes the cut. How can we? We inhabit a continent. Aboriginal Australians have been here for at least 45,000 years, possibly millennia longer. The rest of us have come to Australia from more than 120 countries.

However, that is a very different thing from asserting, as I believe we must, that Australia is a legitimate and central part of the region around us; that we are and have every right – and responsibility – to be a charter member of the region and its institutions. Whether you call this region Asia, or the West Pacific, or the East Asian Hemisphere, or the Asia-Pacific matters much less than our active participation in it, our legitimacy in being part of it.

This right derives in part from geography, but not only that. It springs most particularly from the dense network of interests which bind Australia and our neighbours: the 60 per cent of our trade which goes to East Asia, the tens of thousands of Asian students who have studied in Australia, the long commitment – bindings in our blood and theirs – Australia had made to the security of our neighbours during the Second World War, the Korean War, the Malayan Emergency confrontation and the Five Power Defence Arrangements.

My third conviction about Australia's place in the world was that the times gave us unprecedented opportunities and responsibilities to help shape the world and our region in ways that would help our long-term interests.

In a world in flux, I felt countries like Australia had both the opportunity and the responsibility to help mould the emerging international system. Countries no less than individuals have to be alert to the opportunities they are offered and to know when to take them, when to move.

I had been interested for most of my life in European political history, especially towards and at the turn of the twentieth century, and I had often thought about the reasons for the series of miscalculations and misreadings that led to the carnage of the prolonged European civil war and the tragedies of totalitarianism. None of it was preordained. Our century had been bloodied – and 100,000 Australians had died – because statesmanship had failed.

I thought that what political leaders did at the end of the twentieth century would lay the foundations for prosperity and security in the twenty-first century just as fatefully and inevitably as the actions of Europe's leaders had done a hundred years before. And I felt we had limited time in which to shape the new structures before nations and institutions settled only into ruts from which it would be difficult to dislodge them.

Australia and the Australian prime minister could only be small elements in the reconstruction of the post-Cold War world. We could not determine the outcome, but we could influence it. For a middle-sized country we had a global view and a high reputation. We could punch above our weight, and often did. We had developed well the software of foreign policy. But I was sure that if I was to do anything with the opportunities I had been given, I did not have a second to lose. I did not know how long Labor would remain in office. I had been left with the prospect of winning a fifth consecutive election one year from a poll, and twenty-odd points behind. But however long our time was to be, I was determined to make the most of the opportunity and the responsibility.

In December 1991 much of this lay in the future. I had immediate concerns. Within a couple of weeks I was to host the first visit to Australia in a quarter of a century by an American president. Decisions about the foreign policy agenda had to take on a very concrete dimension.

CHAPTER 2

THE BIGGEST DOG ON THE BLOCK

President Bush's visit to Australia was the first by a serving United States President for twenty-five years. For a new prime minister, it meant a particularly high-profile entrance on the foreign policy stage.

This visit would provide the first chance for me to set out my own views on foreign and defence policy. You're not often invited to leave some messages with the president of the world's only remaining superpower. I was determined that the warm fog of sentimentality that swirls around the relationship between the United States and Australia so easily on these occasions shouldn't obscure the opportunity.

I did not want the President to fly out of Australia having heard no more than rehashed policy positions and familiar catechisms of loyal friendship. It was a long way to come for a few photo opportunities and some high-tone public relations. I wanted the President to leave with some clear, preferably new ideas provided by us.

As I have said, I was very conscious of the sheer malleability of the world in the early 1990s. I could not remember a period when it had been so pliable. A new international environment was emerging which presented Australia with serious challenges: how to preserve our physical security in a more complex world; how to ensure we reaped the benefits of economic globalisation but weren't elbowed out of international markets by larger economies; and how to make certain that Australia could participate in, and benefit from, the new international structures that would have to be created. The United States was critical to our capacity to do all three things. Australia's direct role in reshaping the global order was always going to be limited, but I knew that if we could persuade the United States to the merits of a particular course of action, it was much more likely to be taken.

I have never fully shared the fascination of some of my ALP colleagues with American politics, but Franklin Delano Roosevelt has my vote for the greatest political figure of the twentieth century. And I always felt that he was speaking a literal truth when he spoke of the 'righteous might' of the United States. The mightiness was undeniable. It was the largest economy of the world, and thanks to the rise of the information economy and the collapse of the Soviet Union, the United States found itself at the end of the twentieth century with the level of strategic, if not quite economic, dominance with which it had emerged from the Second World War, nearly fifty years before. In the vernacular, it was the biggest dog on the block.

In the early 1990s, a fashionable line of thought still existed inside and outside America that the United States could no longer sustain its global role and faced inevitable decline. It is interesting from this distance to reflect on that debate. What the 'declinists' did not foresee were the vast changes that were about to flow from information technology. Nor did they understand the way the flexible, inclusive American economic and social environment could take advantage of this technological shift in a way none of the other great powers could match.

Inclusiveness is not necessarily an attribute of great powers. Britain managed an empire without it. But it is a great strength of the United States – and of Australia. It reflects a culture that not only asserts its own norms but draws the best from those of others.

No doubt the United States would eventually face new economic competition, especially from Asia. But within the time-frames Australian policy-makers needed to grapple with, I saw no reason to expect any challenge to the economic or to the strategic might of the United States. And for all its self-absorption and policy errors – for every Vietnam and Bay of Pigs – the United States always had the instinct and capacity for selfless action. Righteousness. This quality had won the Second World War, saved Australia in the great battles of Midway and the Coral Sea, helped a devastated Europe to its feet through the Marshall Plan, and facilitated Asia's miracle of growth by opening its markets to the developing world at a time when the Europeans were closing theirs.

The United States' belief that its own form of democracy had unique virtues made its political rhetoric hard for outsiders to swallow. But I could think of no other great power that I would prefer to see in the dominant position at this period of world affairs.

In late 1991, however, I was worried less about American action in the world than a lack of it. I wasn't concerned about a return to the same sort of US isolationism we saw between the two world wars. But I did not think we could assume that the Americans would necessarily continue to be interested in the world in the same way as in the past or in the form that would most benefit Australia and this region. Quite enough serious political voices were being heard in the United States questioning its international commitments to show how strongly the isolationist (or at least unilateralist) sentiment courses through the veins of the American body politic, and on both its left and its right.

It was, in my view, imperative that the United States should continue to be involved across the Pacific politically, economically and strategically. This wasn't a matter of wanting a big brother to hold Australia's hand or a policeman to patrol the neighbourhood. On the contrary, I saw it as engaging with the country which, for better or worse (I thought for better), was the major ally of Australia, Japan, Korea, and the Philippines, and the major market and source of investment and technology transfer for almost every one of the countries of the region. I believed that this region would be safer and more prosperous with the United States in it. I was always perplexed by the United States' Eurocentricity. I believed it owed it to itself and to others to have a two-ocean policy: one which encompassed the Pacific as well as the Atlantic.

Although (as Roosevelt had shown) the capacity and instinct for American engagement with the world has to be galvanised by political leadership, the direction of American foreign policy would not be shaped by politicians and the political elite alone. As always in the United States, it depended on what the American people thought. And it was obviously going to be harder to engage them in a world shorn of the high moral struggle of the Cold War, where instead the stuff of debate was acronyms like APEC, GATT and NAFTA.

On important issues, the United States invariably moves by consensus. The division of power between the executive and the Congress, and the sheer scale of the place, make this consensus-forming critical. If consensus is present, as it was in the Second World War and the Cold War, nothing can stand in America's way. If it is absent, as it was in the latter stages of the Vietnam War, or even in Kosovo, failure in any global endeavour is in prospect.

I thought this placed a great responsibility on countries like Australia to help galvanise a consensus for involvement in the Pacific. That, in turn, meant providing persuasive reasons for such engagement and, if we could, coming up with ways to facilitate it.

Australia would not be performing much of a service if

we were no more than Washington's antipodean cheer squad. The best contribution we could make as an ally was to put our view in a lucid way, to offer the United States a framework and, above all, to be a source of ideas. Our contribution could be to coordinate our actions in our national interests while keeping the wider interests of prosperity in the Asia-Pacific in mind.

George Bush was one of the most internationalist of United States presidents, and he had a distinguished record of service to his country. However, the political tide was turning against him. Only half a year earlier he had ended the Gulf War with public opinion approval ratings of 80 per cent, the highest ever recorded. But now, the euphoria had abated. Concerned about an economic growth rate stuck at around two per cent, the American people were looking for other solutions and to other leaders.

Officials had prepared a 140-page brief for the Bush visit, but it was briefing for Bob Hawke rather than for me. Much of it was about the bilateral relationship and specific trade matters. Officials could do little more to it than substitute the phrase 'your predecessor' for the word 'you' wherever it appeared. This was hardly surprising; my foreign policy views at that time were, in most respects, publicly unknown.

My office arranged a number of meetings with senior public servants and outside experts to run over the issues for the visit, and I spent a long time thinking to myself about what I could say that would be more than a simple recitation of well-known propositions. I was determined that this would be the moment where Australia re-pointed itself in the new post-Cold War world, where we would enter the game in a more independent way. Useful to the United States but clear in what we wanted for ourselves. I was not going to waste the opportunity.

George Bush was a charming and knowledgeable interlocutor, much more familiar with the global scene than I was. I had met him first in 1971, on a visit with a parliamentary delegation to the United States, when he was the ambassador to the United Nations. I had always been impressed that he had taken the trouble to keep an appointment in Washington with a group of not very senior Asia-Pacific politicians, even though it was the same night the United States lost the China representation vote in the United Nations. It had been a measure of his courtesy.

He and Barbara Bush, along with a party of 475 officials and more than 400 members of the media, had arrived in Sydney on Airforce One in depressingly wet weather on New Year's Eve, 1991. The President was to travel on from Australia to Japan with a group of American businesspeople. United States's public opinion was in the throes of one of its periodic bursts of anti-Japanese sentiment. The main problems were the trade balance and the perception – a legacy of the Gulf War – that the Japanese were not bearing their share of the burden of global leadership. In the eyes of Americans, this meant that Japan was not paying enough to bankroll US operations. It did not imply a desire to see the Japanese strike out with independent leadership positions of their own, a prospect that made Washington decidedly nervous.

I wanted to see the President first in an informal setting and with only one adviser present. I always found this sort of meeting much more productive than the sort of large-scale set pieces into which prime ministers find themselves dragged. Prime ministers are symbolically important in bureaucratic turf-fights and the pressure is always on for as many officials as possible to be present at meetings, so no-one's nose gets out of joint. I resisted this rule as often as I could. So our first meeting was at the Prime Minister's Sydney residence, Kirribilli House, overlooking the world's most beautiful harbour, on New Year's Day, 1992. General Brent Scowcroft, Bush's National Security Adviser, was with him and Ashton Calvert, who had just taken up the position of my foreign affairs adviser, accompanied me.

My main message was that Australia wanted the United States to remain strongly engaged in the Asia-Pacific region so that the liberal democratic views and support for open economies which we both espoused would be reflected in the region's key institutions. I told the President that leadership was currently a scarce commodity in the world and it was important for the United States to hold onto its position. The Gulf War had annealed the US position of undisputed international leadership. But I believed we were at a decisive moment in shaping the world trading system. We had to avoid the risk of the world fracturing into three separate trading blocs in Europe, Asia and the Americas.

'You have the scope to put in place institutions as influential as the post-war Bretton Woods arrangements,' I told him. I spent considerable time arguing that there was no political architecture in the Asia-Pacific. I said that while the Soviet Union had dissolved, the old enmities between the Japanese and the Chinese remained. Taiwan was unresolved, as was the problem on the Korean peninsula. US policy in the Pacific seemed largely run by the US navy – in other words, from a defence perspective – and policy action by the United States hinged on the defence arrangements dictated by the post-war treaties with Japan, Korea, the Philippines, and with Australia and New Zealand.

I told him I believed the United States should be more commercially engaged in Asia. Where American commerce went so, too, did a greater understanding by the American public and a better basis for long-term strategic involvement.

My main new proposal concerned APEC (the Asia-Pacific Economic Cooperation group). Having defined Pacific basin interests at its 1989 inception, APEC could be the foundation for the building of a major piece of political architecture if it was represented at head-of-government level.

The next day in Parliament House in Canberra, with other colleagues present, we went through the broader agenda. We talked about global issues like the future of Russia and disarmament (on which Gareth Evans was particularly strong) and regional political and security developments. The main focus of public attention during the visit, however, was on economic issues.

Unlike almost all other countries in this part of the world, the structures of the Australian and US economies meant that we had a regular trade deficit with the United States. We imported high-tech manufactured goods from them (and were the welcome recipient of US capital investment), but we were competitors in the global markets for many raw materials.

The long-standing subsidies which the United States offered its farmers to improve their chances in export markets, especially the Export Enhancement Program (or EEP) for grains, were a source of great resentment here. And the imbalance in our trade meant that there were few countervailing voices within the Australian business community speaking in favour of the relationship when it came under pressure.

The purpose of the EEP was ostensibly to counter European subsidies, but stray bullets from the subsidisation crossfire were causing serious collateral damages to Australian farmers. Although the ALP had firmly resisted suggestions that we link trading issues and strategic interests by threatening American access to the Joint Defence Facilities (an idea endorsed by the National Party in one of its most brainlessly populist modes), there was no doubt that resentment towards the United States was high. The EEP had become the dominating economic issue in the relationship. And it was clear we had to use the visit by President Bush to bring home the reality of the harm it was doing to Australian farmers.

We arranged for the President to meet in Canberra with representatives of rural groups. They pointed out, as the Government had done earlier, the inherent inconsistency in America's criticism of Japan over market-access issues while it took actions whose consequence, if not intention, was to force Australia out of overseas markets. The President gave the farmers a good hearing and expressed sympathy but made no real concessions.

Although we eventually secured assurances from the Americans that they would try hard to avoid harming Australian interests when they used the EEP, it was clear that the only long-term solution to the problem lay in a resolution of the global negotiations to bring down trade barriers – the so-called Uruguay Round – which were grinding onwards with frustrating slowness.

The Bush visit was judged a success by the media. But although journalists usually report such events as though they are a story complete in themselves, with a beginning, a middle, and an end, the threads of foreign policy are rarely woven into a complete tapestry on a single visit.

For me, however, my preparations for the visit and the discussions during it had given me a clearer sense of what I wanted my foreign policy priorities to be: the building of appropriate multilateral institutional structures in the Asia-Pacific, encouraging an open international trading system and the development of Australia's relations with our immediate neighbours.

It was already obvious that we had one important point of difference with the Bush administration over Asia-Pacific policies. This was about the role and potential of regional institutions. In 1991 and 1992, Washington was expressing suspicion about the emerging Asian regional security dialogue (later to become the ASEAN Regional Forum) in which Gareth Evans and Australian diplomacy had played a major part. Some US officials feared that multilateral discussions about security were a way of containing or constraining US interests. I had asked the President to take a more relaxed view of the emerging dialogue. I told him the United States had no reason to fear negotiations between countries in the Asia-Pacific that were not conducted through Washington.

Only a couple of months earlier, the Secretary of State, James Baker, had likened the US role in the Asian regional security framework to that of a 'balancing wheel', in which Washington was the hub, and the spokes were its bilateral security treaties with its allies around the Pacific basin. The metaphor offered little room for collective dialogue. We were to learn later that suspicion of such multilateral approaches was one of the main foreign policy differences between the Bush and Clinton administrations.

During the course of 1992 the relationship between Japan and the United States continued to deteriorate. Members of the Administration spoke in increasingly agitated and critical terms about the relationship as the elections got closer. The 'hub and spokes' metaphor resurfaced in a different form.

George Bush had made a major speech in Detroit on 10 September 1992 in which he had foreshadowed a 'strategic network of free-trade agreements across the Atlantic and the Pacific and in our own hemisphere'. Back in Canberra, the more we thought about the Detroit speech the more we worried. It seemed to foreshadow a retreat from the region-wide approach that APEC offered to a more limited strategy in which the United States would deal with countries individually. Senior Administration officials were speaking to our embassy of the need to 'encircle' Japan with a network of free-trade agreements. Such an approach was hardly in Australia's interests. Japan was our largest trading partner, and our two-way trade was worth nearly $20 billion. Unlike the United States, we ran a substantial trade surplus with Japan (and a substantial deficit with the United States). We did not benefit from approaches that discriminated against Japan.

It also seemed dangerous to me because it brought closer the possibility of some sort of economic split down the Pacific between a dollar and a yen bloc. And it underlined again the

Administration's scepticism about multilateral solutions. My view was different. I believed that what the region needed after the Cold War was the fullest possible participation by all its members. The magnetic bipolarity had gone; the only thing that could replace it was genuine participation. We could not afford to be exclusive or to encourage division. This wasn't a matter of defending Japan's sometimes selfish, and almost always timid, attitude to economic reform and liberalisation, but a fear that the United States was going in the wrong direction.

In September 1992, I visited Japan for the first time as prime minister. At a lunch in Tokyo I told a business group that 'Australia would see no overall gain from entering into any trading pact which discriminates against Japan, or which in one way or another is directed against Japan.' My comments received colourful press treatment along the 'Keating snubs Bush' and 'PM pledges loyalty to Tokyo' line.

There was a bitter reaction from some in the Administration. A senior White House official penned a note to our ambassador accusing me of 'going after the US'. That was not true (although I was certainly going after one aspect of US policy). But it was true that I wanted to bring home to important partners in the region, and to Australians, the fact that there was a shift in our approach to Asia.

Australia faces a couple of important problems in the area of trade. The first is our size. We are simply not that big. Our economy is the world's 14th largest; we represent little more than one per cent of global trade. In other words, we don't have the weight to achieve things ourselves or to force others to open up their markets. And experience shows that politely asking other countries to do nice things for you won't get you very far in international trade. Our interests lie overwhelmingly in joining our voice to others in a multilateral approach that benefits everyone.

The second problem we face is the structure of our trade. Although Australia is a significant industrialised country, the composition of our trade, with its heavy reliance on commodities, is more like that of a developing country. That is changing quite fast, but it won't disappear. As a result, Australia was disadvantaged by a global trade system conducted under the General Agreement on Tariffs and Trade (GATT) which concentrated on lowering the barriers for manufactured exports but ignored trade in agriculture. Both these problems explain why we put in so much effort over our years in government into the Uruguay Round negotiations.

As Treasurer at the 1985 meeting of the Organisation for Economic Cooperation and Development (OECD) in Paris, I was in dispute with the Europeans over the inclusion of agriculture in the communiqué ahead of the upcoming Tokyo Summit of the group of the seven largest industrialised countries (the G7). This was the precursor meeting to the Uruguay Round. Willy de Clercq, the European Agriculture Commissioner, and the other Europeans were very agitated, even taking the arguments out into the corridors. At the meeting I pressured the United States to hop off the fence and to join Australia to push for the inclusion of agriculture in the round. Without the support of W. Allen Wallis, Under Secretary of State for Economic Affairs in the State Department, we would not have made it. Agriculture went into the OECD communiqué, the G7 communiqué and then into the round. Our main aim was to finally give our highly efficient and unsubsidised farmers some relief from the combined ravages of European dumping and United States retaliation.

It was subsidies for exports rather than direct payments to farmers that caused Australia most harm because subsidies had snatched away markets which we had often put years of effort into building. Australia was much too small an economy to compete in any subsidisation battle. Although there was no way the Europeans and Americans could continue indefinitely to flush money away like this, by the time economic realities finally struck those two mega-economies, Australian farmers might have been irretrievably damaged. The only answer for Australia was to try to work multilaterally. Successive Australian trade ministers, beginning with John Dawkins, had worked very hard against difficult odds to get Australia a place at the table – an effort in which we succeeded.

The Europeans and Japanese fought us all the way. Europe's infamous Common Agriculture Policy had spawned the legendary butter mountains and wine lakes, as European farmers were paid to produce food that was not needed and could only be dumped overseas through massive subsidies. In Japan, the governing Liberal Democratic Party depended heavily on the votes of inefficient rice farmers working pocket handkerchief-sized plots who were protected from market realities by total bans on the import of rice.

Under Dawkins, Australia formed in August 1986 the Cairns Group of free agriculture producers, a new coalition within the GATT negotiations. This was a personal triumph for Dawkins. The Cairns Group brought together agricultural producers from around the world who shared our interest in forcing agriculture onto the international trade agenda. It cut across the GATT's usual divisions and included a number of Australia's neighbours, like Indonesia, Malaysia and Thailand, as well as Latin American and East European countries. It was a good example of the benefits that Australia gains from international coalition-building.

Enormous energy had been put into the Uruguay Round negotiations by a series of trade ministers after Dawkins – Michael Duffy, Neil Blewett, John Kerin and, finally, Peter Cook, who brought it home. I always admired their dedication to this task. It was a good example of the policy unity and corporate view of the Cabinet: all of us pushing in the one direction. Our ministers received impressive support from officials in the Department of Foreign Affairs and Trade. Some, like Peter Field, were among the world's best.

By the early 1990s the Uruguay Round was close to collapse, mainly due to agriculture. If that had happened, the whole multilateral trading system would have been irrevocably damaged. The final success of the negotiations was partly due to APEC's arrival on the scene, and talk at its Seattle meeting of a wider trade agenda. The Europeans thought we were going to walk past them or, worse, put something in place which was exclusive or, in their terms, discriminatory.

When the end was finally reached on 15 December 1993, negotiators had been at work for a mind-numbing seven years, three months and seven days. It was longer and larger, by far, than any of the eight preceding trade rounds since the establishment of the GATT in 1946. The Final Acts and Schedules covered some 6500 pages.

But the outcome opened up new markets for Australian farmers by cutting agricultural tariffs, domestic support measures and export subsidies elsewhere, a point too-rarely acknowledged for Labor by rural organisations in Australia. Our beef market in Asia was preserved from subsidised European exports, we got better access to the Japanese and Korean beef markets, and wedges were inserted in the doors of the Japanese and Korean rice markets.

The round also brought trade in services under multilateral rules for the first time. This was important because the world's fastest-growing exports were no longer physical things like grains or manufactured goods, but services. New opportunities were opened up for Australia's telecommunications, financial services, insurance, business and professional services. New comprehensive rules were introduced to protect intellectual property and to govern disputes in this area. A new World Trade Organisation was set up with more effective mechanisms for settling trade disputes.

The OECD estimated the increase in global economic activity that would result from the implementation of the Uruguay Round at up to $418 billion in the period to 2002. The Industry Commission's estimate for Australia was a long-term increase in exports of more than $5 billion and an increase in GDP of around $3.7 billion. These sorts of figures are obviously impossible to determine accurately, but they showed the general scale of the economic impact.

Even in the retelling, it is not hard to see why ordinary workers might fail to be swept up in the excitement of multilateral trade negotiations. But the long-term benefits which the GATT negotiators delivered to Australia were real and tangible – and today people have jobs and farmers are more likely to stay on the land because of them. Free trade and lower protection were mocked by some in the Australian media as economic rationalism. Better that, I always said, than economic irrationalism. Australia had plenty of that.

The core of the Australia–United States relationship, however, was not about these trade issues, important as they were, but security. The relationship had been cemented in war. We owe a debt in perpetuity to the US servicemen who helped save Australia. An earlier Labor Prime Minister, John Curtin, had laid the foundations for the alliance in December 1941, and it was formalised after the Second World War in the ANZUS Treaty, which was signed in September 1951. By then the Cold War was up and running.

ANZUS was part of a network of global alliances (including the 1954 South-East Asia Treaty Organisation, SEATO, to which Australia was also party) whose purpose for the United States was to cement the western alliance against communist expansionism. Australia's initial purposes were a different matter. We were more worried about the possibility of a resurgent Japan.

Through every conflict of the post-war years – in Korea, in Vietnam, in the Gulf – Australia had stood with the United States. But what did the ANZUS Treaty mean in 1991, in a post-Cold War world? What did the term 'western alliance' signify when the former communist bloc had disappeared while tensions were growing between the United States and its ally, Japan? What was the role of ANZUS now, and how did it serve Australia?

The foundations for the answer to these important questions had already been laid by Bob Hawke, Bill Hayden and Kim Beazley. In the mid-1980s, they had transformed Australia's defence relationship with the United States (and the ALP's attitude into the bargain) by centring it more in the context of our national interests. As a result of Kim Beazley's fundamental work on the 1987 defence white paper, Australia's defence structure was focussed much more centrally on our national capacity to defend the continent rather than on our participation in Cold War-alliance structures.

Our policy emphasised self-reliance but as part of the alliance. (By self-reliance we meant the capability to defend ourselves against any credible attack on Australia without relying on the combat forces of other countries.) Perhaps the meaning of the phrase 'self-reliance within the context of the alliance' didn't stand up to too much detailed exegesis, but it encapsulated perfectly Labor's view that the alliance served Australia's national interests. The result of this work by Kim and others was that while both Australia and New Zealand faced the same domestic pressures over nuclear weapons, Australia managed to make the US alliance more relevant at the same time New Zealand was walking into the mists of its own isolationism.

However, the transformation of the alliance had taken place during the last highly charged days of the Cold War, when the apocalypse (at least to some) seemed imminent. Now, in the early 1990s, the Cold War was over. The security of the country is the principal responsibility of any government, and it was time to review it in the light of the changes that had taken place in the world.

Two critical questions faced us. First, now that the Cold War was over, how far would the United States continue to be involved in Asia strategically? Rising Philippine nationalism after the people power revolution of 1986 had led to the closure of America's long-held military facilities at Clark Air Base and Subic Bay Naval Base. Did this foreshadow a weakening American security commitment to Asia? Would the United States simply drift further and further towards its own shores, until its forces ended up in San Diego? This was a judgement heavy with consequences for all of us. Second, what were the likely strategic consequences of the region's rapid economic growth? If our neighbours could afford better equipment for their armed forces, would they upgrade? And what did that mean for us? We had always taken for granted a technological edge over our neighbours.

We explored these questions in a Strategic Review that the Defence Minister, Robert Ray, issued in early 1994, which looked at our strategic environment over the next three to five years. Then, later in the year, we looked at longer-term approaches to our security and defence resources in a new white paper, 'Defending Australia', which was released in November.

We concluded that the United States was likely to stick around in this part of the world. It would remain the world's strongest military power by a large margin and would continue to play an important strategic role in Asia. But, as I discussed earlier, this did not seem to us something we should take for granted. The United States would not be prepared to carry the whole security burden in Asia. Countries like ours would have to take responsibility for basic elements of security in the region in our own right. And security depended on many more things than enhanced defence capability. It also required the creation of a more peaceful strategic environment.

We assumed that the strategic and military capacities of the nations of Asia would grow as the countries around us became relatively more prosperous, but this did not mean that our region was becoming less secure. On the contrary, with the exception of a few obvious – and serious – problem areas like the Korean Peninsula and the South China Sea, the region was stable, prosperous and dynamic. (Since 1994, the Asian economic crisis may have slowed the pace of regional defence modernisation, but it has not reversed the trend.)

Robert Ray expressed our conclusions: 'The clear message of this review is that Australia's security – like its economic future – lies in and with our region. This means we must be a participant, not an onlooker, in regional security and other areas.' We were looking, in other words, for security *in* Asia, not security *from* Asia. That meant developing defence relations with the countries of South-East Asia based on the concept of strategic partnership.

We felt no tension between our two objectives of defence self-reliance and greater strategic engagement with the countries around us. As I said at the time, in defence policy, no less than in other areas of Australia's engagement with Asia, our efforts to improve our own capacities as a nation and our ability to operate successfully in the region are two sides of the same coin.

Because our defence focus had been on the defence of Australia, the end of the Cold War had fewer consequences for our force structure than it did for the NATO allies in Europe.

In the white paper, we set defence spending at about two per cent of GDP and, for the first time, we instituted a five-year budget commitment. The key defence-structure decisions we made were to raise a fifth regular battalion for the army and to improve the high-technology capabilities of our military. We announced plans to procure airborne early warning and control aircraft, new command, control, communications and intelligence networks, new helicopters for the ANZAC frigates and new minehunters. (As prime minister, I went out of my way to pick up a further eighteen F1-11s decommissioned by the US Air Force to extend the life of our existing squadron. There was no new fighter-bomber on the drawing boards anywhere.)

We were very conscious that the defence environment we were moving into would require the people of the Australian Defence Force to be better trained, more technologically astute and more self-reliant than ever before.

However much we develop our defence relationships with our regional neighbours, the US alliance must remain important to Australia. It is true that ANZUS's reciprocal defence obligations are more weakly phrased than those in NATO. Each member accepts only the obligation to 'meet the common danger in accordance with its constitutional processes'. But the ultimate strength of a treaty like this rests not on a legal interpretation of the words on paper but on the political willingness of the parties at any given time to make the necessary commitment under it. ANZUS is a vital insurance policy for us, complicating the assessments of any potential enemy that may come along.

It seems highly unlikely that Australia will face such a threat over the next fifteen years, and I think the nature of strategic competition in the world is changing, in any case. But within the bounds of reality, defence policy has to be about things you can't foresee. From the collapse of the Soviet Union to the Iraqi invasion of Kuwait, the international environment provides regular reminders of this.

Much more importantly, however, in the day-to-day management of our security in the post-Cold War world, the ANZUS alliance offers us access to technology, intelligence and training which we could neither afford nor develop on our own. The intelligence magnifies our defence capabilities. In the jargon, it is an important force-multiplier for a rather small country.

Our intelligence cooperation with the United States rests, in part, on the local network of facilities like Pine Gap in the Northern Territory and Nurrungar in South Australia, which plays a part in the US international communications and intelligence system, including the early warning of missile launches. Australia has to face the reality, however, that our strategic importance to the United States is diminishing as technology makes our geographic position less relevant. This gives us all the more reason to be politically relevant in the region in which we live; the security-*in*-Asia point again.

At the end of the day, ANZUS's main, and critical, benefit may simply be this: it provides standing for us to have our voice heard in Washington, especially about developments in this part of the world. In the cacophony of sounds which assail any US administration, that is an important plus.

I made my only visit to Washington as prime minister in September 1993 to meet President Clinton. My arrival coincided by chance with the historic meeting between Middle Eastern political leaders Yitzhak Rabin and Yasser Arafat, understandably of greater interest to the White House press corps than a trouble-free visiting Australian. My meeting with the President was rescheduled as a result. Although I was courteously invited to attend the ceremony, this was not a day for a visiting Australian to interlope, so I declined. But we had the distinctly post-modern experience of sitting in Blair House (the President's guest house), amidst the relics of American history, watching on television the famous handshake taking place just across the road.

My own discussions with the President, senior administration officials and congressional leaders were focussed on trying to make these senior Americans realise what was at stake for them in the Asia-Pacific region. One of the important roles of a visiting prime minister is that of the travelling salesman. Success depends partly on selling skills and partly on the quality of what you've got in your sample bag – and for Australia at that time, it was our ideas.

I was impressed by President Clinton whose policy interests, energy, and copious charm led him to embrace an agenda that was outward-looking and inclusive. This was to be very important for Australia and the region – no more hub and spokes, but an effort to create a community in the Asia-Pacific, the ultimate expression of multilateralism.

I had been particularly impressed by two major speeches the President had given during a visit to Japan and Korea a couple of months earlier. At Waseda University in Japan he had urged the creation of a 'new Pacific community' – resting on a revived partnership between Japan and the United States – a progress towards more open economies and trade, and a continuing support for US treaty alliances and its forward military presence. Speaking as much to a US as a Japanese audience, he argued that Asia's vibrancy and Japan's success were not a threat to the United States. He said the 'Pacific region can and will be a vast source of jobs, of income, of partnerships, of ideas, of growth.'

In Seoul, he had reaffirmed his priorities for the security of the new Pacific community: continued American military commitment to the region; stronger efforts to combat proliferation of weapons of mass destruction; support for democracy and more open societies; and, in a major break from the policies of his predecessor, support for new regional dialogues on common security challenges, including the ASEAN Regional Forum.

He wanted a United States that would play a part in the world, not the defensive, inward-looking country promoted by some of his opponents from both sides of politics. I was very keen to encourage this. I promised I would do all I could to help him bring about a successful inaugural meeting with APEC leaders in Seattle later in the year. I was delighted he was prepared to take up the idea and run with it.

To underline my own personal interest in the relationship, I had sent my Principal Adviser, Don Russell, to Washington as ambassador. Don had been a senior treasury official before joining my staff when I was treasurer, and he was an outstanding economist, with outstanding political skills into the bargain. I'm not sure that the Washington diplomatic corps had ever encountered anyone quite like him before, but in a generally youthful administration of 'policy wonks' he made an immediate mark and proved to be an invaluable hand in both Washington and Canberra as we went about the business of reshaping APEC. (At a lunch he gave me in Jakarta, Bill Clinton said that he thought he should get Don a desk and chair in the East Wing of the White House.)

It had always seemed to me that Australia had difficulty getting the tone of our relationship right with the United States. Australian governments, media and the public alike seemed to swing unpredictably between forelock-tugging obsequiousness on the one hand and adolescent resentment on the other. I hope that during this period we got the balance right.

As was to be seen so often in the following years, it was impossible to write the United States out of the Asia-Pacific equation. Nowhere was this truer than in the management of the complex and potentially dangerous situation in North Asia.

CHAPTER 3

THE NORTHERN TRIBES

The countries of North Asia – China, the world's most populous nation; Japan, one of the world's great economies; Russia, a diminished superpower; the dangerously divided peninsula of Korea; and China's increasingly assertive off-shore province, Taiwan – face one another in a complex mixture of national ambitions, economic interdependence, contested territorial claims and bitter historical resentments. This is where Asia's strategic and economic future will be forged.

In 1991, some of the largest questions of the last years of the twentieth century were directed towards this part of the world. How could China finally be brought into the international community? Would Japan, the world's second-largest economy, continue to be, uniquely in history, a strategic client of the largest? Or would Tokyo lose confidence in its alliance with the United States (the Japan–United States Security Treaty) which offered it nuclear protection while it eschewed the development of any nuclear force of its own? The consequences of such a change would be extremely dangerous for us all. As North Korea, the world's most paranoid and isolated regime, sank steadily towards economic chaos, would it make one last disastrous throw of the nuclear dice? As Taiwan moved out of the iron grip of the Nationalist forces that had fled from the mainland after the Communist Party took power, would it be tempted to abandon the One China policy and flex its independence muscles? And what would be the consequences?

Australia had vital economic and security interests in North Asia, but very limited influence. We needed to find some way of leveraging that influence in ways that would protect our interests and, with luck, make some modest contribution to maintaining the region's equilibrium.

I set out deliberately to try to strengthen our links with our North-Asian neighbours.

CHINA

Standing 260 metres high on the observation deck of the Oriental Pearl television tower in Shanghai you have a 360-degree view of a building site. Hectares of farms on the south side of the Huangpu River have disappeared, giving way to jostling skyscrapers, a new financial centre, luxury hotels and factories. More than any of the statistics trotted out about China – and they are myriad – the view from the Oriental Pearl is a powerful reminder of the implications of bringing 1.2 billion people into the world economy.

I first met Zhu Rongji, now China's Premier and one of the world's most capable leaders, in this city in 1988 when he was Shanghai's mayor and I was the Australian Treasurer. 'Mr Keating,' he said, striding to the window and pointing dramatically to the sprawling city outside, 'I have the worst job in the world.' It turned out that he was after a large Asian Development Bank loan for some fundamental sewerage infrastructure in the city and the Australian Treasurer could help. I was impressed by his straightforward approach and happy to oblige. The sewerage project was approved, and in the years that followed I kept an interested and modestly proprietorial eye on the improving shades of colour of the Huangpu River.

The implications made visible from the Oriental Pearl are not just economic – and they won't just affect China. China's sheer size – the third-largest landmass of any country in the world, with nearly one quarter of all the people on the globe – make its entry into the world, and the impact it will have on regional and international institutions, one of the most important issues facing international policy-makers in the first years of the twenty-first century. The shape and health of the whole international system depend on our getting it right.

Even the knowledge that outside of Shanghai much of China is not experiencing growth on the scale of the Yangtze basin and the eastern seaboard only serves to underline the enormity of the problems facing China and their consequences. Those problems include the different rates of development between the coast and the hinterland; high levels of poverty, with 70 million Chinese, especially in rural areas, continuing to fall below the poverty line; huge problems of unemployment as the government begins to reform calcified state-owned enterprises; and dangerous environmental pollution. Already the air quality in Beijing is five times worse than World Health Organisation (WHO) guidelines, and chronic obstructive-airways disease is responsible for more than a quarter of all deaths in China. Only 14 per cent of people in China's rural areas and 40 per cent in the cities have access to safe drinking water. China has less than one-twentieth of the world's fresh-water resources for a quarter of the world's population. It has to feed its people on less cultivated land per capita than Saudi Arabia. In rural areas, land is being degraded by soil erosion, salination and deforestation. And, all the while, an extra 17 million Chinese have to be housed and fed each year.

By the early 1990s, China's economic reforms were continuing in areas like prices, import liberalisation and the extension of open-city status to many interior centres. Beijing's control over the provinces was becoming more tenuous. Entrepreneurial attitudes were emerging, freer of ideology than in the past.

China's economy grew by nearly 13 per cent in 1992, and more and more of that growth was coming from the burgeoning non-state sector. Some coastal areas were growing at more than 25 per cent. This was unsustainable, and it added to the disparities between the coastal cities and the interior.

The task which China's leaders have before them today is unparalleled in its difficulty and complexity. They have to bring this massive nation into the modern economy, while maintaining social stability and equity between regions. They have to find a way of escaping boom–bust growth cycles and plot a development path that can sustain continuing high growth rates. China has to find jobs for its young people and for those displaced by economic reforms. China's leaders have to deal with increasing pressures for openness. And they must do this while working with fewer political and administrative levers than any Australian government has at its command, and with fiscal and monetary instruments which, despite rapid development, are still rudimentary by the standards of the developed economies.

Of all the political leaders who shaped the twentieth century, I can't think of any – Churchill, Franklin Roosevelt, Hitler, Lenin, Gandhi – who will have as much influence on the twenty-first century as Deng Xiaoping, the leader who drove China's opening-up as a 'socialist market economy'. Deng's wisdom and determination will transform China and shape the rest of the world. China faces many difficulties, but any assessment of its problems has to recognise that its modernisation has brought with it a major improvement of the human condition in all its dimensions, including the expansion of choice and privacy. This is a point the journalism of the warm inner glow refuses to recognise. It is an issue that is directly relevant to China's human rights performance.

I should say something at this point about my attitude towards human rights, because it is an important and contentious aspect of the debate about Australia's relations with Asia.

In April 1992, in my first foreign policy speech as prime minister, I said:

> It is sometimes argued that Australia's democratic institutions and traditions of tolerance and open debate somehow disqualify us from forming successful relationships in Asia. My starting point ... is that Australia's democratic institutions and traditions are non-negotiable. Many things have changed and will change in Australia – our ethnic composition and, with it, our culture, our economic and industrial practices, our world view ... But traditions of democracy, fairness and personal liberty, which we have fought wars to defend, will remain this country's guiding principles.

That was more than a rhetorical statement. I believe that if Australia's foreign policy is to be successful it needs to have public support; and to get public support it must be based on a view of the world that is authentically and distinctively Australian. I have never heard any Australian who thinks about the issue argue that our foreign policy should be – or can be – free of a human rights dimension.

I certainly believe, as the Universal Declaration on Human Rights asserts, that we are born 'free and equal in dignity and rights'. These rights are intrinsic to us as human beings. They are set out most comprehensively in the Universal Declaration, which was proclaimed by the United Nations in 1948, and in two relevant covenants which came into force in 1976 – the International Covenant on Civil and Political Rights and the International Covenant on Economic, Social and Cultural Rights.

When Australians talk about human rights they are usually referring to the civil and political rights of the individual, such as freedom of speech, freedom of peaceful assembly and association, freedom from arbitrary arrest and wrongful imprisonment, and so on. These rights are set out in the International Covenant on Civil and Political Rights. The more collective rights covered by the International Covenant on Economic, Social and Cultural Rights – rights to employment, shelter, education and so on – get less attention here, perhaps because we tend to take them for granted, while Asian and other third-world commentators give them greater prominence.

Our ideas about human rights, or at least the emphasis we place on some of them rather than others, change over time. We interpret them in the light of history and experience. No doubt we will continue to do this. Think, for example, about the relatively recent change in attitudes towards women's rights, or the rights of indigenous peoples.

But acknowledging the existence and importance of human rights is not the hard part for governments (almost every politician in the world will do that), nor is applying them domestically. Australia has done this in most cases through legislation. The difficult step is the operational one of deciding how the protection or promotion of human rights should be turned into foreign policy. Should foreign policy principally be about the protection of human rights, as some of the non-government organisations come close to arguing? Which rights? How do you do it? By declaratory statements? By threats? By inducements? If by threats or inducements, how do you prevent a situation arising in which the most powerful countries decide for themselves what the hierarchy of rights is? In any case, how do the moral relationships and responsibilities of states differ from the moral relationships and responsibilities between individuals?

I believed, as Gareth Evans did, that Australia needed to use its voice on human rights clearly and forthrightly. I tried in my own discussions with other governments – whether about Tibet or Timor or Irian Jaya or political prisoners in Vietnam – to speak clearly and persuasively. But I saw no point in staging pieces of theatre for the evening news or in shadow plays designed to buy off domestic political pressure. I saw little advantage in delivering messages in ways that would be counterproductive to the outcomes we wanted.

The most effective long-term human rights policies are, first, the use of constructive and creative policies (including aid) to help build civil society in individual countries. An example is the funding and support Australia provided the Indonesian Human Rights Commission, which was established in March 1993 and thereafter played a positive role in defending and expanding human rights and helping the political transition.

Second is support for a prosperous, mutually reinforcing international community in which a human rights culture can thrive. An example was the effort the Labor Government, especially Gareth Evans, put into reforming international institutions like the United Nations to make them more responsive to the changing international environment. (Article 28 of the Universal Declaration on Human Rights states: 'Everyone is entitled to a social and international order in which the rights set forth in this Declaration can be fully realised.')

Third are direct leader-to-leader, government-to-government exchanges and lobbying of a constructive kind. Fourth come declaratory statements, where the effect is calculated and judged to be positive.

In the life of the Labor Government between 1983 and 1996, many human rights issues were tackled as part of foreign policy: the setting up of the economic sanctions against South Africa and apartheid in which we figured substantially; the accords on Cambodia bringing an end to the epoch of the killing fields in which human rights were so infamously abused; Australia's groundbreaking work in the establishment of the Chemical Weapons Convention, eliminating a whole category of weapons; support for a just solution in Northern Ireland and Sir Ninian Stephen's appointment in the peace process there; our efforts to support peace in Bougainville and greater autonomy in Timor. And of course, at home, the justice of reconciliation with Australia's Indigenes, the inquiry into black deaths in custody and the stolen children.

However, I did not, and do not, believe that a government's foreign policy should only be about human rights. The nation has other equally valid, and sometimes competing, interests and values that have to be protected and nurtured. For example, we have interests in maintaining national security so Australians do not have to go to war. War is the ultimate trampler of human rights. To avoid war, governments need to establish and work on a national security framework which contains its own reinforcing equilibriums; which comprehends all pressures and understands all nuances. Including, and especially, the need to maintain our influence in scores of different countries at the same time. We have commercial interests, too: developing markets for our farmers and other exporters so Australians have jobs and income. We have interests in creating a cooperative regional and global atmosphere in which we can deal with problems such as the environment that can't be handled nationally.

These other interests are valid and important – and they are interwoven. They are also morally serious. The division which some commentators make between moralism and realism in foreign policy is, I believe, completely facile.

Human rights groups are very judgemental of governments. Some of them believe that those who have to deal with governments of a style different from our own are either tainted or suspect, as if the world and all its governments have to have some stamp of approval by western assessors as to whether they meet western social democratic values. This is, of course, arrogant nonsense. Some among them see themselves as being on a civilising mission, hearing voices they believe most of the rest of us can't hear. After the brutality and excesses of Hitler and Stalin and Pol Pot and Idi Amin and their ilk, an emerging international norm for what constitutes civilised and acceptable behaviour. This is one of the encouraging things that has developed in this brutal century. It is a real measure of human progress and a critical one. But to extrapolate from that a requirement that all governments in all places conform to certain nostrums determined by well-fed small 'l' liberal journalists and activists is extravagant conceit.

Unlike such people, governments have to satisfy a wider mandate entrusted to them by their communities. They rarely have the luxury of being able to focus on a single issue or to choose their neighbours, as Britain and Europe found in the 1930s and '40s.

Britain and the United States were philosophically arraigned against Stalin's totalitarianism and were repulsed by his shocking purges throughout the 1930s. But they dealt with him. Had they dealt with him earlier, the course of Hitler's aggression may have been different. Purger and ideologue Stalin may have been, but the neighbourhood watch put him in the picture at Yalta and at Potsdam.

No doubt human rights groups in today's context would be aghast. But Soviet resistance and counter attack on the Eastern Front drained the Nazis, allowing a Western Front to be opened, securing Europe from Hitler. A human rights advance if ever there was one.

Organisations like Amnesty International or the International Commission of Jurists can, and should, have a single focus. Their work is vital in keeping governments up to the mark and in helping to create a global human rights community. But however unattractive or dissembling it seems to the human rights absolutists, relations between governments involve other interests and often require messy, complex and incomplete trade-offs. Governments have no alternative but to pick a careful path among very different, and sometimes contending issues and to try to remain true to national interests and national ethics while doing it.

In 1991, China was still feeling the effects of the global opprobrium that followed the massacre of protesting students in Tiananmen Square in 1989. I had been in Beijing as treasurer just a week or so before the tragedy. Despite the obvious tension in the city, the air was full of a sense of exhilaration. Even senior officials I met felt that the youthful energy of the students would be a transforming influence on the country. Dialogue between students and government still seemed possible.

But the stand-off between them was not resolved and the tanks rolled into the square with tragic consequences. Deng's age and history would not let him countenance a breakdown in the Communist Party grip on the country. His and the Party's response, I believe, set back China's development, not just in losing the energy and enthusiasm of that great reservoir of youth, but economically as well. Australia, like most western countries, had put its relationships with China on hold as a mark of its concern. But shunning China was no long-term strategy, and by 1991 it was emerging from international isolation, bruised but a little wiser, and transforming itself into a major economic power.

In June 1993 I arrived in Beijing on the first prime ministerial visit from Australia since 1986.

Australia's relationship with China had developed well since Gough Whitlam's Labor Government established diplomatic relations with the People's Republic in 1972. From 1949 onwards, the ALP had consistently supported the establishment of relations with Beijing, but conservative Australian governments through the 1950s and '60s failed to take up the opportunity.

Our trade was growing rapidly – up 29 per cent in 1992 (to over $4 billion). It was dominated by commodity exports on our side, especially iron ore and wool, and clothing, textiles and electronic goods on theirs. Investment was also growing. By 1993 about 540 joint venture contracts had been signed by Australian businesses wanting to get into the Chinese market. By no means were all profitable. China is a tough environment for even the most canny Australian business.

In the other direction, according to Chinese figures, Australia was the largest overseas destination for Chinese foreign investment, the most notable investments being the Channar iron ore mine in Western Australia and the Portland smelter in Victoria.

I believed there were areas in which we could integrate our businesses more closely. As China moved towards an annual steel production target of 100 million tonnes, for example, we could encourage further investment in Australia in the extraction and early processing of steel-making raw materials such as iron ore and metallurgical coal. Opportunities also existed to better integrate Australia's wool production and China's textile industry.

But such ambitions required a more transparent and predictable environment in which we could develop our trade. That was one reason why we wanted to see China a member of GATT and the World Trade Organisation, bound by international rules, and why we wanted it in APEC.

I said at the time that I wanted to do away with any notion of a 'special relationship' with China, a trap into which I felt Australia had fallen in the 1980s. I did not believe in such a category in international relations. It seems to me an unhealthy way of thinking about relationships, and does little more than set them up for inevitable disappointment. I wanted Australia to develop with its neighbours solid, tangible, friendly but businesslike arrangements that had a long-term focus. (With its later claim that, unlike Labor, it was no longer seeking a 'special relationship' with Asia the Coalition Government produced yet another straw man from its large store of such artifacts.)

For China, Australia's physical size as well as our mineral resources were part of the attraction in building up the relationship. My conversations with Chinese leaders often seemed to come back to questions of size. One of the first points President Jiang Zemin made to me when I met him in Beijing in June 1993 was that China and Australia were both large countries. Later, at a meeting in Osaka he pointed out that Australia had only 17 million people but an area three-quarters the size of China with massive mineral wealth. 'China can only look on with envy,' he said. I told him there was no need to do so. Australia would share its bounty with the world around it, including China. There was more than we could ever need. The only caveat was the producer's profit, not a large matter, and a smaller one if Chinese companies continued to take large equity positions in Australian enterprises in their own right.

Jiang's comments were typical comments given, I am sure, to most Australian visitors, but they, and others like them, seemed to reflect something more than a statement of obvious geography, but a strategic sense that Australia's physical size and resource base offered us a long-term role in the region disproportionately greater than our population. In fact, it does. I know this and so, too, do the Chinese, as did Suharto.

My visit to China took place in the lead-up to the decision by the International Olympic Committee on the host city for the 2000 Olympic Games, in which Sydney and Beijing were rival candidates. Although this competition had caused advisers in my office some nervousness over the timing of the visit, I found only a realistic understanding of our competitive bids among the Chinese leadership. As I told the Premier, Li Peng, whatever happened we could both agree that the Games should come to the Asia-Pacific.

Australia and China had been developing a human rights dialogue. We had sent parliamentary human rights delegations to China in July 1991 and November 1992 and I invited Li Peng to send a similar delegation to Australia. We were trying to make it clear that Australia was as open to others as we wanted them to be to us, and that human rights issues should be part of the routine discussion of governments.

Tibet was an important part of this dialogue. I had met the Dalai Lama in Canberra in May 1992. He told me that he was not seeking independence for Tibet but 'a tolerant form of the "one country, two systems" approach'. Over dinner in Beijing I questioned Premier Li so closely about the situation in Tibet that his wife intervened to remind me sharply that the premier had recently had a serious heart problem.

We also had a long discussion about Taiwan. In 1949, after his defeat in the Chinese civil war, Chiang Kai-shek had arrived on the offshore island of Taiwan with two million nationalist troops, imposing iron control on a population that had spent the preceding fifty years under a relatively benign form of Japanese colonialism. Both sides of the Taiwan Straits had insisted that there was only One China, but that it was represented by either Beijing or Taipei.

But with the opening up of China, and especially after President Nixon's recognition of Beijing in 1972, Taipei's diplomatic partners had gradually fallen away. In 1991 Taipei had formally dropped its claim to wield legitimate sovereign authority over all of China, and it was moving quickly towards a democratic system. This meant that political power was passing increasingly to native-born Taiwanese who had a stronger sense of independent identity. The issues were becoming more difficult to handle.

Taiwan was also emerging as an economic powerhouse in its own right in the Asia-Pacific and an important integrator of regional economies, including the mainland's. I pressed for Taiwan's presence at the APEC leaders' meeting, despite the opposition of Beijing, because I did not think we could seriously work towards an Asia-Pacific economic community without having Taiwan in it.

On my visit to China, Li Peng went in detail through the 'one country, two systems' formula, which Deng Xiaoping had developed. He emphasised the flexibility of China's position on all questions regarding Taiwan except that of sovereignty, on which it was immovable.

During that time, I became the first visiting western leader to meet a group of leading Chinese newspaper editors. It was a small sign of a more open society. I also visited the Beijing film studio and met Chen Kaige, the brilliant director of *Yellow Earth* and *Farewell, My Concubine*. I wanted to use that visit in part to underline that Australian engagement with China, and Asia in general, was not simply about economics but also about cultural links. If Australians are to reach a deeper understanding of Asia, no doubt the artists, not businesspeople or politicians, will be the most effective interpreters.

Australia was also developing an informal dialogue, at the level of officials, with China on international defence and security issues. As discussed in chapter 2, in the 1994 defence white paper, 'Defending Australia', we expressed our support for greater strategic dialogue with China and for China's participation in regional security.

China's long-term ambition is to be a great power of strategic importance and global influence. That does not seem an inappropriate goal for the most populous country on earth. I believe that the Chinese Government's claims that it has quite enough trouble managing its own vast economy and society without looking for foreign adventures are persuasive.

The time has long passed when it was possible to ask whether China should be brought into the world community. It is here, and I believe we are much the better for it. China's re-entry into the world will have a strong impact on the international community. China's very size allows it to overshadow its neighbours. And it is quite possible that its path to future prosperity will not be smooth.

For this reason we need to have an overarching strategic sense of what we want from, and with, China. We have made mistakes with China in the past (just as China has made them with the rest of the world) and we must not make them again. China has to be permitted to assume its own leadership responsibilities in the region and the world. We must not speak about engagement with one voice and plan for containment with another. The answer for all of us, I believe, lies in encouraging China into the world community and acknowledging the legitimacy of its position in it, but also in ensuring that the world into which it is moving is self-confident and, in ASEAN's term-of-art, 'resilient'.

The Asia-Pacific will be happier and more peaceful if China's neighbours are self-confident, if our own relationships are in good repair, and if all the region's countries feel that they can help shape their future by participating in active regional institutions. This places a heavy responsibility on China's neighbours themselves to maintain their own relationships and to develop solid, working regional institutions. That again is one of the functions of APEC. It is why the leadership meetings are so important.

Nationalism will replace communism as the glue holding China together, but the form China's nationalism will take is not yet clear. It could develop a self-confident and cooperative nationalism, open to the international community, or, more dangerously, a narrow and defensive form which defines itself against the outside world. In the end, the direction it takes will be heavily shaped by whether the other major powers accept that China has a legitimate global role and provide the international space in which it can begin to exercise leadership.

A confident and successful China will sometimes be difficult for the rest of the world to deal with, but nowhere near as difficult as a weak and divided China.

JAPAN

When I became prime minister I knew Japan better than any other Asian country. I had first visited Tokyo in 1976 as the

Shadow Minister for Minerals and Energy. Over the years I had built up friendships with a number of Japanese businessmen involved in the great resources trade between us, including Mr Inayama, the Chairman of Nippon Steel and the business organisation, the Keidanren. These experiences underlined for me the importance of Australia's contribution to Japan's post-war industrialisation, especially after the far-sighted negotiation of the Australian–Japanese Treaty on Commerce, which was signed in 1957, barely a decade after the war's end.

My experiences of Japan in Opposition, and later as treasurer, had given me some idea of the ways in which our two societies were alike – for example, in a basic social egalitarianism, and our support for the rule of law – and the ways in which we differed, especially Japan's reliance on consensus at so many levels, with all the strengths and weaknesses that brought.

Above all, I was in no doubt of Japan's importance to Australia. Japan represented, by itself, nearly two-thirds of the entire East Asian economy. It was a necessary ingredient of the Asian miracle. It took a quarter of all Australia's exports, and it had been our largest trading partner for more than twenty years.

Japan was important to Australia for more than the great commodity trade in minerals and agriculture. It was a growing market for our manufactures and for our emerging service industries. Three-quarters of a million Japanese tourists visited Australia in 1994, for example, and Japan provided six per cent of our overseas students. This had cultural as well as economic benefits. More than 10,000 Japanese and Australian students have studied in the other country. And Japan was also important to us as a source of investment, like the $700 million we persuaded Toyota to put into a state-of-the-art car manufacturing plant in Victoria.

I used to remind Australian audiences that every time Japan's economy grew by one per cent, it increased its size by an amount equal to New Zealand's GDP. So even a small slice of the

Japanese market in areas like housing or food was valuable to Australian exporters and therefore to Australian jobs. But it wasn't entirely a one-way economic street. Australia was Japan's third-largest source of imports. If oil was excluded, we were its single largest supplier of energy.

In the early 1990s, the Japanese economy and political system were in a state of flux. The 'bubble economy' of the 1980s had burst and the economy was moving into the rolling slump that would last through the rest of the decade. This wasn't a cyclical decline from which it would quickly recover, but a structural one, as significant for markets as the Depression of the 1930s. For the Japanese, it was scarifying. Calls for reform of the Japanese political system were growing, especially from those who argued that the elected politicians should seize back policy-making powers from the hands of the powerful bureaucrats, especially in the Ministry of Finance.

New security problems increased the atmosphere of uncertainty in Japan. The Soviet Union had disappeared as a military threat in the North Pacific, leaving questions about the strategic balance in the region. And after the Gulf War, American pressures were growing, especially from Congress, for Japan to take a greater share of the international security burden (although any signs of genuine Japanese strategic independence caused nervousness in Washington). Japan's post-war constitution defines it as a pacifist state, with its military confined to a self-defence role. In 1992, after intense public debate, the Diet passed a new law permitting Japanese participation in United Nations peacekeeping operations. Its first forces were sent to Cambodia.

The crisis Japan faced was not simply economic, but political as well. The nation's long-standing social contract was coming unstuck. Japan had been governed for most of the years since the Second World War by the Liberal Democratic Party (LDP). The LDP had, in effect, conscripted the whole post-war generation in

Japan to save in order to support Japanese business and its export drive. But the result was poor social infrastructure, rabbit-hutch housing and too few social amenities. Now this system was reaching the end of its life. Demographics alone would ensure that. Almost one-quarter of Japan's population is now aged 65 and above, and its population size will peak in 2005 at 128 million. Unemployment, unknown in Japan before the early 1990s, was steadily edging up and none of the remedies being applied to the economy seemed to work. The emerging younger generation wanted something more. But if they were to get it, Japan had to realise that the best market it had was at home, and to turn itself from a nation of savers into a nation of spenders. It was a hard metamorphosis.

From Australia's point of view, I thought a couple of things were clear. First, we needed Japan, as the world's second-largest economy, to throw its weight behind reform that would open world markets, including its own agricultural market. Japan had preferred to hide itself in the smoke of the battle over agriculture between the United States and Europe, hoping questions about its own rice market could be ignored. The 'managed trade' solutions being sought by the United States – essentially another term for import targets – presented serious risks for Australian exporters. And it was vital for security reasons that these trade disputes between Japan and the United States be kept in perspective and not allowed to corrode the strategic relationship between the two countries. If Japan lost faith in the Japan–United States Security Treaty and sought the protection of its own nuclear forces, the security consequences for Asia and the world would be extremely dangerous.

Second, as the rest of Asia began to grow rapidly from the 1980s onwards, Australia's economic relationship with Japan was changing from a strictly bilateral one, in which they imported Australian inputs for their own manufacturing, to one of shared interest in broader Asian growth. Japan had already moved a quarter of its manufacturing production offshore to East Asia and demand for some of our core export items – materials associated with steel production, for example – had probably peaked. So although the overall importance of Japan to Australia was unlikely to change much, it would become more indirect. This increased our interest in drawing Japan and the rest of the region into co-operative institutions like APEC.

I made the first of my four visits to Japan as prime minister in September 1992, at the height of one of the periodic bursts of trade frenzy between Japan and the United States. The Prime Minister was Kiichi Miyazawa, a distinguished and courteous politician I had known for nearly a decade. We had met as Japanese Finance Minister and Australian Treasurer at countless international meetings.

On this first visit, I wanted to underline Australia's community of interest with Japan in dealing with the uncertain international trading environment. My aim was to tie the Japanese into APEC and energise it as a force for trade liberalisation, or if that was too ambitious a goal, at least to encourage it to move in the right direction. I spoke strongly about the need for Japan to change its total ban on rice imports into tariffs, however high they might initially be.

I also wanted to reinforce the understanding in Japan that its bilateral trade links with Australia were a principal sinew of regional trading arrangements. This led me to make the commitment, discussed in the last chapter, that Australia would not enter any trade arrangement that was directed at Japan.

In return, I sought and received assurances from the Japanese that in any third-party arrangements to diminish the trade imbalances in Japan's favour (or, put more bluntly, if the Americans put the screws on the Japanese for greater access to their market) it would not be at Australia's expense.

At the end of the visit we took the unusual step of issuing a joint statement by the two prime ministers, setting out the way in which Australia and the region were moving.

'More than on any previous occasion,' our embassy reported after the visit, 'the changing nature and focus of Australia were brought home to a wide range of people in the Japanese elites.' That was exactly what I set out to do.

Prime Minister Miyazawa returned the visit to Australia in April 1993. Just two months later, however, a crucial bloc of Liberal Democratic Party members led by Ichiro Ozawa and Tsutomu Hata, the former finance minister, deserted him and he lost a vote of no confidence in the House of Representatives. Ozawa and Hata then formed a new party, Shinseito. Other politicians also abandoned the LDP to set up political shop on their own. Morihiro Hosokawa formed the Japan New Party in order to press for electoral reform.

When Miyazawa was forced by these unprecedented political ructions to call a snap election in July 1993, the 38-year-old LDP Government was defeated and replaced by a coalition of eight opposition parties under Hosokawa's leadership. He became the second of the five men who would be Prime Minister of Japan during my period in office.

By January 1994, Hosokawa had succeeded in partially opening the rice market and in introducing an electoral system which included single-member parliamentary constituencies for the first time. The importance of this reform lay in the hope it offered that Japanese legislators would be forced to become more responsive to the needs and aspirations of voters rather than to the party bosses who determined their fate under the existing system of party lists.

But internal dissension within the coalition over tax changes and a proposed Cabinet reshuffle forced Hosokawa to resign in April 1994. He was replaced, in turn, by Tsutomu Hata at the head of a minority coalition government. Hata only lasted eight weeks in office before the LDP returned to power as part of one of the most unlikely alliances of modern politics in a coalition government with the party which had become Japan's permanent Opposition, the Japan Socialist Party. The Socialists' price for participation in the coalition was the prime ministership for their leader, Tomiichi Murayama.

Japan's political foundations seemed to be moving. The great earthquake centred on Kobe in January 1995, which took 5500 lives, and the poison gas attacks on the Tokyo subway by the Aum Shinrikyo sect a couple of months later, reinforced a sense of fragility and uncertainty for the Japanese people. Local elections in April 1995 resulted in some startling victories for outsiders as governors of Tokyo and Osaka.

In May 1995 I made a protocol-encrusted 'official' visit to Japan. I told Prime Minister Murayama that my reception in Japan by the head of one of the ALP's fraternal parties was one of the truly unexpected events of my political life.

Murayama, with his bushy white eyebrows and avuncular manner, was a man with whom I enjoyed dealing. My visit coincided with the 50th anniversary of the end of the Second World War, and the Prime Minister's genuine compassion and kindness, and the sensitivity with which he handled the issue of the war, were important at this time for the outside world.

Japan was defining an international role for itself, but the people of the Asia-Pacific region, and the Japanese themselves, needed to feel comfortable with that role. The first step towards this had to be a full understanding within Japanese society of the history of the Pacific War. History hangs heavily over Japan's relationships with its neighbours. That history has not been fully faced, so Japan and the countries that were its victims during the Second World War have been prevented from achieving a full psychological settlement for the past as Germany was able to do with the rest of Europe.

Within a few weeks of taking over as prime minister I said at a commemoration service for the Battle of Australia in Darwin on 19 February 1992:

> Among the countries of the region, a common awareness of the history we share will strengthen the basis of trust and cooperation in our relations. In Japan's case, more candid recognition of responsibility for past actions will enhance the wider acceptance and legitimacy of its emerging leadership role in the Asia-Pacific region.

Demands that Japan should apologise for the war always seemed to me to be less important than this 'candid recognition of responsibility'. A great deal of attention was given to the precise nuance of Japanese comments about the war, to weighing expressions of 'deep remorse' against 'heartfelt sorrow'. In August 1994, Murayama issued a strong statement of 'profound remorse' that Japan's 'acts of aggression, colonial rule and the like caused such unbearable suffering and sorrow for so many people'. He went on to say that 'it is imperative for the Japanese to look squarely at our history'. And he announced a ten-year program worth $US1.4 billion to support historical research and exchange programs.

But Murayama was from the minority, and traditionally pacifist, Socialist Party, and he was just one man. Others continued to express different views. Just the year before, the Justice Minister in the Hata Government was forced to resign after claiming that the Rape of Nanking, in which hundreds of thousands of Chinese were slaughtered by Japanese troops in December 1937 and January 1938, was a fabrication.

In any case, what the Japanese said to others did not seem nearly as important to me as what they said to their own young people. I felt the same way about this as I did about Australia's facing up to the truths of our own history and the terrible dispossession of our Indigenous people. I told students at Keio University in Tokyo: 'We ignore history at our peril. I don't believe we can deliver a secure future to our young people without coming to grips with the realities of our past. This is a lesson I think we are learning in other contexts in Australia.'

It was not a matter of distributing guilt but of understanding and acknowledging what human nature is capable of doing, of looking history squarely in the face so we would not repeat it.

On the same visit in 1995, I visited the beautifully maintained Hodogaya War Cemetery, about 30 kilometres from Tokyo. The 280 Australians buried there are just a few of the 17,000 who died at the hands of the Japanese, almost half of them as prisoners. My uncle had been one of them.

I said there:

> We will never forget the evil that was done to our fellow Australians. And we believe Japan should not allow these events to be forgotten. We believe our friendship will be stronger if the truth about these events is known to the Japanese people – and we are pleased the Japanese Government has taken steps to make it known.

But I also paid tribute to those who had the vision and the faith to build a partnership between our countries because they saw that their duty to the dead was a duty to the living.

The commanding officers and around 125 other personnel from HMAS *Hobart* and HMAS *Success* – Australian ships which were then making goodwill visits to Japan – formed an honour guard at this memorial ceremony. It underlined how far we had come in fifty years.

A major objective of my official visit was to reaffirm the success of the relationship we had built up over those fifty years. To mark this, we negotiated a 'Joint Declaration on the Australia–

Japan Partnership', a document which set out in a formal, and quite revealing, way what the nature of the relationship had become. The declaration said:

> Fifty years on from the end of the war, Australia and Japan have a relationship of unprecedented quality. The governments of Australia and Japan reaffirm the importance they place on the close relationship of goodwill and cooperation that they have built up over the post-war years. They pledge to build on that foundation an enduring and steadfast partnership.

In a signal of Japan's attitude towards Australia's position in the region, article six stated:

> As partners in the Asia-Pacific, the two governments are determined to work with other countries in the region in promoting prosperity, reducing tension and enhancing political cooperation. Individually, and in partnership, they will play an important part in achieving these objectives. The Government of Japan welcomes Australia's decision to create its future in the region and reaffirms that Australia is an indispensable partner in regional affairs.

The phrase 'an indispensable partner in regional affairs' came to the heart of what we had been trying to do as a government. It was a very welcome acknowledgement from Asia's most powerful economy that we had an intrinsic role to play in regional affairs.

Japan's future still lies in the balance. It is a country of enormous strengths. In their quiet, unassuming way, the Japanese have built a mighty economy while rebuilding their society. The Japanese say little but stand for much. To write Japan off as a pinnacle of achievement that has been eclipsed is to not understand Japanese unity, determination, and its ceaseless innovation. Japan does have to change, and its political system must change, but I simply believe that it will. It will struggle with the age of information, but it will get there.

The reaction to the Kobe earthquake in January 1995 showed how tough, resilient and dignified the Japanese people are in their response to adversity. Japan's greatest asset at a time of challenge and change is its social cohesion. But in a globalised world, Japan cannot afford to wait for a broad national consensus to form down to the last elderly fisherman in Hokkaido. Unless real progress is made towards opening up its economy to new competitive forces and deregulating it, I fear the current loss of confidence inside Japan will be needlessly prolonged.

The health of the international system as a whole requires the world's second-largest economy to play a more substantial role in the world. Australia has supported, and should support, Japan in living up to its economic significance.

KOREA

Many Australians knew Korea essentially from the experience of the civil war. Seventeen thousand Australians served in Korea with the United Nations forces between 1950 and 1953 and more than three hundred had died there. The result of the inconclusive outcome is a peninsula still dangerously divided forty years after a cease-fire had been proclaimed.

By the early 1990s, almost without either side being aware of it, we found ourselves with increasingly close economic links. By 1992 our two-way trade was over $5 billion. South Korea was our fourth-largest export market, and just three years later it would surpass the United States to become our second-largest.

This had come about as a result of South Korea's economic growth, one of the most impressive elements in the entire Asian miracle. After fifty years of Japanese colonialism and a devastating civil war, the economy of South Korea in the early 1960s was poor and agrarian in nature. Thirty years later it had comprehensively outpaced the economy of the communist North, and it would soon receive the ultimate accolade of developed-country status – membership of the Organisation for Economic Cooperation and Development (OECD).

The political environment in the South was also changing in the early 1990s. In December 1992, Kim Young Sam, a long-time democratic opponent of the successive military regimes that had governed the country, had been elected as the Republic of Korea's first democratic president for thirty years.

At the same time, the end of the Cold War and the South's spectacular economic growth had made the relationship between the North and the South even more fragile. The isolated and paranoid regime in Pyongyang depended on the 'southern threat' to maintain control.

Just forty kilometres north-west of Seoul, the Demilitarised Zone (DMZ) stretches across the peninsula and roughly represents the positions held by the opposing United Nations and combined North Korean and Chinese forces when the war ground to a halt. It is a strip of land about four kilometres wide. North Korea – the Democratic Peoples' Republic of Korea – is probably the world's least understood, and therefore most unpredictable, regime. By the early 1990s it had comprehensively lost the economic competition with the South. The aging dictator, Kim Il Sung, who died in June 1994, was preparing to hand over power to his son, Kim Jong Il. With the loss of Moscow's aid after the fall of the Soviet Union, the economy was in ruins, with malnutrition, and even starvation, rife. The North's other principal ally, China, normalised relations with Seoul in August 1992, and trade was growing strongly. North Korea had defaulted on its loans to the West and its credit rating was among the world's worst. Meanwhile, 20 per cent of its economy was being spent on defence.

The issue of the North Korean nuclear program was becoming increasingly worrying. The signs that Pyongyang was trying to develop nuclear warheads were clear from intelligence, and it already had a delivery system – the Nodong rocket – capable of covering South Korea and parts of Japan and China. It was developing this technology fast and sharing its secrets with other of the world's least attractive regimes.

In 1993, Pyongyang refused to permit inspectors from the International Atomic Energy Agency to examine its nuclear holdings as it was required to do under the Nuclear Non-Proliferation Treaty (NPT), and announced it was withdrawing from the NPT. Presumably this was because the inspection would have identified discrepancies caused by the diversion of plutonium to weapons manufacture.

The security implications of the North's behaviour were very serious. A nuclear-armed North Korea would upset peninsular, regional and global security. Not only was it possible that a regime as desperate and possibly irrational as Pyongyang might decide to gamble on a nuclear strike against the South, but Japan and China would feel threatened by its nuclear weapons and would want to respond. If Japan's faith in the US nuclear umbrella weakened, the pressure to develop its own nuclear program, or (as has since happened) to seek anti-missile defence technology, would grow greater, and this would further complicate regional security.

The Americans, on whose military commitment to the South the security of the peninsula rested, were trying to address the danger. They persuaded the North to suspend its withdrawal from the NPT, and after a series of difficult diplomatic confrontations, to sign an 'agreed framework' in October 1994. Under this agreement, North Korea agreed to freeze and eventually dismantle its existing nuclear program and return to full compliance with its international nuclear obligations, in return for the construction of two light-water reactors (which had only minimal weapons application) and the provision of heavy fuel oil which would replace its existing reactors and meet its electricity needs. The Republic of Korea and Japan were the main external donors to the special fund established to help do this – the Korean Peninsula Energy Development Organisation (KEDO). But because the security stakes were so high for all of us, Australia also agreed to make a substantial contribution.

Korea will eventually be reunified, and on the South's terms, but the North can still do a lot of damage on the way there. It is the manner of Korea's inevitable reunification – that is, whether through negotiation or the collapse of the North in chaos or, in the worst case, as a result of military conflict – which is the most significant issue. The management of this endgame will require skill and finesse on all sides.

I visited South Korea in June 1993. I wanted to give our bilateral relationship greater breadth to match its economic strength. The best symbol of that economic strength, and of South Korea's astonishing growth, was the Pohang Iron and Steel Company, POSCO, which I included as part of my visit. In just twenty-five years POSCO had become the second-largest steel company in the world, and Australia had been there from the beginning. BHP had assisted with an independent assessment of the original feasibility study for the company, and Australia now supplied half the plant's iron ore and coal requirements. In the preceding year, these exports had been worth around $1 billion to us, making POSCO the single largest customer for Australian goods anywhere in the world.

That trade would continue to be valuable for us, but we also wanted South Korea to see Australia as a source of technology-oriented goods and services. I told President Kim Young Sam that South Korea and Australia were 'a natural fit' and that we wanted to do more with them, especially in the areas of industrialisation of research and development, and investment. It was becoming clear globally that trade no longer followed the flag, as the old saying had it. It followed investment. We were keen to improve our performance there.

Kim and I were able to take this further when he visited Australia in November 1994. During the year since I had been in Seoul, our bilateral trade had grown by another 16 per cent, but investment was still lagging. We agreed to establish a joint fund worth $1 million to help industrial technology projects in areas like information and clean energy. We also arranged a new science-and-technology agreement as another way of broadening the relationship. Nor did we forget the circumstances under which the modern relationship had been forged. We each agreed to contribute to the cost of a Korean War memorial to be built on ANZAC Parade, the ceremonial road in Canberra leading to Australia's National War Memorial.

These visits and my other discussions with Korean visitors underlined for me how many things we had in common. Our economies were roughly the same size, although its population of 44 million was more than double ours. As with Japan, China and Taiwan, South Korea's trade with Australia had a strategic character. Australia provided the raw material inputs for Korean industry: the coal, alumina, iron ore, non-ferrous metals, uranium, wool and cotton. This complementarity did not mean it was always an easy economic relationship. We faced export barriers to our beef, dairy and horticultural products. They complained about our anti-dumping measures. Korean thinking – though not at the most senior levels – contained a strong streak of North Asian mercantilism. We heard constant complaints about our $2 billion trade surplus, together with hints that it was our responsibility to reduce it. I pointed out that Australia's trade deficit with the United States helped to fund Korea's much larger trade surplus with the Americans.

We had something of a national style in common with the Koreans, too; a certain directness, sometimes to the point of bluntness. Those Australians who believed all Asian cultures were characterised by the reserve and obliqueness of Java or Japan had never met a Korean.

As Australia looked out into the region, we found that we shared important foreign policy interests with South Korea. We each had an important alliance relationship with the United States, and we wanted to keep the Americans engaged on this side of the Pacific. We could see the value of trying to get all the regional great powers – the United States, Japan and China – involved in a multilateral framework.

These were all reasons why South Korea was an important ally of ours in developing APEC. Bob Hawke had launched the idea of APEC in Seoul, and in 1991 Korea hosted the third APEC ministerial meeting at which APEC's founding principles were formulated.

Soon after I became prime minister a very senior Japanese politician had asked me what I thought of the Chinese leaders, and whether I thought China would attack Japan. This very experienced leader had never met his Chinese counterparts. Given the stakes in North Asia, these were worrying questions to hear. It was in large part because of the contribution APEC could make to resolving all the contending pressures in that part of the region that I was now trying to take APEC from a discursive, purely economic body represented by trade and foreign ministers to something which had trans-Pacific political might.

CHAPTER 4

BUILDING AN ASIA-PACIFIC COMMUNITY

The idea that a broader institutional framework was needed in the Asia-Pacific had been around long before APEC. In the early 1970s, Gough Whitlam had spoken about the idea of a comprehensive regional organisation, and other, now-forgotten or little known acronyms like ASPAC, PAFTAD, PECC and PBEC lay scattered around the regional landscape.

The most effective of the existing regional organisations, the Association of South-East Asian Nations (ASEAN) had been operating for more than twenty years and it had proved its success, at least in political terms. But it was confined to South-East Asia. Other bodies, like the United Nations Economic and Social Commission for Asia and the Pacific (ESCAP), were too broad in their geographic coverage and too unfocussed in their aims to be effective. An important step forward had been taken in January 1989 when Bob Hawke proposed in a speech during an official visit to South Korea that a new Asia-Pacific economic grouping should be established.

The importance and originality of the Asia-Pacific Economic Cooperation forum – APEC – lay not so much in its function, which was trade and economic cooperation, as in its scope. It covered the rapidly developing economies of East Asia (Japan, Korea, the three Chinese economies – that is, China itself, Hong

Kong, and Taiwan – and the ASEAN countries – Indonesia, Thailand, the Philippines, Malaysia, Singapore and Brunei), Australia and New Zealand and the two North American economies of the United States and Canada. In other words, it was, if not from conception, then from shortly afterwards, a trans-Pacific organisation, which made it less likely that the United States would turn inwards, economically and politically, to its own hemisphere, as the new North American Free Trade Agreement (NAFTA) gave it the potential to do. APEC gave the smaller countries of the Asia-Pacific a say in the nature of the trading arrangements and in its strategic organisation.

By November 1989, after some skilful Australian diplomacy involving, among others, Richard Woolcott and John Bowan, the first APEC ministerial meeting was held in Canberra. The timing was right for the establishment of a regional organisation like this. The twentieth century had been dominated by global struggles. Imperialism, Marxism's claims for world revolution, two world wars, and the ideological battle of the Cold War had all taught us to think about the world and its problems in essentially global terms.

During the Cold War, countries in this part of the world had seldom identified themselves principally by region. The Non-Aligned Movement, or the communist movement (Beijing or Moscow branch) or, in some cases like Australia's, the British Commonwealth were the prime external groupings with which we associated ourselves.

That was now changing. One advantage of the great spurt of economic growth in Asia from the mid-1980s onwards had been the growing consciousness of Asia as a region. If an economic miracle was happening in Asia, everyone wanted to be Asian.

The economic models adopted by each of the East Asian countries had been very different. Even two such culturally and geographically similar economies as Hong Kong and Singapore had taken very individual paths to growth; the first a model of laissez faire entrepreneurship, the second shaped by the strong engagement of government in most areas of the economy and society. But what was common to all the economic paths – and what set this region apart from much of the rest of the developing world – was that the regional governments had taken enthusiastic advantage of the movement towards economic globalisation. East Asian economies had worked hard to integrate themselves with the world. The disadvantages of such integration, when not properly managed, would surface later.

For Australia, one of the most important consequences of globalisation, was the way it brought developing countries into the world economy in a different and more dynamic way. Over the decade from the mid-1980s to the mid-1990s, the trade of the developing countries grew as fast as for the developed countries as a percentage of their economies, and their share of global foreign direct investment rose to two-fifths of the total.

But it was the East Asian economies that grew fastest and were most integrated into the global economy. In the first half of the 1990s, for example, East Asia accounted for almost one-third of the world's total growth of imports. By 1994, the import market of the three Chinese economies, Korea and the ASEAN countries was two-and-a-half times that of Japan and marginally larger than that of the United States. On all the major indicators of integration with the global economy – trade ratios, foreign direct investment, and share of manufactures in exports – East Asia came in well ahead of other regions.

This was an important factor in APEC's development because globalisation also increased the incentives for governments to work more closely together. Businesses were increasingly structured across different countries and started demanding the simplification and harmonisation of the various national regulations and standards which increased their costs as they shuttled product from country to country. Governments encountered new problems. How would they deal with transfer pricing by companies seeking to lower their tax obligations? Or with the consequences for their tax receipts as competition for foreign direct investment became more intense? These issues, too, could best be dealt with through some form of multilateral cooperation.

As we have seen, the end of the Cold War gave a new boost to regional cooperation. Local disputes in Central America or Afghanistan or Angola no longer constituted a metaphor for a wider global and ideological struggle. They could be addressed on their own terms. The potential membership of regional institutions expanded. Vietnam could join ASEAN and all three Chinese economies were able to participate in APEC, an outcome that would have been impossible during the Cold War.

Regional organisations already existed, of course, but they had usually been subordinated to the broader global competition. The multilateral defence pacts of the 1950s like SEATO and CENTO were an example; institutions like the Organisation of American States were designed in part to strengthen regional capacities against Communist threat. Even the development of regionalism in Europe through the European Economic Community (EEC) was driven by the need to strengthen Western Europe against the Soviet threat (as well as by the desire to contain Germany within a broader structure).

Regionalism's cause was also helped by the rapid growth in the number of members of global organisations. With more than 180 members, the sheer scale of the United Nations and other large multilateral bodies meant that dialogue and debate inside them tended to fall into the hands of formal negotiating groups, or those relatively few countries with the human and economic resources to commit to the task.

Smaller, more flexible regional organisations could address

the growing number of issues that were too large for the nation-state to handle and too small for global action, and which often required a quick response.

For all these reasons I believed that we had an unprecedented opportunity to generate new ideas, subsume old enmities, and establish new ways of doing things within a regional framework. But only if we knew what we wanted and where we were heading.

Australia had economic, political and strategic interests at stake. We had taken the hard decisions ourselves on opening up our own markets to competition. We hadn't cut tariffs for the benefit of others but because we knew it was necessary to give Australia a sustainable economic future. But now it had been done, we needed to find ways of keeping the pressure on our neighbours to open up their markets further. There was only up-side for Australia here and, we believed, for our neighbours as well.

We also faced an uncertain future with the Uruguay Round of global trade negotiations, which had dragged on for six years at that stage. It was by no means clear that we would get a successful outcome. The Europeans were completely intransigent on agriculture, which was vital to Australia. We had to have something else up our sleeve in case the global system started fracturing. A grouping which included our largest and fastest-growing export markets served the purpose.

Politically, we also needed to find a multilateral framework that would enable us to expand our dialogue with our neighbours. And, as I have discussed, strategically, we needed to find ways of strengthening communications and contact across the Pacific, encouraging an outward-looking United States with a foot in both the Atlantic and Pacific oceans and a healthy triangular relationship between China, Japan and the United States.

All my thinking about these various interests kept leading me back to APEC. By early 1992, APEC had been in formal existence for a couple of years. It was developing steadily. Its structure was based on annual meetings of foreign and trade ministers, supported by senior officials, and a series of working groups covering different industry areas. It was making slow, modest progress. By the time I became prime minister it had become a familiar, useful, but not yet particularly high-profile, part of the regional scene. Its principal virtue was that it had defined its own constituency. But in its present form it would not have been able to fulfil the hopes I had for it.

Within a couple of weeks of becoming prime minister I had hosted the presidential visit of George Bush. I had been determined to put to him some structural thinking about Australia and the region that went beyond the bromides of praise for the bilateral relationship and the specifics of our various trade disputes. As I recounted in chapter 2, I decided to float with him the idea of restructuring APEC; of changing it to a more political and powerful organisation represented at head-of-government level.

I knew that the involvement of heads of government would provide the locomotive to drive a more ambitious APEC agenda. But in addition there were compelling strategic reasons for such a gathering. This was the only significant part of the world in which no structure existed to involve heads of government in regular dialogue. European, African, Latin American, South Pacific leaders met routinely. Regular summits were held by leaders of the Atlantic alliance. But in the Asia-Pacific, we stared at each other across a void, often suspiciously. The Prime Minister of Australia was more likely to have a close personal relationship with the Prime Minister of Zimbabwe or Jamaica than the President of Indonesia or Korea, simply because they met regularly at Commonwealth Heads-of-Government Meetings. This was a real impediment for Australia, but when it meant that the President of the United States and the President of China, or the Prime Minister of Japan and the President of Korea had no chance to meet outside the very irregular, formal pageantry of bilateral visits, I regarded it as disastrous.

It was not that I was besotted by the idea of personal diplomacy. But we were missing out on both the personal knowledge of other leaders, which would improve our capacity to make judgements about what drove them, and the easy familiarity that made it easier to pick up a telephone to resolve a problem or avoid a misunderstanding. We were also missing the opportunity to learn from one another's experiences.

I had received a non-committal response to my proposal from President Bush at the time, though his National Security Adviser, General Brent Scowcroft, seemed quite taken with it. The issue was left open and I said I would write to him about it. On 3 April 1992 I did just this, recalling our discussions in Canberra and setting out the benefits which I believed a pattern of regional meetings of heads of government would provide for the United States and the rest of the region. I acknowledged that such meetings were no panacea for regional problems, but I said I believed their absence would have consequences for us all over time. I said I wanted to put the idea on the regional agenda to encourage further discussion. I was looking at this stage for his reaction or advice.

I wrote in similar terms to the Prime Minister of Japan, Miyazawa and President Suharto of Indonesia. We chose these leaders because if we encountered outright hostility from Japan, or from Indonesia as the largest ASEAN country, it would mean that we faced an uphill task.

I floated the idea of the leaders' meetings publicly in my first foreign policy speech on 7 April 1992:

> Another way of promoting cooperation in the Asia-Pacific region would be to establish a process of periodic heads-of-government meetings, say every two or three years. The absence of such a process is conspicuous in a region whose

weight in global affairs is steadily increasing. Various formulas for participation are possible, but I personally would find most attractive a mechanism based on APEC membership, because it embraces the most important economic linkages throughout East Asia and across the Pacific.

President Bush wrote back to me on 29 April. It was a warm letter, but reading between the lines it offered only a glimmer of hope. It read pretty much as though the views of cautious officials had prevailed. The basic message was that the United States ought to stand well back from the proposal but that if I could get any interest going with other leaders the United States would be prepared to hear back from me.

Over the next few months I wrote to the other APEC heads of government and the replies started to drift back in. They were mostly politely favourable, although cautious about whether we could bring it off.

An obvious problem from the start was the political dilemma of how you could have a meeting like this involving China, Taiwan and Hong Kong without coming up against the sensitive problem of sovereignty. The agreement on the participation of Chinese Taipei and Hong Kong in APEC rested on the basis that this was a meeting of economies, not countries. China would certainly refuse to sit down with the Taiwanese President at a heads-of-government meeting because of the implications that would have for China's sovereignty over Taiwan.

Gareth Evans canvassed our proposal at an ASEAN meeting in August 1992 and received encouraging responses. But he was worried about the 'conceptual incompatibility' between using APEC as the basis for a heads-of-government meeting and the sovereignty issue involved in the three Chinas. I was not convinced it couldn't be resolved. I told him I thought there was nothing wrong with working over time towards an outcome where China and other sovereign countries participated at head-of-government level and Taiwan was represented by an economic minister. Gareth doubted this compromise would fly. He thought it would be best to work towards some sort of stand-alone meeting with a looser association with APEC.

For me, however, APEC was central to the proposal. I wanted to use the heads-of-government meetings to give it more political and institutional weight. I thought free-standing regional heads-of-government meetings would not necessarily lead anywhere. In any case, I did not want to compromise before we even began by watering down the connection with APEC. This was an idea to develop over time. And Gareth set to work on it.

I discussed the dilemma a month after my conversation with Gareth with the Prime Minister of Singapore, Goh Chok Tong, who was an early and consistent supporter of the proposal. I said I thought the problem would eventually be resolved. I believed Taiwan, which was an important part of the regional economy, should be allowed to participate, but that it would eventually agree to representation by someone other than its president, and that China would also agree to attend.

From the beginning we assumed that the most likely first date for such a meeting would be 1994 – when Indonesia was due to take over as Chair of APEC, a position that rotated each year – and that subsequent meetings would be held at two- or three-year intervals.

In Singapore in September Senior Minister Lee Kuan Yew, who had been part of the South-East Asian scene longer than anyone, gave me excellent advice. He told me that if President Suharto agreed to the meeting, in his opinion it would be on, but that Suharto was cautious and not comfortable with the spotlight. He was more comfortable with bilateral than multilateral arrangements and would only want to meet multilaterally if a substantial outcome could be assured.

By the beginning of 1993 the government's trade agenda was well-developed, but we wanted to push it forward again, and APEC was to be its booster engine.

While we knew that the global 'everyone in' approach of the General Agreement on Tariffs and Trade (GATT) and its Uruguay Round of negotiations could deliver the best outcome for Australia, and economic modelling work confirmed it, we thought we could improve on global benchmarks by reaching our own agreements in the Asia-Pacific. Agreements that would be good for the region, but would also strengthen the global system. What we were looking at was what we called a GATT-plus arrangement.

In February 1993, I made the scope of our aims explicit. I said:

> We should continue to rely on GATT outcomes to move us towards greater integration in the production of goods, while supplementing those outcomes with regional agreements in some sectors. At the same time, we can act regionally to remove administrative, legal, bureaucratic and infrastructural impediments to trade and investment.
>
> In other words, we should seek as our goal an integrated market which includes Australia and New Zealand, the ASEAN countries, the three Chinese economies, Korea, Japan and North America – a market of two billion people producing half the world's output, bound together with harmonised trade rules, harmonised investment rules, harmonised standards and certification, and an agreed way of settling disputes between members.
>
> It would be a market where trade between its members already accounts for two-thirds of their own trade and where total exports of the region already account for 40 per cent of world exports.

I said this should be an integrated regional market that had a place for inner markets like the Australia–New Zealand Closer Economic Relations (CER) agreement and the ASEAN and North American free-trade areas, but which worked towards 'commonality and minimum restriction in all the areas in which it could sensibly be advanced'.

I pointed to particular areas on which we should work over the next few years – harmonised standards for motor vehicles, telecommunications equipment and pharmaceuticals, harmonisation or mutual recognition of food standards, consumer electronics and labelling, and mutual recognition of professional and trade qualifications.

I proposed that we should discuss a framework agreement which would set our goal of establishing an 'open economic association in the Asia-Pacific region, in which its economies were by degrees integrated to create the world's most dynamic zone of production'.

That ought to provide some sort of an agenda for an APEC leaders' meeting, I thought. We could never have been accused of not being ambitious.

Luck was running with us in a number of ways, but nowhere more than in the election of President Clinton in November 1992. I wrote to the incoming president a letter that was more than the usual formal congratulations. I said, in effect, 'Have I got an idea for you!'

The Bush administration had been quietly supportive of the idea of a regional heads-of-government meeting, but it had not claimed ownership in any direct way. So the proposal became a fresh idea for an incoming administration looking to make its mark in foreign policy. The timing could not have been better, in that, under normal rotational arrangements, the United States would be the chair of APEC in 1993. Whatever intrinsic value the idea of leaders' meetings may have had, the weight of the

United States was essential to getting it operating and overcoming the natural reluctance of some members to participate.

Meanwhile, as I continued to make the argument as persuasively as I could in my selling trips around the region, others were becoming more attracted to the proposal. During a visit to Canberra in April 1993, Prime Minister Miyazawa of Japan discussed the question of 'your baby'. He said he was 'more and more sold on the idea' of an APEC leaders' meeting. Japan wanted a multilateral body to meet and discuss affairs with its Asian interlocutors, especially China. It already had bilateral arrangements with the United States but not a thing with anyone in North Asia.

I had discussed the idea during visits to South Korea and China in June. President Kim Young Sam had expressed support, and I had lengthy conversations with the Chinese Premier, Li Peng and the Vice-Premier, Qian Qichen. The Premier had insisted to me that it would be 'inappropriate' for Taiwan and Hong Kong to participate in the leaders' meeting, but he conceded that this was China's present policy and that the Australian and Chinese foreign ministers could look at it further. In response, I pointed to all the advantages APEC offered China. APEC needed to include Hong Kong and Taiwan, I argued, if it was to remain fully representative of the economies of the Asia-Pacific region. Separating the leaders' meeting from APEC would be the beginning of the end for APEC. Later in the visit, Vice-Premier Zhu Rongji came back to the subject in my meeting with him. This seemed to be another indication of Chinese flexibility.

It was reasonably clear by now that only the Malaysian Prime Minister, Dr Mahathir, would have any real problems with the proposal. This was because he was pursuing an alternative model for regional cooperation, an East Asian Economic Group (EAEG), which would comprise only the countries of East Asia, under the general leadership of Japan. Australia and New Zealand were pointedly excluded from his formulation. So, too, was the United States.

By late June 1993, the US Administration had formally decided to have a go at the proposal. President Clinton let me know that he would be prepared to issue a formal invitation to APEC leaders following the scheduled ministerial meeting in Seattle in November, provided there were enough positive responses. My job was to get as many as possible, especially President Suharto and the Chinese, to say yes. The United States sent its embassies out to canvass views.

I wrote formally to President Clinton on 1 July expressing my personal support, recounting my conversations with regional leaders and offering to push as hard as I could.

I also wrote to President Suharto, urging him to respond positively. I knew that Indonesia's response would be critical. Its attitude would be decisive within ASEAN and, as it was APEC's incoming Chair, any follow-up work would fall on its shoulders. In my letter I addressed directly the concern Suharto and his colleagues had that APEC might detract from ASEAN's standing. I said I did not believe that would be the case. I said I hoped that the meeting in Seattle could be followed up the next year with a meeting in Jakarta. The Americans were portraying the meeting only as a one-off exercise, but I knew that we would only get the benefit from it if it were to become regular, and that meant keeping Indonesia interested. The natural drumbeat would be for a second, follow-up leaders' meeting to be held in Indonesia. But the first task was to have Suharto agree to attend Seattle.

One of my concerns throughout this period was to do what I could to help keep relations between the United States and Indonesia on an even footing. Pressures in the bilateral relationship were continuing to emerge over issues like the link between Indonesia's performance on workers' rights and a renewal of the preferential trade arrangements between the two countries, and over congressional threats to restrict arms sales because of human rights concerns. Indonesia was becoming increasingly less relevant to Washington, a fact that would be brought home clearly a couple of years later during the Asian economic crisis.

I urged the importance of Indonesia on President Clinton and on congressional leaders during a visit to Washington in September 1993. At the joint press conference after our meeting, the President described Indonesia as 'one of the most underestimated countries in the world'. Speaking mainly about Americans, I suspect, he said 'most people have no idea how big it is ... that it is a vast, enormous, potential partner in a global economy'.

At the end of July, ASEAN ministers had met in Singapore and decided to try to resolve the complication of Malaysia's proposal for an East Asian Economic Group by supporting it, but only as a caucus within APEC. The EAEG became an EAEC. This was an obvious improvement and, in part, a face-saving device for Malaysia, but it did not resolve the key question: whether it would weaken APEC by turning it into a more adversarial forum, in which East Asia would range itself against North America.

A number of our Asian friends were asking now if Australia might join such a grouping, if this could be sorted out. Japan, in particular, was obviously uncomfortable about being squeezed between Malaysia and Australia, and about the United States's attitude towards the group. I cabled Gareth Evans in Singapore, expressing my agreement with the line he had been taking there:

> Of its essence, and certainly at this stage, the EAEC is a racially based concept which has the added danger of excluding the United States, the largest customer of most of the EAEC constituency. Were the EAEC to succeed as its author proposes – that is, with Japan and others enthusiastically embracing it – the decision of whether we should join it

or deal with its constituents bilaterally is one we should decide only on very mature reflection. Leaving the United States institutionally disconnected from the Western Pacific with an important ally (Australia) joining the EAEC to its exclusion, is not a policy we should embrace without a great deal of forethought.

I passed this message on to the Japanese Ambassador personally.

In September, after my own visit to Washington, President Clinton wrote again to other APEC members setting out his hopes for the leaders' meetings. The name had sensibly been changed now from a 'heads-of-government meeting' to an 'APEC leaders' economic meeting', which was less threatening and helped to overcome the sovereignty sensitivities. He began his letter to me gracefully, by saying: 'Following our discussions in Washington, I wanted to give you credit again for your idea of holding an informal meeting of APEC leaders.' He said the goal was 'to share informally perspectives on the region's economic future in a quiet, secluded setting. Together we can examine ways to promote sustained growth and address issues of global concern. Just as important, I want the opportunity for all of us to develop the personal relationships that are essential for our ability to work together cooperatively.' He ended by kindly acknowledging that 'Australia deserves great credit for its contributions to the emerging structures that will chart the future of the Asia-Pacific region in the post-Cold War era.'

By this stage it was clear that the meeting would go ahead, and that was an important start. But there was now another pressing issue. What would be the outcome? What would we discuss?

I was travelling to Cyprus in October to attend the Commonwealth Heads-of-Government Meeting (where I had another useful discussion with the Prime Minister of Singapore, Goh

Chok Tong, about the tactics for the APEC meeting). I decided that I would travel back via Jakarta to reinforce my representations to President Suharto. I had one-and-three-quarter hours with him, almost all the time spent discussing APEC. It was clear that Suharto was well-disposed towards the organisation – indeed he was probably slightly ahead of his own foreign ministry on the matter. He saw its potential for involving the large regional countries and the smaller ones constructively in the development of the regional economy and for constraining raw American, Japanese, and Chinese economic power within a multilateral framework. Suharto was a shy and introspective character, but he could think and he would take risks.

I had sought and received from Bill Clinton during my visit to Washington the previous month an assurance that if there was to be a further APEC leaders' meeting in Jakarta the following year, he would attend. This was important for any ongoing arrangement. After some gentle pressure, Suharto agreed that if a consensus in favour of another meeting emerged in Seattle, he would be prepared to issue the invitations to leaders to come to Jakarta. He was clearly concerned about Malaysia, however. By this time, Dr Mahathir had advised the United States that he would not attend the Seattle meeting. I assured Suharto that Australia would be sensitive to this issue, but that the Malaysian Government was no more entitled to veto APEC's development than was France to stand in the way of an outcome to the Uruguay Round. I told him no road map existed for what we wanted to do – precedent and official advice would not be sufficient to guide us in what lay ahead.

Back in Canberra, as the meeting got closer, we were trying our hands at what a leaders' statement might look like and sharing the results with the Americans, especially Sandra Kristoff who, in various policy positions dealing with East Asia on the National Security Council staff and in the State Department during this period, was a formidable advocate for APEC and for United States' interests in it. Our excellent embassy staff in Washington, with Don Russell, the Ambassador, were actively involved in prodding and pressing the various parts of the sprawling American system.

At the APEC ministerial meeting in 1992, an Eminent Persons Group had been commissioned to prepare a report about the future that would challenge the APEC economies. It was an excellent idea. The group was chaired by the indefatigable Fred Bergsten, the distinguished American trade economist.

The Foreign Affairs and Trade department's recommendation for Australia's nominee was a well-known academic with a notable record of achievement in the area of regional trade. When I turned the nomination down and asked the former New South Wales premier and now businessman, Neville Wran, to take on the job I was met with surprise and a measure of umbrage. What would happen, was the unspoken subtext among some officials, if trade policy became tainted with politics and politicians?

But my reasons were very clear. I was sure APEC was moving into a new phase of its existence and that the critical thing was not so much to get the economics right – at base, it was clear enough what that was – but to get the politics right. We needed to sell the idea to a whole variety of different constituencies, including politicians and businesspeople, and to understand those dynamics and to wrap them into a challenging framework. I could think of no-one better to do this than Neville.

In October, the Eminent Persons Group came up with its report: 'A Vision for APEC – Towards an Asia-Pacific Economic Community'. It was a strong document, focussed around what it called 'the creation of a true Asia-Pacific Economic Community'.

It recommended that APEC set a goal of free trade in the Asia-Pacific (and move towards announcing a specific date for it), and that it begin the process by launching an ambitious trade facilitation program; that is, a program of harmonising regulations and standards and taking other steps to make it easier for companies to import and export goods and services within the region. Other useful proposals included the establishment of an Asia-Pacific Investment Code, work on effective dispute-settling procedures, and regular meetings of APEC ministers responsible for macro-economic and monetary policy. It also suggested a modest institutionalisation of APEC. It was exactly the sort of report that could only have come from outside the system, and it helped set the agenda for the leaders' meeting.

President Clinton had proposed Seattle as the venue for our meeting because it was the centre of the new industries – aerospace with Boeing, and information technology with Microsoft and others – which were so important to US commerce in Asia. The meeting was held against the background of the successful approval by Congress of the North American Free Trade Agreement (NAFTA), which brought Mexico and Canada into a common market with the United States.

The regular ministerial meeting held before the leaders arrived took a couple of decisions that disappointed me, especially in extending APEC membership to Mexico, Chile and Papua New Guinea. In fact, this decision didn't just disappoint me, it infuriated me. My opposition to expanded membership had nothing to do with any antipathy to these countries, but to the belief that if APEC got too big, or its membership became more diffuse – for example, by drawing in Latin America – we could not achieve what we wanted to do strategically. Chile was an open economy which wanted to increase its links with Asia, but its strategic and security concerns were not caught up in this nearly as much as ours were.

The differences in opinion about membership lay in conceptual confusion about whether APEC was a Pacific-Rim body, or an Asia-Pacific one. A number of APEC's antecedents like the

Pacific Economic Cooperation Conference (PECC) had been Pacific-Rim bodies, and this shaped some of the official thinking about APEC. At the same time, Malaysia was enthusiastically encouraging new members, presumably because it made its own East Asian Economic Caucus seem a more workable alternative. Its lobbying for the entry of these countries should have been seen for what it was: an attempt to make APEC ineffective before it had really begun. Many members privately shared our feelings about a rapid expansion of membership, but the moves were too far advanced to stop. Warren Christopher, the US Secretary of State, was still referring to APEC as 'OPEC' at ministerial meetings. We did have our problems.

In a speech at a stop-over in California on the way to Seattle, I talked about the sort of Asia-Pacific economic community we were looking for. I said we did not want 'an upper-case "C"-style Community like the familiar European one, complete with an upper-case "E"-style Eurobureaucracy, and aggressive protectionism against the rest of the world, but a lowercase "c" community, marked by the comprehension of common and enduring interests.'

The meeting was held on 20 November 1993 on Blake Island, a 475-acre island in the waters of Puget Sound about a twenty-minute boat ride from Seattle. It was a cool and overcast day and a remarkably informal venue – an exhibition centre that was a showcase for the culture of the Native Americans of the Pacific Northwest. There were no officials or interpreters in the room. One of the things I had tried to insist on was a genuinely discursive meeting without officials. I wanted to keep any APEC leaders' structure away from the pre-cooked approach of the G7 or OECD countries. Each of us was to have one assistant on the island who could listen in to the conversation but could not see it. This proposal at first appalled a number of officials in the region. What would become of the world if political leaders were left to their own devices? But the format went to the essence of what the meeting was about. APEC's formal work was the responsibility of the preceding ministerial meeting. This left the leaders without formal agendas and free to focus on APEC's goals and longer-term strategic issues. It was easily the most valuable thing about the meeting.

As I looked around the log cabin at the thirteen other leaders sitting in a semicircle of easy chairs, I reflected on how inconceivable this meeting would have seemed just a few years earlier. I was still apprehensive about the course of the day's events. It was still not clear as we met one another – I introduced Bill Clinton to the President of China, Jiang Zemin, at the hotel – whether we would simply have an enjoyable picnic, or whether this was the beginning of a more important structural change.

Bill Clinton's thoughtful, creative chairmanship was essential to the success of the day. It could not have been carried out better. He set out a proposal for an informal discussion of what economic challenges the APEC countries faced. The idea, which worked very well, was to get a sense from each of us of how inter-related were the problems we faced despite the differences in the size and development of our economies.

As the day went on, the discussions became increasingly frank and open. With few exceptions, the interventions were unscripted. People were enjoying it. The Asian leaders were able to hear the representatives of the developed countries grapple with the problems of growth without employment. Jean Chrétien, the Prime Minister of Canada, was particularly strong on this. It was good to be in favour of open trade, he said, but people were afraid their jobs would no longer be there. He was wrestling with the dilemma that people felt worse off, and they were. Somehow, our people had to understand that growth in the Pacific meant something for them.

In the other direction, the representatives of the developed world could hear at first hand about the struggle of leaders of developing countries to raise the living standards of their people. President Suharto made a cautious but positive intervention emphasising the different development levels of the APEC countries. He emphasised APEC's potential role in helping strengthen the base of development. He saw APEC as a pioneer of genuine north–south cooperation. He was worried about the outlook for the Uruguay Round and suggested an emergency APEC ministerial meeting to prevent the situation worsening if the round failed.

The encouraging thing was the increasingly strong sense of the region's interdependence that came out of the discussion as the day went on.

I said APEC was already a highly integrated region but we were running into a new generation of problems. We could not assume that growth would continue indefinitely. I spoke about the need for better vocational education and public sector reform. Asia had come a long way and the growth rates were spectacular, but the resource base, the infrastructure, and the savings rates would all face limits. APEC had been set up to deal with these long-term problems, and this was a chance for the Asia-Pacific to get its act together.

After discussing the problems, we went on to talk about what might be done about them. We agreed on a statement which envisioned 'a community of Asia-Pacific economies'. For reasons I never quite understood, the Australian media had seemed consumed by whether APEC changed its name from Asia-Pacific Economic Cooperation forum to the Asia-Pacific Economic Community. It was an issue on which I had no strong views, and which I did not speak about in any official conversation I held before or during the meeting. What mattered to me was not the name of the thing but what it did. We agreed that APEC should continue to expand its dialogue and work program and work to deepen and broaden the outcomes for the Uruguay Round, including in the trade facilitation area.

We announced the establishment of an APEC finance ministers' meeting to consult on broad economic issues, and we set up a Pacific Business Forum in which business leaders would identify issues APEC should address. Business, which had after all been instrumental in establishing regional economic linkages well before APEC arrived on the scene, was an important and deliberate part of the APEC agenda. I had held a round-table meeting of Australian business leaders in the Cabinet Room before coming, and Australia's first representatives on the Business Forum, Philip Brass and Imelda Roche, would go on to provide an invaluable service to the government and their own business constituency.

At the end of the day, and as a result of an agreement we had teed up in advance, Kim Young Sam proposed that President Suharto convene a meeting in 1994 to follow up this one. Goh Chok Tong immediately supported him. Suharto accepted. It was a beginning.

CHAPTER 5

BOGOR AND BEYOND

In Seattle, the meeting was the message. It was enough that such a gathering of leaders from the region had taken place. But if APEC was to become a lasting feature of the regional scene, with all the advantages that gave Australia, we had to keep pressing on with the development of an agenda serious enough to warrant the attention and the attendance of heads of government. I often commented that while the Group of Seven, the exclusive club of large industrialised countries, could afford meetings that fluctuated in value and achievements, at this stage of its development at least, APEC operated like a ratchet. Unless it kept climbing, it would fall back all the way.

The Uruguay Round had finally been completed hurriedly but successfully at the end of 1993, partly as a result of APEC's implicit threat to the Europeans that Asia and North America had somewhere else to go. After seven years of effort, trade officials lay in an exhausted heap all around the world. On the global trade front, nothing was likely to happen for some years. Still, we had to find ways of keeping up the pressure for the implementation of the agreements we had reached with the Uruguay Round. APEC could help with that.

I was worried that the American commitment to APEC would remain relatively thin. Those in the Administration who supported it and understood the opportunity it presented were few. Its multilateral complexion did not appeal to a lot of the unilateralists in Washington. Trade disputes between Washington and Tokyo continued to drag on peevishly. If you are as big as the United States, the temptation to get what you want by simply throwing your weight around must be almost overwhelming. In the North American Free Trade Agreement, the United States had in place, if it wanted, a ready-made western-hemisphere approach to trade. If APEC was to change minds in Washington, it had to show it could deliver the goods. That was not something that could be left until a few weeks before the next leaders' meeting.

By February 1994, officials from the International Division of the Department of the Prime Minister and Cabinet were advising me that we faced real problems in keeping up the momentum for progress in APEC in the year ahead. Warning signs of foot-dragging by officials had already emerged in the couple of months since Seattle. That sounded right. I held a meeting in my office on 18 February to review the situation. I said I thought we had to fast-track the trade liberalisation agenda in APEC. The only answer for Australia was not to slow down but to keep pressing for even larger, more concrete, outcomes from the next leaders' meeting in the following November; for a policy explosion. Trade facilitation – that is, smoothing out the pipelines of trade – was important, but we also had to build larger pipelines. For this, we needed to reduce tariffs and other formal barriers to trade.

Two days later, I wrote to President Suharto outlining Australia's priorities and offering my support for an ambitious agenda. It was the beginning of a very busy year. I said earlier that all prime ministers make their own choices about where, out of all the possibilities, they wish to focus their efforts. In a year which also included the government's white paper on unemployment, 'Working Nation'; the establishment of an Indigenous Land Fund; the arts and information technology statement,

'Creative Nation'; and dealing with the consequences of the worst drought for a generation, APEC was only one focus of mine. But some idea of the priority I attached to the success of the Bogor meeting can be gauged from the fact that in the nine months between the meeting in my office on 18 February and the leaders' summit on 15 November, my diary records around thirty-six meetings or telephone calls, mostly with other APEC heads of government, focussing on the meeting, and seventeen letters to other leaders about APEC. This was in addition, of course, to the constant work done by Trade Minister Bob McMullan and Gareth Evans with their own colleagues and the enormous effort put in by the public service and my own office.

On 9 March I wrote to Prime Minister Goh Chok Tong and President Kim Young Sam, two of the regional leaders whose views were closest to Australia's, outlining what I thought we should be trying to achieve in the year ahead with trade liberalisation through APEC, and enlisting their support. Both replied positively, including supporting trade liberalisation efforts. But all of us were conscious that trade liberalisation raised many ticklish issues. What were we talking about? Were we thinking about creating a preferential APEC trade bloc like the European Union, in which we lowered barriers with each other, but maintained them against the outside world? Or were we talking about liberalisation on what was called a Most Favoured Nation (MFN) basis, under which our tariffs would be unilaterally lowered to all other countries? Would it be better to tackle trade liberalisation on a sectoral basis – that is, industry by industry – rather than across the board? What if some members wanted to move ahead but others did not? Did we need to get unanimity from all APEC members?

In any case, what did 'free trade' mean? Did it mean zero tariffs? I did not think it did, because as I said at the time, 'Once you are down to these sorts of levels of tariff protection, the daily exchange rate fluctuation is worth more than the five per cent tariff. So I don't think there is any point [in arguing] about zeros and fives, but there is a lot of point about forties, and sixties, and hundred-and-twenties, and two-hundred-and-forties.'

Bob McMullan had seen President Suharto in mid-March and reported back that the President had told him that he saw trade liberalisation as one of the main priorities for APEC. Suharto wrote to me and other leaders in April, previewing his hopes for the year ahead. He said he was appointing Professor Bintoro Tjokroamidjojo as his Special Assistant to work with the other leaders to help ensure the success of the meeting at Bogor at the end of the year. He asked me and the others to appoint a personal representative of our own.

As I discovered at our first meeting, Professor Bintoro was an engaging, talkative and excitable academic, and a former ambassador to the Netherlands. He had a background in public administration, and good access to the President. I could think of no better person to appoint as my own representative than Michael Costello, the Secretary of the Department of Foreign Affairs and Trade. This was not because of Costello's formal position but because he was one of Australia's best public servants, an energetic and experienced official whose negotiation techniques had been fully tested over the 1991 Cambodia peace settlement. He was committed to APEC and to Australia's engagement with Asia. The work he did (with David Ritchie from the Prime Minister's Department, and Peter Grey, the Deputy Secretary in the Department of Foreign Affairs and Trade who was responsible for so much of the work at the officials level) critically helped to bring about success at Bogor.

From the beginning, it was clear that Suharto saw what might emerge from Bogor as one of the important building blocks of the emerging Asia-Pacific community. It was equally clear, however, that his own hopes for the meeting in November were a good deal more ambitious than many of his ministers and officials wanted. He had appointed the Coordinating Minister for Trade and Industry, Mr Hartarto, to be responsible for Indonesia's year in the chair. Hartarto was a strong supporter of APEC, but many of his colleagues were taking a far more cautious approach, and the activities of Indonesian officials at APEC meetings did not always match what we knew the President wanted.

Left to its own devices the official machinery of APEC – the APEC Senior Officials' Meeting – would not move beyond agreements based on the lowest common denominator. In March, Australian officials were reporting that leaders' initiatives from Seattle were being smothered in APEC committees, and that progress was very slow. Not all of this was bureaucratic jealousy. In a number of the other countries the level of support for rapid movement in APEC was less than in Australia, and we encountered the usual amount of concern that the Americans were trying to push others too fast. Not all the countries responded to President Suharto's efforts to appoint leaders' coordinators because they did not want to see another (and by implication faster) level of decision-making in APEC. But gradually, most fell into line and in the end this off-line process was a key to Bogor's success.

To deepen our apprehension at this stage, a meeting of APEC trade ministers held in the sidelines of a World Trade Organisation gathering in Marrakech in April 1994 was a dispiriting affair for anyone hoping for fast progress. It was not all gloom. APEC finance ministers had met in Honolulu in March, one of the first practical outcomes of the Seattle meeting.

I visited Jakarta in June 1994 and had a two-hour meeting with President Suharto. Much of the discussion was about APEC. He suggested a fifteen- to twenty-year time frame for free trade in the region, and outlined ways in which this might be approached. Suharto kept underlining the importance of taking into account the differences between the developed and developing countries and the need for developing countries to benefit from free trade. But his bottom line was that there should be open competition. 'The important thing is to nurture a mental attitude which eliminates fear among the Asia-Pacific countries,' he told me.

I replied that the meeting at Bogor offered an opportunity to take an historic step towards consolidating APEC as an organisation by setting a goal for all APEC members of free trade by a certain date. I suggested that the goal could be reached on a phased basis, by using a formula borrowed from ASEAN that we called '18 minus X'. This meant that of APEC's 18 members (Chile, Mexico and Papua New Guinea had now joined), those who were ready to do so could move ahead quickly, and the others could join progressively, perhaps by set interim dates. All would have to be in by the agreed end date.

I suggested that the question of exactly how free trade might be achieved — and in particular the question of whether it would be on a Most Favoured Nation or preferential basis — should be put to one side for the time being. I doubted we could resolve it before November. Instead, we could agree to undertake liberalisation 'on a GATT-consistent basis', a phrase which would cover either option. The important thing for me was the commitment to free trade by a certain date.

Suharto wrote to me after our meeting that 'Australia, which played a leading role in the birth of APEC, now also plays a pivotal role in the common endeavour to strengthen economic cooperation in the region'. This pleased me because I was investing a lot of effort in that common endeavour.

I was gradually selling the message to other APEC leaders, including Prime Minister Chuan and Deputy Prime Minister Supachai during a visit to Thailand, and Vincent Siew, Chairman of Taiwan's Council of Economic Planning and Development, who had been Taipei's representative at the Seattle meeting. In Thailand, Supachai suggested that we think about establishing linkages between the Australia–New Zealand Closer Economic Relations and the ASEAN Free Trade Area (AFTA). I welcomed this idea and wanted to keep it in play, not necessarily because it was the best option for Australia, but against the prospect that something went wrong on the larger global trade scene. We had the first AFTA–CER trade ministers' meeting in September that year.

By July, we had clear aims in mind. We wanted to see the next leaders' meeting deliver substantial progress on the Seattle initiatives, including a commitment to achieve free trade in APEC by a certain date. This date should not be so close as to be unrealistic or so distant that it would not represent a serious commitment. A phased approach would have to be adopted that would allow those members who were able to do so to move ahead, with others following progressively. The process would have to be GATT-consistent and to begin with a standstill – that is, an agreement by all APEC members not to increase existing trade barriers or to introduce new ones. We also wanted to see some concrete progress on trade facilitation. Australian officials had prepared an outline of what a leaders' statement might look like and we were sharing it with the Indonesians.

I knew that if the argument turned into one about Most Favoured Nation versus preferential trading arrangements, we would get lost in it. In any case, given the length of time we were looking at, the questions were largely academic. They would inevitably be subsumed by another global trade round. But I knew that we had this very rare chance to get a commitment to free trade in the Asia-Pacific while Suharto was in the chair, and probably only under these circumstances. We needed him, Bill Clinton and a reasonably neutral position on the part of the Japanese. Then we would get it.

In August, Fred Bergsten and the Eminent Persons Group delivered another useful report, 'Achieving the Vision', which kept the public pressure on. I did not agree with all its conclusions, but it played an essential role in preventing any tacit conspiracy to sweep the hard issues out of sight. It recommended that APEC adopt a long-term goal of 'free and open trade and investment in the region', with a start date of 2000 and an end date of 2020, with a general recognition that more advanced members should eliminate their barriers more quickly than the newly industrialised and developing countries. But all countries would have to begin liberalising at the same time; that is, we would all leave the starting blocks at the same time.

I spoke to Bill Clinton by phone on 16 August, to run through my own recent contacts and to try to explain what I hoped could be done. He seemed enthusiastic about the prospects and assured me that the United States would be there at the end. Then in September, I made a two-day trip to Japan essentially to try to sell a deal at Bogor. I saw Prime Minister Murayama, my old friend Ryutaro Hashimoto, who was now Minister of International Trade and Industry and a critical figure in this, as well as a number of former politicians and senior businesspeople, all of whom were important in forming a Japanese consensus. Sporting metaphors are far rarer in my experience among Japanese ministers than their Australian counterparts, but Hashimoto assured me that 'all Japan's efforts will be devoted to joining the scrum in November, and even though the ball might be hard to handle, Japan will be there at the end'.

By the end of September it was becoming clear that most APEC members supported, or at least accepted, the idea of leaders making a broad political commitment to a free-trade goal by a specific date. The remaining hold-outs seemed to be China and Malaysia. China was keen to use this issue to help resolve its long-standing difficulties with the United States over trade policy by insisting that all APEC liberalisation should be automatically shared with other APEC members, and to generate support for China's accession to the World Trade Organisation. Malaysia was opposing any institutionalisation of APEC because of its continuing support for an East Asian economic body. It did not want to see APEC develop as a free-trade bloc. However, with Malaysia's ASEAN partner, Indonesia, in the Chair, Dr Mahathir had stopped short of specifically ruling out a free-trade goal or date.

More pressure for trade liberalisation came from the private sector in mid-October, when the business leaders in the Pacific Business Forum issued their own report calling for a plan to liberalise regional trade by 2010.

The draft of the leaders' statement was circulated by the Indonesians at the beginning of November. It proposed that APEC adopt the long-term goal of free and open trade in the Asia-Pacific on a GATT-consistent basis by 2010 for developed countries and newly industrialised economies and 2020 for developing countries. It was what we were putting around privately and was as good as we could have hoped for. Suharto and I had had a couple of phone calls over the 2010 and 2020 end-points, and the need for all to leave the starting blocks at the same time, with different speeds over the track. If we could get it accepted in close to that form, it would represent the policy explosion we had been looking for.

Now, however, trouble was emerging from an unexpected quarter. Despite President Clinton's positive comments to me only a couple of months earlier, we encountered a massive outbreak of nervousness in Washington as the meeting drew closer. This was partly fear that Congress would never accept a declaration in which China, as a developing country, was seen to be given a ten-year break over the United States, as a developed one. Having driven the agenda hard, the Americans were now suggesting that all countries be subject to the 2020 date, but with the addition of some wording acknowledging the principle of phasing in for developing countries. The US Treasury and the domestic political areas of the White House seemed the key problems.

We knew that any compromise on a staged commitment would be unacceptable to Suharto and APEC's developing-country members and unfair to them as well. We now faced the danger that as each country found elements it did not like, the whole package would unravel. The most useful thing we could do was to help Suharto repel boarders.

I spoke to Suharto on the telephone again on 7 November congratulating him on the draft leaders' statement. I urged him to keep the specific dates in it. Without them, an agreement on free trade would be no more than a vague statement of aims. Its strength would disappear. Suharto said he fully agreed. I said I would stick with him no matter what the United States decided, but I believed if we stared the others down we would get the statement agreed.

I told him of my recent activity, including a long personal letter I had written to Dr Mahathir about APEC and the way it could help Malaysia. I said I was confident the Japanese would go along with the statement, but that I was worried about the Americans.

That night I asked Ed Perkins, the United States Ambassador, to come and see me. I told him that the United States and Australia each had very open economies, so neither of us would be giving away much to secure a free-trade goal. The real objective for us was to bring down the other barriers in the region. From what I could see, the problem in Washington was not a technical or policy problem but one of perception. I told the Ambassador it was not hyperbole to say we would never get a chance like this again. China was not quite confident enough to say no; the Japanese were not quite politically secure enough to say no; and we had this proposal for free trade before us from one of the leading developing countries. If we only had one end date, we would lose the signal that the developed countries were prepared to make a contribution to trade liberalisation. I understood the President's domestic problems with Congress and its concern about giving China what was seen as a 'free ride', but the cost of dropping the 2010 date would be horrible.

I said that I and others had been running around Asia for two years now, talking about the importance of continuing to engage the United States in Asian trade and investment. I feared that if the United States said 'no thanks' on this statement, the Asians would start heading their own way.

The ambassador reported the conversation to Washington, but Bill Clinton had other things on his mind, including the mid-term congressional elections. He was unlikely to think about APEC until he boarded the plane for Jakarta.

Those mid-term congressional elections in the United States were a comprehensive defeat for the Democratic Party, and delivered control of both houses of Congress to the Republicans. President Clinton's decision to meet his promise and fly all that way to Jakarta, despite obvious physical exhaustion, was a notable contribution to the creation of an Asia-Pacific community. He flew out within a day of the elections.

But as I arrived in Jakarta on 13 November it was not at all clear what the outcome would be. I had meetings in the following twenty-four hours with the Prime Minister of Canada, Jean Chrétien, Dr Mahathir of Malaysia, President Jiang Zemin of China, Thai Prime Minister Chuan Leekpai, and President Ramos of the Philippines. Bill Clinton hosted me to lunch, a relaxed and very friendly affair at the US Ambassador's residence.

My meeting with President Suharto was the last he had scheduled. I had asked that we meet late on the day before the meeting began so I could pass on the impressions I had picked up from my meetings with other leaders.

Suharto said the good news, as I had already heard directly, was that President Clinton would support the draft declaration. But another problem had come up. Having earlier given approval to the document, President Kim Young Sam, who was experiencing political problems in Seoul over parliament's ratification of the Uruguay Round outcome, now wanted Korea placed in a new category for newly industrialised countries, with a deadline of 2015. Suharto believed it was very important not to reopen the document at this stage and said he had asked Prime Minister Goh to help as well. We also discussed concerns about the document that Dr Mahathir had expressed to President Suharto and to me that morning.

We agreed that the only way we could get agreement was if no changes were made to the draft. I told Suharto that the reason so many countries were wobbly was that it was an historic declaration. People cared about it. I said he could rely on me if he faced a difficult situation in the meeting room. 'I collect APEC arguments like some others here collect postage stamps,' I told him.

I did not want to take more of the President's time and said I had told others he was as tough as old boots. The President laughed, although Foreign Minister Alatas and State Secretary Moerdiono who were with us looked startled. I explained that I meant he would hang on and not let go. I thanked him for the leadership he had shown. I told him not to let the declaration out of his hands; not to surrender any part of it.

Australia's position in the alphabetical order has disadvantages. One is that I was the first of the leaders to set out on the fifty-kilometre drive to the Presidential Palace at Bogor, in the hills south of Jakarta, where the leaders' meeting was to be held. As I was driven with my foreign policy adviser, Allan Gyngell, along the eerily deserted highway, I was still apprehensive. I thought the declaration would be agreed but I could not be sure. And in what form? I understood how international meetings went. From bitter experience I knew how hard it was to end a meeting with the words you began with. But I knew that the future of APEC and its impact on the region depended on getting the declaration through.

The setting at Bogor was much more formal than at Blake Island, reflecting the different styles of the two leaders and two cultures. As one of our embassy officials pointed out, what is a relaxing environment for a US president or an Australian prime minister can be intimidating for an Asian leader from a different generation.

The meeting was held in a large, high-ceilinged reception room of the palace, which had been the official residence of the thirty-eight Dutch governors-general during the colonial period. President Suharto welcomed the leaders and explained that the draft declaration they had each been given reflected the results of the consultations which had been going on through the leaders' assistants. He said that perhaps the concept had not met everyone's needs, but it could be accepted as a flexible consensus. This was essential if we wished not to stifle dynamism. If the majority of APEC members were ready to cooperate, they should do so even if the others were not ready. 'Bogor is a continuation of the process of response to global change,' he said.

The leaders then spoke one by one. President Jiang Zemin was the fifth speaker. I was anxious to hear what he had to say, because China's views were so important. He talked about the 'complex state of flux' which characterised international relations at present and spoke of the need to enhance peace and regional stability into the twenty-first century. Diversity and interdependence were what gave the Asia-Pacific the opportunity to grow.

This was a particularly interesting intervention because it showed that APEC could cope with an agenda broader than economic cooperation, something that in our terms was fundamental to the APEC process.

President Jiang spoke positively about APEC's future and about trade liberalisation, and although he emphasised the need for APEC to accommodate different pacing and modalities among its members he did not question the Bogor draft. I was very relieved.

President Kim then spoke and, as we had heard the day before, expressed his concerns about the specific implications of the 2010 date for Korea. While emphasising his support for the declaration, he wanted to change its terminology.

Dr Mahathir was called. He said that he had some reservations about the document and wanted to put these in an annex. His main argument was that it was not fair to commit future generations of leaders without allowing them to modify agreements. I thought this was curious reasoning that would effectively rule out any sort of long-term international agreement at all. He said he feared that developing countries might not be able to compete in a free-trade environment. And even if Malaysia were to become a developed country by 2020, as it wanted, free trade would still only be fair if economies were the same size. He then circulated his document. Malaysia would accept the 2010–2020 dates, but only if they were on a 'best endeavours' basis and were conditional and non-binding. In addition, APEC decisions should be based on consensus – in other words, unanimity – rather than majority agreement. He concluded that apart from these concerns, he was quite happy to go along with the document.

Well, yes. But it was a fairly big proviso.

The next speakers, however, all swung the debate in a more positive direction. Jim Bolger, the New Zealand Prime Minister, made a strong statement in favour of the declaration; Malaysia's

ASEAN partners, Brunei and Thailand, spoke positively; and Bill Clinton made a thoughtful intervention. He said that in every country during this period of rapid change there was a struggle going on between stability and growth, between protection against chaos and freedom. All countries answered this in their own ways. There was no perfect balance and we all had to keep moving. The leaders' document struck as good a balance as we could get at the moment. If we made a grave mistake, our successors would correct it. But our people needed to have confidence in our ability to resolve these problems.

At that point the meeting broke for lunch. I spent much of the lunch period talking about Dr Mahathir's proposal and President Kim's problem. It was clear that any formal annex of the sort Dr Mahathir proposed would effectively render the Bogor declaration meaningless. The media would have discounted it, and with it the whole of the APEC process. We also needed to find some way of preventing President Kim's problem from leading to the document's unravelling.

I was the third speaker after lunch. I thanked both Suharto and Clinton for their work in bringing us to this place. I said we had only been able to get a document like this together because of the authority which the leaders' meetings had brought to the APEC process.

I pointed out that the debate about the north–south dialogue – that is, about the economic relationship between the developed and the developing world – had been going on for most of the political lives of all the leaders in the room. The proposed agreement gave expression to that dialogue by recognising the different levels of development in APEC and the way the needs of developing countries could be buttressed. Australian economic modelling had shown that the benefits to the APEC countries under free trade would be greater by three times than those of the Uruguay Round outcome alone.

I said the leaders' declaration was very firm. With regard to free trade it used words like 'commit', 'achieving the goal', 'agreement', 'completion', 'decision'. In other words, leaders were not passing decisions to ministers to make but were telling them what was intended so the ministers could facilitate it. The declaration had a political advantage for each of us, I said, in that all the APEC economies would be liberalising together. Such joint action would reduce the political costs of economic restructuring in individual countries by enabling us to point to what was going on elsewhere.

I then said I agreed with President Kim's suggestion that the phrase 'developed and newly industrialised economies' be changed to 'industrialised economies' (which made South Korea's status more ambiguous). The change did not seem to me to alter the central meaning. In any case, President Kim had noted that South Korea would be an industrialised country well before 2010.

Prime Minister Goh spoke after me, again with strength and clarity, about what the APEC declaration meant for us all.

The meeting ended with a discussion of Prime Minister Mahathir's reservation. President Suharto was implacable. In his quiet Javanese, but utterly determined manner he said that we would never finish if we included reservations. He hoped the statement could be issued as drafted, with the exception of the replacement of the phrase 'industrialised economies'. Otherwise it should remain as it was. On the question of an annex, he had taken this to include simply the proposals that had come up during the day for new initiatives such as meetings of telecommunication and agriculture ministers. It should not be something that would diminish the weight and content of the declaration. So it would be better if he had the approval of the meeting to issue the statement as it was. He would say that views were expressed by leaders and the document had been approved by consensus. Dr Mahathir replied that he did not see his annex as part of the declaration, and did not expect it to be appended to it. He would be asked about the declaration and he would explain his reservations in his own way. These were just clarifications. He thought it should be part of the official documents but not part of the declaration. Suharto simply said the declaration was approved by consensus.

It was an outstanding performance by Suharto. The leader of one of the world's largest developing countries had, at no little cost, committed his own country, and because of Indonesia's size and influence, the rest of South-East Asia, to a free trade agenda and an open international trading system. It was a very important message. He had chaired the meeting with great dignity but also tactical astuteness. There were plenty of people in his own government arguing for caution; who resisted greater economic liberalisation and saw the world much more in terms of north–south divisions between the developed and developing countries. This was no less one of Suharto's concerns, but he knew that free trade was the best way of improving the position of the people of his own and other developing countries.

The APEC Declaration of Common Resolve, which was the result of those months of work, reasserted a vision for the community of Asia-Pacific economies. The declaration described the open multilateral trading system as 'the foundation of our market-driven economic growth'.

Leaders declared that the 'goal of free and open trade and investment' in the Asia-Pacific was to be

> ... pursued promptly by further reducing barriers to trade and investment and by promoting the free flow of goods, services and capital among our economies. We will achieve this goal in a GATT-consistent manner and believe our actions will be a powerful impetus for further liberalisation at the multilateral level to which we remain fully committed.

> We further agree to announce our commitment to complete the achievement of our goal of free and open trade and investment in the Asia-Pacific no later than the year 2020. The pace of implementation will take into account the differing levels of economic development among APEC economies, with the industrialised economies achieving the goal of free and open trade and investment no later than the year 2010 and developing economies no later than the year 2020.
>
> We wish to emphasise our strong opposition to the creation of an inward-looking trading bloc that would divert from the pursuit of global free trade. We are determined to pursue free and open trade and investment in the Asia-Pacific in a manner that will encourage trade and investment liberalisation in the world as a whole. Thus the outcome of trade and investment liberalisation in the Asia-Pacific will not only be the actual reduction of barriers among APEC economies but also between APEC economies and non-APEC economies.

The declaration committed the APEC economies to speed up the implementation of their Uruguay Round commitments and to a standstill (through a 'best-endeavours' basis) to any reversal of free trade. Progress was also made through trade facilitation and on building up APEC's economic development dimension, especially with human resources.

It was a tip-top result. The approach was, in a number of ways, unique. This was the first time developing countries had not just participated in, but had led a major trade liberalisation process. Secondly, and in complete reversal to the approach of traditional trade negotiations, APEC had set the end goals it wished to reach – free trade and investment in the region by 2010 and 2020 – and proposed to work towards achieving them. Traditionally, end points were never agreed and trade ministers would do their utmost to give as little away as possible. By nominating and agreeing end points, APEC turned the traditional approach on its head. The statement was very good: everything about it was ambitious.

For Australia, the commitments we adopted under the declaration did not pose any great problem. By the time of the Bogor meeting, the effective rate of industry protection in Australia was about one third of what it had been in the early 1980s, while during the same period our exports had expanded from less than 14 per cent of GDP in 1983 to 22 per cent of GDP. In 2000, a full decade before we were required to achieve free trade under the Bogor commitments, our average trade weighted tariff would be just 2.9 per cent – a testament to the Labor Government's belief in turning Australia into an open market economy. Even in industries traditionally regarded as highly protected, our tariff barriers would be coming down to modest levels.

Modelling by the Office of National Assessments and the Industry Commission estimated that under APEC free trade, Australia's real output would rise by 3.8 per cent and real national income by 1.2 per cent. This would include a 27 per cent increase in Australian exports and a 20 per cent projected rise in imports. Once the effects of APEC trade liberalisation had fully flowed through, we could expect a permanent increase in employment of over 200,000 jobs.

Over a sashimi dinner that night with my wife and personal staff and the Australian officials who had put such effort into delivering this outcome, I reflected that this had been one of the most satisfying days of my political life.

Back in Australia, I told the House of Representatives:

> With Bogor . . . Australians can say for the first time that the region around us is truly 'our region'. We know its shape; we have an agreed institutional structure; we share with its other

members a common agenda for change ... Just as the Bretton Woods agreements after the Second World War established structures in the IMF and the World Bank, which enabled the world to grow and prosper, so in APEC we have established a model which will serve the interests of the post-Cold War world.

I knew we had a very long way to go before the Bogor declaration could be implemented, but it had already served a useful purpose in acknowledging the interdependence of the countries in this part of the world and establishing a collective commitment to free trade. It had given us a much clearer notion of an Asia-Pacific community. It gave Australia a seat at the largest table we had ever sat at.

We had agreed in the Bogor meeting to hold another leaders' meeting in Osaka, Japan the following year. We were off and running. This would institutionalise the leaders' meetings more quickly and more regularly than I had anticipated a couple of years before. As happened after Seattle, it would be necessary to start discussion soon after this meeting ended. The momentum had to be maintained. It was a bit like the bicycle. You had to keep pedalling or APEC would fall over.

Now that the goal had been set at Bogor, we needed to achieve a blueprint to get there. Japan would be the place to deliver an action plan on how to achieve free trade. I knew we couldn't continue to press the trade liberalisation agenda at the same pace in 1995 as in 1994. Australian aims had been incredibly audacious. After taking such a large leap, the APEC economies would want to catch their breath. In any case, the decision-making style of the Japanese made it unlikely that they would move the agenda fast. Bureaucratic divisions were more marked and harder to breach than they had been in Indonesia. We knew we could expect effective management, but particularly with a relatively new prime minister in a weak political position Japan would not be able to push other members hard.

APEC members would also have to demonstrate that their expectations were not unrealistic. In particular, with Republican majorities in both houses of Congress and the 1996 presidential election drawing closer, the US Administration was going to be thinking about trade policy increasingly in terms of domestic politics. Latin America was also edging back into the US agenda because of a perception that the United States had more to gain there economically. The word we were getting from officials' discussions in Washington was that the Administration would not seek to push the trade liberalisation aspects of Bogor for at least the next two to three years. We encountered continued American cynicism, not all of it misplaced, about how fast Japan and China would be prepared to move, although in my view this attitude only increased the importance of APEC. I knew President Clinton was positive about APEC, but at the senior officials' level in Washington there were few champions. Still, notwithstanding Japanese caution and American uncertainty, we thought we would be able to sustain the momentum of Bogor, provided we kept up the pressure.

Now that the Bogor goals were established, APEC slotted into more regular policy-making patterns in Australia. We established an ad hoc committee of Cabinet to deal with APEC matters, and in February 1995 Bob McMullan presented a comprehensive strategy for the year ahead.

We agreed that Australia would seek to support whatever mechanism seemed most likely to deliver an early result. The approach that seemed most promising was called 'coordinated unilateralism'. Under this plan, APEC members would prepare unilateral work plans showing how and when they intended to meet the Bogor commitments, and these would be subject to negotiation and discussion with the other APEC economies. This was far from the all-in approach of the Uruguay Round, but it was in line with what the Asians might be prepared to accept.

Australia would insist that the coverage was comprehensive. In other words, we would not agree to others deciding to opt out of agriculture, for example. The plans would have to balance members' interests to ensure that all benefited from trade liberalisation. At the same time, the developing countries should be required to begin liberalising at the same time as the developed countries, even if they did not reach the end point until later. All away at the starter's gun. This was a big and, as far as I was concerned, immutable point.

As the year went on the Americans were getting more nervous about 'concerted unilateral liberalisation'. It was the antithesis of trade legalism. It was far from the usual American approach to heavily reciprocal trade strategies.

In May 1995, I was travelling to Japan. I rang President Suharto before I left because I wanted to have his views when I spoke to Prime Minister Murayama. Suharto's pride in the Bogor agreement was always evident. He expressed intense irritation at some white-anting of Bogor that one of the other ASEAN members was reportedly engaged in at the time. He asked me to convey to Murayama as strongly as possible the fact that the Osaka meeting was to be a continuation of the process begun at Bogor, and that Osaka should produce 'concrete results and operational schedules to undertake the Bogor commitments'.

Japan and the United States were in the middle of another spat on auto parts. I said to Murayama that Japan needed a strategy to deal with the United States that would reach over these interminable trade irritants, and that its best option was to try to build APEC liberalisation. A big result at Osaka would make it much more difficult for the United States to engage in unilateral pressure. I handed over a two-page outline of Australia's views on the forthcoming Osaka meeting, a sort of blueprint for the Japanese to study.

Our efforts during this period were directed towards retaining the comprehensive nature of the Bogor commitments against the efforts by many – not least the Japanese farm lobby – to back away from it. On 19 October I told a delegation of Liberal Democratic Party parliamentarians who were engaged in some special pleading for Japanese farmers that we were not prepared to have the principle of comprehensiveness watered down. Every member of APEC had its own sensitive sectors and if all were to seek particular exemptions the whole process would unravel.

I pointed out that by 2000 Australia would have cut its average effective rate of assistance across all manufacturing 40 per cent in the 1970s to just five per cent. Japan had been a major beneficiary of those tariff cuts. Similarly, the Australian farming sector had suffered enormously from the vagaries of a distorted world agricultural market; a quarter of our farms had disappeared and farm employment had fallen by 20 per cent. We had not responded by protecting our farmers. I said it was unthinkable that Japan, the second-largest economy in the world, should be trying to wind back commitments made at Bogor under the leadership of Indonesia, a developing country. Unthinkable.

The Osaka meeting was held on 18 and 19 November 1995. President Clinton did not turn up in the end because of the standoff between Administration and Congress over the budget. It was certainly an important time for him politically, but the decision to not go was essentially one in favour of presentation in domestic politics over substance in international relations, and was therefore very much to be regretted. I was disappointed and made my position clear to Vice-President Gore, who came in his place, in a private meeting. 'You make me feel like a skunk at the picnic,' he said ruefully. One good thing about Clinton's absence, however, was that the focus shifted to Japan's role.

The Osaka meeting showed that APEC had reached a critical mass, and that even under difficult circumstances – the absence of the US President and political difficulties in Japan – APEC was able to continue making progress towards its goals. Out of the meeting we got a declaration and an action agenda; it gave further definition to the closer integration of the regional economies. There was no backing away from the 'unwavering resolve' to free and open trade in the APEC region by the 2010 and 2020 dates.

The Osaka action agenda set out the principles that were to underpin the process of trade liberalisation in the Asia-Pacific. The eight principles included WTO consistency, comparability, non-discrimination, transparency, standstill and a commitment to move together on the liberalisation process. We got what we wanted on comprehensiveness. This was an acid test of APEC's relevance not just to Australia but to developing agricultural producers like Thailand and Indonesia.

In addition to the principles, a process was agreed for liberalisation. Leaders directed ministers and officials to prepare 'concrete and substantive' action plans for the following years' meeting. The process, vital in its own right, bolted the principles down even tighter. We created a Pacific Business Council, as a new and permanent APEC business forum, and made some modest but credible down payments to speed up the Uruguay Round outcomes.

After Osaka, we knew where we were going. We had an end point we wanted to reach – free and open trade and investment in the APEC region – and a process – concerted liberalisation – for getting there. It was another very good result. Murayama and Hashimoto together looked like the cat who had swallowed the canary.

Just four years after I raised with George Bush the prospect of upgrading APEC to a heads-of-government meeting, and six after Australia had hosted the first APEC ministerial meeting, the organisation was powerfully established as a feature of the regional landscape. Year by year the leaders were able to meet, easily and without formality, and to deal effectively in their bilateral and group discussions outside the meeting with political and security issues as they emerged.

In the years that followed, APEC was to be damaged by the addition of new members who took it away from its core competencies and made easy and informal discussions more difficult by increasing the number of people sitting around the table. It also failed to act sufficiently early and coherently on regional financial pressures. Nevertheless, the story APEC had been telling the region about itself through its declarations, its regular meetings, its business connections was powerful and persuasive. It was a story of interdependence, openness and free trade. So when the Asian economic crisis came in 1997, with its pressures for governments to close up and look inwards, the significant thing was that APEC's free-trade goals and aspirations remained in place. The plot-line of the region's story did not take a sudden turn. That was a striking achievement.

CHAPTER 6

OUR LARGEST, NEAREST NEIGHBOUR

I knew with certainty, well before I became prime minister, that one of my priorities in the job would be to try to develop the full potential of Australia's relationship with Indonesia.

I said as much in media interviews during my leadership challenge to Bob Hawke in mid-1991. But my belief that this was Australia's great underdeveloped relationship went back much further than that. Travelling on the train from Bankstown to the city to work at the Sydney County Council in 1965 and 1966, I distinctly remember following newspaper accounts of the turmoil of President Sukarno's Year of Living Dangerously and the violence that followed. The drama of those events always kept my thinking focussed on Australia's relations with those around us, especially with Indonesia.

This vast, complex country of around 210 million people – the fourth most populous in the world – is an archipelago of more than 13,500 islands stretching for 5000 kilometres across Australia's northern approaches. Around 60 per cent of Indonesians live on the island of Java. But the people on the arc of outer islands come from more than 300 other ethnic and cultural groups. And although nearly 90 per cent of Indonesia's people profess Islam, making it the largest Moslem country in the world, Moslems co-exist with significant Christian, Hindu and Buddhist communities. Even within the Moslem community, pre-Islamic traditional beliefs persist alongside Islamic faith and practices.

Such diversity means that national unity in Indonesia has to rest on a foundation of tolerance for difference. Conscious of this, President Sukarno, the flawed, charismatic leader of the new Republic, set out in 1945 a guiding philosophy for the nation. The philosophy was expressed as five principles, or *Pancasila*: belief in one God; justice and civility among peoples; national unity; democracy through deliberation and consensus among representatives; and social justice for all. The precepts are vague, but that is part of their strength. They helped all the people of the archipelago, whatever their cultural or religious background, define themselves as Indonesians.

The question of how Indonesia sees itself is a matter of central importance to Australia. Contact between the two countries goes back well before the first European explorers saw our shores. Generations of fishermen from Makassar in the southern Celebes regularly travelled to Australia in search of sea cucumbers. Throughout the nineteenth century, Batavia – now Jakarta – was a regular port of call for ships travelling between Europe and Australia. And Indonesia's strategic importance to Australia was brought home with brutal force during the Second World War, when Australian troops fought against the Japanese in Timor and Ambon.

When the Dutch tried to take back control of their former colony after the war, the young Indonesian revolutionary movement resisted and Australian trade unions, the public and the Labor Government became directly involved in the independence struggle. Australia brought the Dutch 'police action' – the anodyne term for its attempt to seize back control from the infant republic – to the attention of the recently established United Nations Security Council, and we represented the new Indonesian state on a committee which was set up to try to mediate between the Dutch and the nationalist leaders. In 1950 we co-sponsored

Indonesia's admission to the United Nations. The Chifley Government's decision to help marshal international support for Indonesian independence rather than acquiesce in the return of the colonial power marked perhaps the first fundamental turning point in the development of an independent Australian foreign policy.

But the early goodwill did not endure. It was dissipated by the opposition of the Menzies Government to Indonesia's efforts to regain control over West Irian, territory which had been part of the former Dutch East Indies, and by President Sukarno's increasingly erratic actions. In 1963, Sukarno launched a policy of 'confrontation' against the newly formed state of Malaysia, which amalgamated the former British colonies of Malaya, Singapore, Sabah and Sarawak. Australia took diplomatic and military steps, including stationing Australian armed forces in Borneo, to help defend Malaysia. In this period lay the roots of a persistent Australian suspicion of Indonesia as a military threat.

Sukarno's romantic nationalism, incompetent economic policies and dangerous international adventurism had plunged Indonesia into a desperate economic crisis. In September 1965, an abortive communist coup attempt, whose origins and significance remain a contested subject among historians, resulted in the murder of six senior Indonesian generals. General Suharto, then head of the Army's Strategic Command, led the military response and quickly seized back the initiative. In subsequent vengeful score-settling perhaps 250,000 people were killed in a terrible nation-wide outbreak of communal violence. In the aftermath of this horror Sukarno was forced from power in March 1966 and General Suharto took over the presidency as head of a 'New Order' Government. He had the backing of the armed forces and, ironically as it might now seem, the support of students and urban intellectuals who were reacting against the chaotic style, risk-taking policies and economic disasters of the Old Order.

Under President Suharto, Indonesia turned essentially

inwards. The new government's slogan, as it tried to dig its way out of economic turmoil, was 'economics first, politics later'. For people living in squalor and housed in places in cardboard shanties, it underlined the importance of economic growth. It abandoned Sukarno's international posturing. The results for the country's economic and social progress were striking. Between 1966 and 1991 Indonesia's real GDP expanded by 450 per cent. Until the Asian economic crisis of 1997–98, its economy had been growing at a steady rate of around six per cent each year, and the growth was well spread. At the time, the World Bank estimated that poverty alleviation was greater in Indonesia than in any other country it had studied. Under Suharto's Government, the number of Indonesians living below the poverty line fell from 60 per cent of the population to 13 per cent in 1994. Infant mortality more than halved, literacy rates doubled and life expectancy rose by 17 years. In human terms it was a watershed.

The coming to power of the New Order Government was arguably the event of single greatest strategic benefit to Australia after the Second World War. Without an Indonesian Government that was focussed on economic and social development and committed to policies of cooperation with its South-East Asian neighbours, Australians would have faced three decades of uncertainty, fear and, almost certainly, massively greater defence spending. And ASEAN and APEC, two foundation stones of regional cooperation, could not have developed.

There was, therefore, every reason for a warm and deep relationship to develop between Australia and Indonesia. But that was not the way it worked. In the years after 1966, bilateral relations had sometimes gathered speed for a while, but had then lost momentum. Committed people in both countries had worked hard to build friendship, but despite their efforts the relationship remained a thin foreign policy crust covering a disappointingly hollow core.

Significant misunderstandings persisted on both sides.

Research we commissioned in 1994, for example, showed that fewer than one in five of the Indonesians surveyed saw Australia as a modern or advanced society and only two per cent were aware of Australian manufactures and mining products. A depressingly large two-thirds believed the White Australia Policy was still in operation. On Australia's side, there seemed an equal level of ignorance about modern Indonesian society that was not much altered by decades of package tours of Bali. Suspicion of Indonesia as a long-term threat to the country persisted. In both directions, the situation was a reminder of how the images we have of other countries, once struck, endure.

The problem with the relationship, in Gareth Evans's good phrase, was that it had no ballast. As a result, it was easily driven off course by any passing political storm. For several years Gareth had been working closely and productively with Ali Alatas, the urbane and skilful Indonesian Foreign Minister, to create such ballast. We could not have hoped to have two more able or committed foreign ministers working on the problem. But foreign ministers could not do the job alone. I believed the fundamentals of the relationship could only be changed by an effort led by the two heads of government, involving the whole of the government. The ballast had to come from the economic and social policy departments of government and, more importantly, from outside government, from business people, professional organisations, students and community groups. From the people of both countries.

My objective as prime minister was to weave a web of relationships with Indonesia so strong that if one part was under stress or torn, we could repair it while the other filaments held the web intact. This meant encouraging ministers to develop direct links with their Indonesian counterparts so we could identify areas where our mutual interests would be served by working together. It also meant encouraging the development of stakeholders in the broader community. Ordinary Australians had to see what was going on in the Indonesia–Australia relationship as relevant to their own interests. (The potential for a relationship was there: according to public-opinion polling, 60 per cent of Australians agreed or strongly agreed that a close relationship with Indonesia was very important to Australia.)

At the end of 1991, as so often before, the storm clouds blowing the relationship off course seemed darkest over East Timor. The circumstances and consequences of Portugal's abandonment of its former colony and the subsequent Indonesian takeover in 1975–76 had haunted Australia–Indonesia relations ever since. Timor has loomed far larger in Australia's consciousness than other, longer struggles for autonomy within Indonesia, like that of Aceh in Northern Sumatra. A number of factors shaped this Australian response: Timor's proximity to Australia, the history of unstinting help given by many Timorese to Australian soldiers during the Second World War, the links with the Catholic Church and, perhaps most significantly, the shooting of five Australian journalists by Indonesian troops during the military action there, a matter which subsequently became a cause célèbre among the Australian press. More ignobly, our response was also fanned by a persistent strain of anti-Indonesian sentiment among a core group of Australian journalists.

Indonesia faced, in 1975, the sudden abandonment by Portugal of a colonial enclave occupying half of the island of Timor in the middle of the Indonesian archipelago. Portugal was surely one of the world's most incompetent colonial powers: at the time it walked out, after 300 years, the literacy rate among the East Timorese was just five per cent.

Civil war had broken out between local groups who wanted independence and others who favoured integration with Indonesia and were supported by Jakarta. The main pro-independence group, Fretelin, was tied up with the Portuguese Communist Party. This was the height of the Cold War, and the political and military leadership in Jakarta was alarmed about the possible emergence of a pro-Russian or pro-Chinese state deep within its own territory. After initially providing covert support to the pro-integration faction, Indonesia eventually used its own forces to invade the territory in December 1975. In July the following year it declared East Timor its 27th province.

Indonesia created most of its own problems in East Timor. In two similar cases involving Portugal's residual colonial empire, India had marched into Goa and taken it over in 1961, while in Macau, China had simply never budged from its claims of sovereignty until Portugal negotiated for the colony's return in 1999.

East Timor was a long way from Jakarta and to a highly centralised administration it was remote and relatively unimportant. Its population of around 800,000 seemed a drop in the ocean among 210 million others. The administration was left largely in the hands of the military, which developed significant and profitable economic interests in the province. Outsiders dominated the bureaucracy. Sometimes Jakarta's actions had been well-intentioned. East Timor certainly received a disproportionately large share of central government development funds, although not all those funds went to the people they were destined for. More often, however, Indonesian policy combined insensitivity, brutality and incompetence. The result was that Indonesia's own actions fathered successive new generations of resistance among the East Timorese.

Timor had a particular relevance at the time I became prime minister because on 12 November 1991, unarmed civilians had been massacred in the Santa Cruz cemetery in Dili by Indonesian troops. The massacre was the result of an appalling lapse of control by individual security forces on the ground in Dili rather than deliberate policy instructions from Jakarta. But it raised again the deeper question of why the Indonesia authorities maintained such an intense military presence in East Timor, and how much control the government exercised over its operations. The estimated ratio of military forces to the civilian population was one to 50 in East Timor, compared with one to 850 through the country as a whole.

Australians had been shocked by the massacre, as were many Indonesians. Gareth Evans was given the difficult job of going to Jakarta just before Christmas to express Australia's concerns and to urge that the National Investigation Commission, which had been set up by the Indonesian Government, hold an internationally credible inquiry. He was on this mission, which he accomplished with great dignity and skill, on the day that I became prime minister.

I discussed in chapter 3 the general question of human rights in Australian foreign policy. In the case of Indonesia, I believed that Timor, and dialogue about it (as well as other Indonesian human rights questions) were an important element in our relationship. I held few conversations with Indonesian leaders in which I did not raise Timor or Irian Jaya, but I was not prepared to make the whole of our complex relationship with 210 million people subject to this one issue. Like previous Australian governments we accepted the incorporation of East Timor into Indonesia. We regarded this as the best potential outcome for Indonesia and the East Timorese. A quirk of European colonialism, not an ethnic or geographical division, had determined that a line would be drawn down one half of one particular island. But we could see, and worried deeply about, the way Indonesian policy, through its emphasis on military solutions, was itself building a sense of East Timorese nationalism. We urged the Indonesians to abandon the military approach and to acknowledge the distinct cultural and religious identity of the East Timorese by giving them greater autonomy. I believe that policy, applied earlier, would have worked to the advantage of all Indonesians and the East Timorese. Claims were regularly made by Australian supporters of East Timor that Australian policy was somehow shaped by Australian economic interests in the oil of the Timor Gap. Similar claims were routinely made in respect of Bougainville about the reopening of the copper mine there. In fact, at no point in any of my discussions with colleagues or foreign governments did the issues of any Australian economic interest shape, let alone determine, the government's thinking about the proper policy to follow on either of these questions. I cannot recall, in all my time in government, a single conversation about East Timor or Bougainville in which the commercial advantages or disadvantages for Australia with regard to developments there was even raised.

Although I was being urged from some politically cautious quarters not to risk an early visit to Jakarta following the massacre in Dili the previous November, I decided to make Indonesia the destination of my first overseas visit as prime minister. No direct contact had taken place between the Indonesian and Australian heads of government for nearly a decade, a situation I thought extraordinary between two neighbours. With Indonesia's economic growth, new opportunities were opening up for Australia. Trade, transportation links and visitor numbers were all growing. But the official infrastructure needed work. I announced my intention to go there in the middle of a media flurry about a Portuguese protest ship that was trying to sail to Timor from Darwin.

I arrived in Jakarta on a typically sweltering day in April 1992. We were to visit Jakarta, Surabaya and, as a deliberate signal of respect for the rich culture of our neighbour, the magnificent ninth-century Buddhist temple in Borobudur, near Yogyakarta in Central Java.

At a banquet on the evening of my arrival I spoke about my hopes for the relationship. President Suharto made a formal response that seemed pre-emptively cold. 'We will open-heartedly receive all kinds of suggestions and even criticism that are given in a spirit of friendship,' he said. 'But comments and criticism that are lodged mainly for the purpose of magnifying existing shortcomings in our national development and with the tendency of interfering in our internal problems are another thing.' The speech caused a minor flurry in the Australian party. Were we being sent a message about the next day's talks? We finally concluded – with assistance from Ali Alatas the Indonesian Foreign Minister – that the language simply represented the foreign ministry's pro forma speech for such occasions and that nothing beyond the words should be read into it.

I had my first formal meeting with the President the next day at the Istana Negara, the presidential palace in Jakarta. The palace is an old Dutch building, light and airily proportioned, its walls hung with large paintings in the elaborate style of Indonesian baroque favoured by the former president, Dr Sukarno. I came to know it well during the next four years.

For me, the important thing about this first meeting was the opportunity to listen, to try to get Suharto's measure and work out what our governments might be able to do together. I wanted to keep the meeting small. The President had with him his longstanding interpreter, Mr Widodo, and Ashton Calvert, my foreign policy adviser, accompanied me.

The meeting began formally. President Suharto ran through an account of Indonesia's history, culture, and the development plans he had for the country. He talked about the Borobudur temple. He spoke of the importance of regional resilience in ASEAN. He addressed directly the issue of the political succession, saying that Indonesia's constitutional arrangements and the philosophy of *Pancasila* would ensure that the succession went smoothly. This insistence on constitutional forms, I would discover, was one of the most consistent elements in Suharto's conversations. (It accounted, in part, for the way he eventually left office.) The account he gave was obviously one that other visitors in my position had received before, but what interested me about it was the care he put into explaining what he was doing and why, and his mastery of detail.

On the bilateral relationship, Suharto was quite specifically trying to reassure me that Indonesia did not pose a threat to Australia. For my part, I said I wanted my choice of Indonesia for my first overseas visit as prime minister to make clear to Australians the priority I meant to attach to the relationship. Australia did not threaten Indonesia. Australians had fought many times in war, and in many parts of the world, but never for the purpose of adding to Australian territory, only to protect others.

We talked about regional developments and I repeated to him, as I had over dinner the night before, my arguments for meetings of APEC heads of government. Suharto did not seem persuaded by the urgency of my tone. He agreed such meetings could eventually take place, but suggested they would need 'careful preparation' – ominous code words in Asian diplomacy. He pointed out delicately that it had taken nine years for ASEAN to hold its first summit meeting. I said I believed this would be too long for APEC and explained why. I asked him to consider the proposal further.

As at almost every meeting we held, I spoke to him about East Timor and human rights. I said this issue detracted from the fabric of all the New Order Government's accomplishments. To be traduced internationally by one of the most appalling colonialists, Portugal, made it worse. I offered whatever help Australia could provide to deal with the issue, including direct aid to Timor and participation in its economic development, a step which would have been unprecedented for Australia. I told him Australia would jointly develop the province further with Indonesia if Indonesia believed this would be of value and would work. Suharto listened but did not respond.

The meeting lasted more than two hours. It convinced me that Suharto was completely strategic in his thinking, naturally cautious but willing to act when necessary. In particular I was confident that, like me, he thought the relationship between Australia and Indonesia was important and should be developed. He always showed an alert and patient understanding of Australia. I think he believed that, fundamentally, the relationship could be sound and that, given time and patience and some goodwill, it would come good – good for us, good for them.

My first visit to Indonesia was a success as these things go. But I knew there was no point in simply mouthing words about the importance of bilateral relations in speeches that would be forgotten soon after they were uttered. The only way I could be sure the words were translated into action would be by returning to Indonesia often. I wanted to show by my presence that I meant all I said about the value of the relationship.

I returned five times over the next four years, more than the total number of visits to Indonesia by all my predecessors since the Second World War. Thanks to the APEC leaders' meetings I was able to meet President Suharto in Seattle and Osaka as well. My visits were mostly short and as protocol-free as possible, designed to develop a habit of consultation between Australia and Indonesia.

The criticism was sometimes made that I over-personalised the relationship with Indonesia, placing too much weight on my own relations with the President. It is true that I liked him and valued the friendship. But I was always conscious that no relationship between states can rely on evanescent personal contacts. I knew that I would not be around forever and neither would he. The consistent message of all the Australian official briefing I was receiving through that period was that the New Order institutions were coming under strain, that criticism of Suharto and his family would grow, but that he was likely to be in power until at least the 1998 elections. And so it turned out to be. My aim was to use my relationship with Suharto, for so long as we were both there, to try to develop structural changes that would outlast us both. I made this point directly to him.

Media pundits, anxious to belittle me, claimed that I addressed Suharto as 'Bapak', an Indonesian honorific meaning 'Father'. This is as untrue as it is absurd. I had far too much regard for the standing of the office of Prime Minister of Australia to call him anything other than 'Mr President'.

In my first meeting with the President I proposed the establishment of a ministerial forum that would meet regularly and would involve at least two economic ministers from each side as well as the foreign ministers. I had in mind something like the Australia–Japan Ministerial Committee, which over many years had exposed Australian economic ministers, including me, to the broad issues in the Australia–Japan relationship.

Suharto agreed and the Ministerial Forum met for the first time in the following November. It provided the impetus we hoped for. In the three years to June 1994 we had 35 ministerial visits between the two countries, nearly four times the number in the preceding three years. I was very pleased, after leaving office, to hear Indonesian ministers talk with obvious satisfaction about the results of the Ministerial Forum in October 1996, a meeting which included six Coalition ministers. The forum was just one of several ways we worked to build the number of stakeholders in the relationship over the next four years.

In 1995 we marked the 50th anniversary of Indonesia's independence by setting up a new scholarship scheme – the Australia–Indonesia Merdeka Fellowships. These were designed to promote mid-career exchanges between outstanding young Indonesians and young Australians. I hoped that over time we could build up personal links between our most able young people in the way the Rhodes scholarships had done with Britain, or the Harkness or Fulbright fellowships with the United States. I hoped we could bring about a situation in which the brightest young Indonesians would want to study in Australia as much as in the United States or Europe. It remains an aspiration worth pursuing.

We worked hard and successfully to get Australian newspaper and media correspondents back into the country. This has been important in strengthening public (and media) understanding of Indonesia.

Trade between our two countries was also growing rapidly, rising at a trend rate of 22 per cent in the early 1990s. So when I visited Indonesia for the second time in June 1994, it was for a major trade promotion and in the company of representatives of over two hundred Australian companies, the largest trade mission ever to leave Australia. The promotion was not only designed to boost trade, but to help overcome some of the misconceptions about Australia that the survey we had commissioned earlier had revealed. When I launched the promotion a couple of months before, I said, for the first time: 'No country is more important to Australia than Indonesia.' This careful formulation was designed to position Indonesia in a triumvirate of central relationships with the United States, our major ally (and an important economic partner), and Japan, our major trading partner. I was not saying that Indonesia was our most important relationship, though my words were sometimes misinterpreted in this way in the media. But I was signalling that the Indonesian relationship needed to be thought about and worked on with the same care and intensity we gave to the United States and Japan.

I was not after a 'special relationship' with Indonesia, a phrase I never used, and a category of international relationships in which, as I have already discussed in regard to China, I did not believe. But I did want a relationship appropriate to two neighbouring countries of our size and with our potential for development. And we did not have it.

The relationship wasn't all plain sailing. As a government, we disagreed with Indonesia over the legal right of East Timorese to self-determination and over East Timorese refugees, over Irian Jaya, over the burning of Indonesian flags by demonstrators in

Australia at the time of the 50th anniversary of Indonesia's independence. But we were making progress.

So by 1995, when another of these crises blew up, I felt we had made the hoped-for transition to a relationship in which we could disagree without putting everything at risk.

The Indonesian Ambassador throughout most of my time as prime minister was Sabam Siagian, a combative and articulate former journalist and editor who had been a popular representative of Indonesia in Australia, not least because of his un-Javanese directness in dealing with the media. However, in 1995, his posting had come to an end and the Indonesian Government nominated as his successor General Herman Mantiri, the former chief of the Indonesian army.

There is no doubt that the Indonesians saw the appointment as a mark of the importance of the Australia–Indonesia relationship. General Mantiri was a highly regarded military officer who had done much to improve discipline in ABRI, the Indonesian armed forces. But in defending his men against public criticism he had justified the actions of the Indonesian military during the Dili massacre although he had nothing to do with the massacre personally, and his reported comments aroused controversy and protests in Australia.

On the Australian side, we did not handle the issue well. We should have been more alert to the problems at an earlier stage of the process, and we should have discussed them with the Indonesians. But after a good deal of behind-the-scenes activity, Suharto decided to withdraw the nomination in July 1995. He did not like doing so. He did not immediately nominate a replacement which, in the circumstances, was hardly surprising, but the affair generated a spate of hysterical press coverage and overblown rhetoric from the Opposition about the fragile state of relations with Indonesia.

A couple of months later, in September, I met Suharto again in Bali. I had flown directly from Papua New Guinea, mainly to discuss with him the handling of the Osaka leaders' meeting. Suharto raised the Mantiri nomination and said he had been trying to convince his people that they should not lose patience over small incidents and allow them to harm the solid basis of the relationship between the two countries. He said we needed to 'deepen the relationship in the minds of the people'. General Mantiri's appointment might have jeopardised the relationship, so he had withdrawn it. He agreed with me that the public in both countries were finally realising the importance of the bilateral relationship. Throughout the period of the dispute over the Mantiri nomination, we had good evidence that Suharto himself intervened in support of the relationship with Australia to cool the emotions of some of his more hot-headed officials.

The main outcome of the visit to Bali, however, related neither to ambassadors nor APEC. It was the unexpected culmination of something I had by then been working on for a couple of years – a security agreement with Indonesia.

Defence cooperation between Australia and Indonesia had been developing well. We saw it as an important element in developing trust between the two countries. Already, Australia was the most significant source of foreign military training for the Indonesian army. We were careful to avoid some sensitive areas that could involve human rights issues, but we believed that the Australian Defence Force had much to teach ABRI about military professionalism that would benefit the Indonesian people. Successive commanders of the ADF during this period – General Peter Gration, Admiral Alan Beaumont, and General John Baker – worked hard to develop personal links with their Indonesian counterparts and to intensify dialogue on defence issues and regional cooperation. I believed this to be a good thing, but I also thought Australia and Indonesia needed to widen the focus of our defence relationship from military-to-military cooperation to strategic cooperation. That is, we needed to move beyond cooperation between our military forces to build a foundation of shared security perceptions and commitments in the region.

Back in February 1994, during the Security Committee of Cabinet's consideration of the Defence Strategic Review, I had raised the possibility of our seeking to negotiate a security agreement with Indonesia. The Strategic Review had concluded that, 'More than any other regional nation, a sound strategic relationship with Indonesia would do most for Australia's security. We should seek new opportunities to deepen the relationship in areas that serve both countries' interests.' I agreed with this objective, but I thought the recommended measures to achieve it were inadequate. We had security treaties and agreements all around Indonesia, but not with it.

I believed a formal agreement with Indonesia would complement our other regional security relationships. These included the Five Power Defence Arrangements which linked us to the security of Singapore and Malaysia and which had originally been put together with concern about Indonesia in mind, our relationship with New Zealand through ANZUS, and our Joint Declaration of Principles with Papua New Guinea. Indonesia was the only one of our immediate neighbours with which we had not tried to build some sort of strategic relationship, and it was the biggest country of all. My Cabinet colleagues agreed that the feasibility of such an agreement should be examined, although I didn't detect much enthusiasm or confidence around the table that anything would come of it. They weren't the only sceptics. My own staff were cautious, not about the aim but about the chance of bringing it off, given Indonesia's historic commitment to non-alignment and its suspicion of defence pacts.

Gareth Evans, separately, had been working with Ali Alatas for some time on the idea of an umbrella agreement between Australia and Indonesia – a broad political declaration that would cover basic principles of the relationship in all its dimensions, including defence. The main argument for such an agreement was that it would put a 'roof' over the relationship.

When the proposal was raised with me, with its political and cultural references, I was decidedly unenthusiastic about it. I thought that what the relationship between Australia and Indonesia needed was not a roof but a stronger strategic foundation. I believed the sort of document Gareth and Ali Alatas had in mind, which would assert a number of basic principles Australia and Indonesia held in common and proclaim that relations would be based on mutual respect for 'shared and unique values', begged more questions than it answered. I felt that by trying to assert common values between two very different cultures, such a document might make the resolution of future difficulties between us *more* difficult, not less. I was always distinctly worried by declarations that went to other people's ideas of civil society, especially in such a religiously and ethnically diverse place as Indonesia.

The sort of agreement I was after did not need to be lengthy or complex; nor did I want anything that begged questions about internal matters. Indeed, the simpler and more straightforward it was the better. It was the commitment that mattered. After the Cabinet decision, I asked my foreign policy adviser, Allan Gyngell, to seek some confidential advice from the public service about a defence agreement. Some very useful preparatory work was undertaken in the International Division of the Department of the Prime Minister and Cabinet by Michael Thawley and his colleagues there, and the first internal draft of what such a document might look like was ready a month later. It drew strongly on existing agreements like the United Nations Charter, the Five Power Defence Arrangements, the Australia–Papua New Guinea Joint Declaration of Principles and ANZUS, as well as the work Gareth and Ali Alatas had done on an umbrella agreement.

At this point, the senior public service committee on strategic policy was brought fully into the discussion. It prepared a paper on defence relations with Indonesia that canvassed various options. It came out in support of the idea of a defence agreement but again expressed doubts about whether it could be done.

At the same time, the Minister for Defence, Robert Ray, was getting cautious advice from defence department officials who were suggesting a less ambitious approach. (In general, the government received great support from Defence and the ADF for closer engagement with Indonesia. But a mostly unspoken thought continued to lurk in the collective bureaucratic mind of the Defence department and could not be expunged: how could public support for the defence budget be maintained without the implicit threat of Indonesia?) The judgement about whether we could get the sort of agreement I wanted was not one I was prepared to give up on.

I was due to visit Indonesia again for the trade promotion in June 1994. I decided to use this opportunity to sound out President Suharto. Suharto was an early riser and our appointment was fixed for 9 a.m. on 28 June in the now-familiar surroundings of the presidential palace. We again met for two hours and spoke for another hour over an official dinner that night.

The President himself brought up the subject of defence cooperation. In the course of the usual review of bilateral relations, he said he believed Australia and Indonesia could establish closer defence relations. I responded that Australia now saw the beginning of strategic trust between Indonesia and itself. 'We are willing to put our cards on the table, face up, and make a clear declaration that such trust exists,' I said. If we could declare this reality in some way, it would send a very strong message to our neighbours, whose interests it would serve by making the entire region stronger. Australia was prepared to think about some more formal arrangement. This would not be an agreement in which we would commit ourselves automatically, but one in which we would declare our common strategic interests and agree to consult in the event of any strategic threat.

The President listened carefully. He was cautious about a more formalised defence agreement but, importantly, he did think schematically and he did not rule it out. Finally, after I had pressed him politely but firmly, he agreed we could discuss the matter further. We agreed that he and I would be the principal conduit for such discussions because he had to be given the opportunity to handle what would be difficult matters on the Indonesian side. I said I would consult Robert Ray about the appointment of a prime ministerial emissary to carry the work further. I already had someone in mind for this job: the retired chief of the Australian Defence Force, General Peter Gration. General Gration was one of Australia's most distinguished soldiers. During his period as chief he, more than anyone else, had been responsible for reorganising the structure of the Australian Defence Force. His thoughtfulness, judgement and personal commitment to closer defence relations between Australia and Indonesia had long impressed me. I knew his reputation in Jakarta would help reassure the Indonesian armed forces – ABRI – as well as the Australian defence establishment about what we were trying to do.

In September, General Gration visited Jakarta with Allan Gyngell to meet State Secretary Moerdiono, who was Suharto's nominated contact point on this matter, and to outline what we were, and were not, trying to do. At this meeting Moerdiono asked for a non-paper – the diplomatic name for an informal document which can be disowned if necessary – setting out the concepts we had in mind. This was prepared in Canberra and handed to him by our able Ambassador in Jakarta, Allan Taylor, early in October 1994.

The non-paper began by stating:

> Australia and Indonesia share similar strategic concerns. We share an interest in each other's security. Neither is a threat to the other. An agreement or understanding on security

cooperation between Australia and Indonesia would benefit us both. It would also strengthen the stability and strategic resilience of the region. An agreement would be consistent with our strong and broadly based bilateral relationship. It would demonstrate the trust and confidence each has in the other. It would have a beneficial impact on public attitudes in both countries. It would provide a formal basis for our more active defence relationship.

We emphasised that we were not proposing a non-aggression pact. That would imply we saw one another as a threat, which was not the case.

Then came an unexpected glitch. Gration and Gyngell returned in November 1994 to discuss the non-paper, only to discover that their contacts seemed to have left town. Moerdiono failed to confirm an appointment tentatively put in place by the Ambassador, and was uncontactable. We did not know what to make of this. Was it a Javanese signal that we should not go ahead with our proposal? Did it mean that the Indonesian side was not ready to make a decision? Was it simply administrative confusion? We decided it probably reflected difficulties on the Indonesian side. We had always known it would be hard for Indonesia to take such a decision because of its traditional non-alignment. I decided not to press the matter further by raising a fuss over Moerdiono's non-attendance. This was the sort of arrangement that was only worth having – and could only be got – if each party was comfortable with it and had time to discuss it informally.

For the next nine months we heard nothing more from the Indonesian side, though we heard word it was being discussed. Then unexpectedly, at the end of our meeting in Bali in September 1995, President Suharto himself referred to the proposal and suggested that Indonesia was now in a position to look at a draft text. I was pleased he had come back to it himself.

Gration and Gyngell flew to Jakarta on 15 November to negotiate the text with a wider Indonesian group that now included ABRI and foreign ministry officials. As in all their earlier meetings, they were joined by Ambassador Taylor. The main problems the Indonesians identified were not with the content of the proposed agreement but the presentation. In particular, they wanted to avoid any suggestion that this was a military pact. Phrases like 'defence agreement' and 'external threat' raised sensitivities for them. In response to the Indonesian concerns, we agreed to call the document the Agreement on Maintaining Security and to substitute the phrase 'adverse challenges' for our drafted 'external threat' to show that we wanted the agreement to cover not only military contingencies but the full range of external problems that might affect both countries and benefit from common action. The underlying force of the agreement lay in recognition by Australia and Indonesia that each had a fundamental interest in the security of the other, and was prepared to cooperate to protect this interest.

Agreement was reached on all but a couple of areas. Gyngell flew straight from Jakarta to Osaka to join me at the APEC meeting, where I was due to see Suharto. Suharto and I met on 18 November 1995 and endorsed the draft text, subject to a meeting that night between Moerdiono and Gyngell to resolve a couple of minor issues of language.

The final agreement was just over a page long. The preambular paragraphs placed its provisions in the context of the United Nations and noted that nothing in it affected the existing international commitments of either party. The three key operative paragraphs provided for Australia and Indonesia to:

- consult at ministerial level on a regular basis about matters affecting their common security and to develop such cooperation as would benefit their own security and that of the region

- consult each other in the case of adverse challenges to either party or to their common security interests and, if appropriate, consider measures which might be taken either individually or jointly and in accordance with the processes of each party
- promote, in accordance with the policies and priorities of each, cooperative activities in the security field.

After my meeting with Suharto in Osaka, I returned to Australia to put the agreement to the full Cabinet. On 13 December, the evening before I was to do this, I personally briefed the American Ambassador, Ed Perkins, of what was coming. It was, of course, essential that we advise our closest ally, but I had been relaxed about the timing. I knew from many conversations with senior Americans, dating back to my first talks with George Bush, that they attached importance to the building of our relationship with Indonesia and would not see the agreement as any sort of caveat to the alliance. On the contrary, I always had the sense from the Americans that they were comfortable with Australia managing its own relationships within the region.

On the following day Cabinet endorsed the agreement and I walked out into the ministerial courtyard in Parliament House to announce the proposal to the media. In an age when government leaks are a dime a dozen, the fact that this had been kept confidential until the announcement was a source of great satisfaction to me, and corresponding irritation to some in the press.

General Gration and senior government officials then fanned out around the region to explain the agreement to our friends and neighbours, including China. We wanted to deflect any suggestion that the agreement was part of some plan to 'contain' China.

Within Australia, the Opposition expressed its support for the agreement. Some journalists, however, suggested that I had negotiated the agreement and planned its timing with domestic political considerations in mind. This revealed a strange understanding of Australian politics. I had not pursued the agreement because I thought there might be domestic advantage in it. If anything, I thought there might be some short-term disadvantage for Labor, given the long tradition of public wariness of Indonesia and the likely attitude of the pro-Timor groups, including within the ALP. But I believed that getting the agreement in place was important to Australia's interests, and that this was a risk worth taking.

One did not need to be a political scientist or military historian to know how important the Indonesian archipelago was to Australia. The Japanese had, in 1942, advanced towards it down the Malay peninsula, overtaking Singapore. We had fought them in Ambon and Timor. Similarly, Papua New Guinea was the place where the Japanese army was first defeated, at our hands and with the United States. The waters around Papua New Guinea was the place from which Japan sought to launch its attack on Australia, and where (in the Coral Sea) they were thwarted.

An arc of friendly countries across Australia's north provided Australia's best protection against threat from any country within the arc or beyond it. The recognition by Indonesia that we shared a strategic interest in this part of South-East Asia and its readiness to say so and to consult were it to be threatened was a highly important step forward. For us as well as for them. We had an interest in Indonesia's bulk, its 210 million people. They had a defence interest in our professionalism, our capacity to train forces and provide material.

Suharto, who was the only person capable of delivering such an agreement within Indonesia, understood this well. He intuitively understood that when I said we had no strategic designs on Indonesian territory, I meant it and it was true. He put trust in that view, as I did in his that Indonesia had no territoral designs on Australia.

In Australia, the manner of the agreement's negotiation was

also criticised. Claims that the agreement was somehow illegitimate because it was announced after a process of consultation between the two countries were taken up by journalists and interests traditionally hostile to Jakarta. This was a 'secret' agreement, fulminated the critics. But it was secret only to those who had not been paying attention to the government's statements about defence, or who assumed that I did not mean what I was saying in almost all of my speeches about Indonesia.

The general direction of the government's policy towards Indonesia was well known and had been debated in Parliament. The 1993 Strategic Review said specifically: 'More than with any other regional nation, a sound strategic relationship with Indonesia does most for Australia's security.' In March 1994, to take just one of many examples, I had said publicly:

> Changes in Australia and Indonesia and in the world since the end of the Cold War should compel us to take a fresh look at our strategic relationship. I believe great potential exists for further defence cooperation between Australia and Indonesia ... If we are to turn into reality our policy of seeking defence in and with Asia, instead of against Asia, Indonesia is the most important place it will have to be done.

An earlier announcement of the fact and details of the negotiations would not have delivered an agreement. It is impossible to negotiate something like this in the public view, because until just before the announcement was made we did not know whether the Indonesian side would want to go ahead or whether those in its own constituency had had the time and the private space to consider its implications fully. That is why in the Westminster system the treaty-making function has always been the responsibility of the executive. It has never been otherwise. And in this case all the proper processes of the executive were followed. Every treaty becomes subject to public debate in the process of consideration and ratification by Parliament. And that is when it should happen. In this case, that step was implemented by the Coalition Government that succeeded Labor in 1996.

On 18 December 1995 I flew to Jakarta for the signing of the agreement. I took with me – with deliberate symbolism – the most senior Australian delegation ever to visit another country. The Deputy Prime Minister (Kim Beazley) was present along with the Foreign Minister, the Minister for Defence, and the Chief of the Australian Defence Force. I had particularly wanted Kim to be present as a signal of continuity. I knew that, sooner or later, he was likely to succeed me as Leader of the Labor Party.

I felt proud of what had been accomplished and what it revealed about the progress we had made in relations with Indonesia. I shook Suharto's hand. It was the last time I was to see him as prime minister.

The following year I was out of office and life became steadily more difficult for Suharto. His wife died unexpectedly in 1996. It seemed to me that this was a bitter personal blow. It affected his political judgement as well. His children became relatively more important in his personal life, and this seems to have blinded him further to the effect their commercial dealings were having on his political reputation and, increasingly, on the Indonesian economy.

Then, from the middle of 1997, the Asian economic crisis presented Indonesia with the sharpest economic decline in its history, one of the steepest anywhere in the world in modern times. The economy shrank by 20 per cent. Unemployment more than doubled. Inflation soared by 80 per cent.

It was a crisis unlike any Indonesia had faced in the past, because it was taking place in a country that had been transformed. In 1966, when Suharto came to power, agriculture made up half the economy; now it was just 20 per cent. A large middle class of perhaps 15 million people had grown up. Most importantly, community expectations had changed. As a result of thirty years of development, the people of Indonesia expected their own lives, and the prospects for their children, to steadily improve.

As in Thailand, Indonesia's problems began when the government was unable to sustain the informal currency peg it had established between the rupiah and the US dollar. Indonesia had benefited greatly from this link. But although it helped bring in foreign investment, it also generated a huge offshore debt burden. Indonesian businesses borrowed US dollars at US interest rates rather than at the higher Indonesian rates and did not hedge their borrowings because they assumed they faced no exchange risk. The offshore debt was around $US74 billion. Three-quarters of it was unhedged, and it was mostly short term. Suharto told me later that his government had no idea of the size of this private sector borrowing.

As the economic crisis intensified, nervous capital, including capital from the local Chinese community, started leaving the country, capital inflow slumped and confidence evaporated in the local market. Problems everyone had known about and lived with, like corruption, a weak banking sector, a general lack of commercial and governmental transparency, poor prudential controls and the political direction of investment decisions were put under greater scrutiny.

The Indonesian Government realised it did not have the resources to defend the rupiah. (In Thailand most of the reserves of the central bank had been thrown away in a fruitless attempt to defend the baht.) So in August 1997 – quite early in the crisis, and to the applause of the international financial community – the rupiah was floated. But the economic collapse continued. An extensive deregulation package in September did not restore market confidence, nor did an IMF package in November which the Indonesian Government was praised for seeking in a timely way. In fact, as the International Monetary Fund (IMF) subsequently acknowledged, the measures made matters worse. The closure of sixteen banks helped create a run on the entire banking system.

In January 1998, Indonesia's annual budget was brought down. Its handling was another illustration of growing political ineptness on the part of Suharto's Government. Despite some strong points, the budget's credibility was undermined by out-of-date economic assumptions. Indonesia was forced back to the IMF to negotiate another, even larger $US43 billion package of support.

By that time it was clear that the future of the Indonesian economy had become caught up in judgements about its political system. One of the consequences of Indonesia's opening up had been an enormous increase in the influence on its economy of the finance and currency markets of New York, Frankfurt and London. I don't think Suharto fully understood this.

A presidential election was due in the following May. Markets want certainty and the Indonesian political timetable was unable to deliver it. The United States, which had been a staunch supporter of Suharto during the Cold War, had largely lost interest in South-East Asia, or at least the degree of interest it had before. In Washington's collective mind, Indonesia had become an issue rather than a country.

It seemed to me that the necessary step to resolve the situation was a clear sign from Suharto that he would step down at a specific point. The times required directness and clarity from Indonesia's leadership, but what we were getting was Javanese obliqueness. Although I was now a private citizen, I felt I owed it to Suharto as a friend to tell him this myself. If he took no action, I feared for the way things would go in Indonesia.

Inside Indonesia and in South-East Asia, there was a great reluctance to speak frankly to the President. This was partly

President Clinton. It was, in my view, imperative that the United States should continue to be engaged
the Pacific.

One of the benefits of the APEC leaders' meetings was the opportunity they provided for personal contact. Seattle brought President Clinton and President Jiang Zemin of China together for the first time.

Zhu Rongji, now Premier of China. We first met when he was Mayor of Shanghai.

Australian commodity exports helped underpin Japan's industrial development. In 1993, I toured the Toyota factory with the Chairman, Mr Toyoda, soon after the company had announced a major manufacturing investment in Victoria.

With Emperor Akihito of Japan. In the 1990s Australia and had developed 'a relationship of unprecedented quality'.

very informal setting of the first APEC leaders' meeting at Blake Island, near Seattle, in November 1993.

President Suharto and his interpreter on the eve of the Bogor Summit. The summit was an outstanding rmance by Suharto.

At the magnificent ninth-century Buddhist temple of Borobadur in Central Java on my first visit to Indonesia in 1992.

Hellfire Pass on the notorious Burma–Thailand railway. The site of such horror during the Second World War, but also where one of the truly great Australians, 'Weary' Dunlop, did so much to ease suffering and inspire faith when it was most needed.

Singaporean Prime Minister Goh Chok Tong was a firm ally in our attempts to develop APEC and our relations with the region. He hosted an impromptu birthday party for me during what was to be my final visit to Singapore as prime minister in 1996.

...rst meeting with the Prime Minister of Malaysia, Dr Mahathir, in 1993. My disagreement with his policy ...ved around a quite different view of what Australia's role in the region should be.

Australian peacekeeping troops in Cambodia ...92. The Cambodia peace agreement was a ... achievement for Australian diplomacy and ...ularly for Gareth Evans.

The ceremony in 1995 making me an honorary chief of the Oro people was a symbolic reminder that Australia and the people of the Kokoda region were linked forever by the sacrifices made there during the Second World War. This was where Australia had been saved.

I wanted my young daughters to see something of the extraordinarily rich culture of Papua New Guinea.

Surveying the moonscape surface of the phosphate mining areas of Nauru, one of the many environmental challenges facing the South Pacific.

and, at the grave of my relatives. My great-
[grand]parents had come from Tynagh, which I
[visited] in 1993.

The crowd at the 1993 Gaelic football final at Croke Park in Dublin sang along to the words of 'Waltzing Matilda'.

[In fron]t of the Charlottenhof, designed by Karl Friedrich Schinkel, near the German city of Potsdam, which has
[seen s]o much good and evil in European history.

With President Mitterand outside the Elysée Palace in Paris in June 1994. Mitterand was already ill but he still had a forceful presence and a complex, engaging mind.

Labor believed that a real and mutual sense of reconciliation with Indigenous Australians, one of the oldest civilisations on earth, would bring immense national dividends.

because of Asian cultural preferences to avoid confrontation, partly because of Suharto's own political style. Some who had tried in the past to raise the issue of his succession, or of the behaviour of his children, had suffered politically for their temerity. And he was unlikely to take much notice of the chorus of voices in Washington and Europe now demanding his head.

I telephoned a regional leader whose advice I valued about what I proposed to do. He encouraged me. 'After all,' he added, with an accurate but somewhat unnecessary frankness about my own position, 'if I tell him he may hate [my country]. If you tell him, he will just hate you.'

So when I arrived in Jakarta, I was not looking forward to the task ahead. I saw Suharto on 15 January 1998, the morning he was to sign a new, $US43 billion, package of support with the IMF (the occasion later remembered for photographs of IMF Director General Michel Camdessus standing with folded arms as Suharto signed the papers). Even on this busy morning he received me warmly and listened intently to what I had to say. I stayed three-quarters of an hour. He even suspended his interpreter to make better use of the time available. He repeated back to me several of the points I made to ensure he understood. But as subsequent events showed, he did not take the advice. The last thing I said to him as I left the door of his home was, 'Mr President, if you wait until March [when the Parliament was to meet to elect the new President] you will wait until it is too late.'

The January IMF package surprised almost all observers with its comprehensiveness. It involved extensive economic restructuring, including fundamental reform of the financial sector and the dismantling of most government monopolies. 'Sweeping away the restrictions' was the way the IMF put it.

But nothing was going to work. The IMF's demands included not just measures to allow orderly economic adjustment but a complete reordering of the Indonesian economy. It seized the opportunity to impose an extensive and intrusive agenda of change. Some of the reforms were badly needed and would strengthen the Indonesian economy when it recovered. But, as even the IMF later admitted, they made that recovery more difficult by changing Indonesia's political dynamics and imposing goals that were politically unachievable and subsequently had to be renegotiated, thereby delaying the restoration of confidence.

Despite Indonesia's rapid development, it was a developing economy with serious administrative shortcomings. Implementation of government policy was always difficult. Now it was being asked to put in place a package of reforms so extensive that Australia, with a smaller population and much better communications, could not have done it in the time required.

Even before the ink was dry on the January agreement, prominent voices in the United States and Europe were casting doubt on Indonesia's willingness to comply. The currency was plunging, inflation was soaring. Perfectly reasonable efforts by Indonesia to explore other solutions, like the use of a currency board to underpin the rupiah, were sneered at in Washington as 'snake oil remedies'.

What happened in Indonesia was an unnecessary tragedy. Whatever the country's political or economic problems, the social dislocation and suffering caused to ordinary Indonesians by the economic collapse could not be justified. The Asian Development Bank estimated that 10 million Indonesians were thrown back into absolute poverty. The international community's approach meant that the political and economic problems facing Indonesia had to be dealt with simultaneously, making both harder to resolve.

To make matters worse, Suharto reacted by digging in. After his re-election as president on 10 March 1998 by an acquiescent parliament, he appointed a cabinet that got rid of some of the better independent thinkers and replaced them with cronies and children. Politics and the economy were locked together in a mutual downwards spiral.

The next time I saw Suharto, in Bali in April 1998, the hotel he was staying at was ringed by loyal troops. He seemed disconnected from the gathering storm. I urged on him the importance of avoiding physical harm to the student demonstrators who were then out in the streets of Jakarta. He said he agreed. But a month later students were shot after widespread protests. On 21 May 1998 Suharto stepped down in order, he said, to avoid further bloodshed. His recently appointed Vice-President, B.J. Habibie, took over. Dr Habibie told me afterwards that the decision had been as unexpected for him as for everyone else.

I returned to Jakarta in November that year to deliver a speech. I took the opportunity to meet President Habibie, the commander of ABRI, General Wiranto, opposition figures like Mrs Megawati Sukarnoputri and the leaders of the student demonstrators. I also called in on the former president at his relatively modest suburban house in central Jakarta. The students were again on the streets, demonstrating in favour of faster moves to democracy, and calling for investigations into the Suharto family's wealth. His house was surrounded by ABRI troops. Stories had been circulating in Jakarta the previous night that he had fled the country.

Suharto looked well and, as always, he seemed calm. But there was, for him, an angry edge to some of his comments about the current political scene. He said Indonesia's growth and its stability had been hampered. He had believed the only way for Indonesia to get to prosperity was through security. Now people wanted to get to prosperity through democracy.

He raised the opposition claims that he had used his position to enrich himself and that he had money stashed overseas. He said he was becoming a target but he would not run away from his responsibilities. If he were brought to court he would face that eventuality. He had nothing to hide, and no overseas bank accounts. His opponents could not identify such money because there was none. Claims that he used money from charitable foundations which he, or people close to him, controlled, were wrong. That money was not his.

Suharto said Indonesia was a tolerant society, but the problem was its leaders. Great kingdoms had been established through these islands, but they had crumbled because of the selfishness of the leaders. The Dutch had colonised the country by playing on that selfishness, pitting one against the other. Now Indonesia would go back to the multi-party bickering of old.

Even Islam was splintered, Suharto said. He believed that those who strove to establish an Islamic state in Indonesia would find opposition from inside the Islamic community as well as outside it. Islam had been freer under the New Order. Fanatics would ask him why Indonesia should not be an Islamic state. After all, they would say, we are the majority. He had told such people that if they tried to achieve this they would bring destruction to Indonesia.

We are too close to the Suharto era to see it clearly and historians' judgements about it will be shaped by what comes next in Indonesia. Many of the criticisms are accurate. He stayed too long and by the effluxion of time believed himself to be indispensable. His political views were shaped by the poverty of his youth and by the experience of Indonesia during the chaotic parliamentary period of the 1950s and Sukarno's guided democracy. He failed to understand the ways his own achievements had transformed Indonesian society, so that if there had been force in the original New Order slogan of 'economics first, politics later', the 'later' part was well overdue. He failed to respond to the demands of richer, better educated people for more control over their own lives. The commercial activities of his family and friends distorted the economy and undermined his legacy. Committed from his revolutionary days to a united, secular

Indonesia, he could not bring himself to change a harsh and unworkable policy in East Timor. He was for keeping an archipelago and a sense of nation together at all costs. And the costs were high, for others and also for him.

Against that, however, he had an enduring sense of the sort of country he wanted Indonesia to be – one that was growing and in which the lives of the rural poor, in particular, were improved. With great single-mindedness and consistently hard work he pulled Indonesia out of poverty and into development, leaving a legacy that will outlast the current downturn. He managed the fissiparous tendencies of Indonesian politics in a way that preserved unity and developed a sense of national identity. He opened up the Indonesian economy. He made regionalism possible with ASEAN and APEC. He steadfastly believed in the importance of the relationship with Australia. And, in the end, rather than risk further violence, he stepped down voluntarily and constitutionally. The record may be flawed but it is very substantial.

In contrast to accusations that he was a figure like Mobutu in Zaire, plundering his country for personal gain, nothing I saw of him in any of our conversations over many hours led me to think that his principal motivation was other than his conception of the best interests of Indonesia and its people. Nation-building was really his mission in life. His family certainly made money and wanted too much of it, but greed was not what drove him.

The Suharto period in Indonesia is over, even if the consequences are still being played out. Indonesians are searching for a new vision of what their country means, how it operates, how it is structured, whom it includes, and how it fits in to the wider international community.

Indonesia's national motto is 'Unity in Diversity'. How much diversity and what form of unity will be matters of continuing debate, but the power of that national commitment will be as important to Indonesia's future as to its past. And the way it resolves the debate will be critical for South-East Asia, too. I don't believe it is possible for the rest of the region to prosper if Indonesia is uncertain and unstable.

It is unlikely Indonesia will again have a leader with Suharto's degree of control, and it does not need one. Rather than a powerful president, Indonesia will benefit from a more decentralised parliamentary system in which regions and groups have clearer representation. Power is steadily flowing outwards, from the presidency to parliament, from the national parliament to regional assemblies. Islam will also have more of a role to play, and over time the military will have less. Some pent-up nationalist energy will be expended as the political system develops. The coming Indonesia will be less predictable, less centralised, but ultimately stronger economically and more robust socially.

Ali Alatas once made the point to me that the view in some quarters in Australia that Indonesia was an aggressive and expansionist country was a serious misperception. Indonesia's real problem, he said, was that it was not outward-looking enough. It had a low number of students studying abroad and few expatriate businessmen. The more I saw of Indonesia the more I came to believe this was right. Indonesia's size and population give it the option of turning inwards in a way that is available to few countries. I saw the things I was trying to do in our bilateral relationship and through APEC as part of an effort to encourage Indonesia to look outwards.

By 1999 relations between Australia and Indonesia had again sunk to new levels of hostility and suspicion following the mishandling on many sides of the East Timor issue. Crude stereotypes re-emerged in the press of both countries and politicians pandered to them. I was surprised and disappointed that the Howard Government so easily acquiesced in the stated abrogation of the Agreement on Maintaining Security by the Government of President B.J. Habibie at the height of the crisis.

Senior ministers of the Coalition Government were on record a number of times about the value of the agreement. At the third Indonesia–Australia Ministerial Forum held under the auspices of the new Coalition Government in Jakarta on 24 and 25 October 1996, the joint press statement recorded that ministers 'highlighted the entry into force of the Australia–Indonesia Agreement on Maintaining Security in July 1996 as a significant milestone and noted that the Agreement set out the common interests of both countries in the peace and security of the region.' In 1998, the Defence Minister Ian McLachlan described it as 'an umbrella under which we can talk more openly'. But despite these words, the Coalition Government had not tried to use the agreement to build common perceptions of regional security, presumably because it arose from an initiative of the Labor Goverment.

Under pressure from journalists with questions relating to the Timor crisis, John Howard described the agreement as 'irrelevant'. The agreement, of course, was not designed to deal with issues like Timor. It was directed at our mutual security in the broader region. However, in an atmosphere of anger and humiliation the Indonesian Government then announced on 16 September 1999 that the treaty was being abrogated. President Habibie's spokesperson, Dewi Fortuna Anwar, cited Prime Minister Howard's remarks as the principal reason for this.

It was a measure of how far the relationship had fallen. I regarded Howard's dismissal of the agreement and his failure to challenge the Indonesian decision as being recklessly indifferent to Australia's interests. While the agreement might not have been his, I believe his complicity in losing it as an instrument of Australian security and as an explicit declaration of our trust between two countries was taking partisanship to absurd lengths.

However, as those who had earlier worked on the relationship between Indonesia and Australia over fifty years knew, the only thing to do in the face of such setbacks was to continue the slow, patient efforts to build a deeper relationship. This is a relationship that needs to grow not only in the statements of governments but in the attitudes and actions of ordinary Australians and Indonesians. I can see no alternative to the policy we followed in those years – efforts to build the number of stakeholders in the relationship and to develop trust and understanding. Indonesia's importance to Australia will not diminish. Neither one of us will float away to another location.

Neither Indonesia's future nor the future of our bilateral relationship will be without difficulty. We will encounter problems and misunderstandings. We are different societies with different cultures at different stages of development. Can we sustain a relationship of depth and worth across this divide?

We can and we must.

CHAPTER 7
THE ARC AROUND US

South-East Asia is where Australia's national foreign policy interaction with Asia began during the Second World War and after it, as the peoples of the band of European colonies around us struggled, often painfully, to become sovereign states. The region dominated the debate about Australian security during the 1960s and '70s when conservative Australian governments assured us that collapsing dominoes would open a path for the downward thrust of communist expansionism. It was the Asia most Australians knew best and where exchanges of people, especially students, had been most intense.

By the first half of the 1990s, both the region at large and the individual South-East Asian countries had entered a period of transition. Each of them would come out of this period changed in some important way, economically, politically and strategically.

Looking at the political and economic confidence of contemporary South-East Asia, even after the economic crisis of the late 1990s, it is very easy to forget how uncertain its future looked just over thirty years ago. In 1967, when the foreign ministers of Indonesia, the Philippines, Thailand, Malaysia and Singapore met in Bangkok to form the Association of South-East Asian Nations or ASEAN, the Vietnam War was raging. Thailand and the Philippines were battling active communist insurgencies. Indonesia's policy of confrontation against Malaysia had only formally ended in August 1966, after President Sukarno's fall from power. Tensions within the newly formed Malaysia had led to Singapore's splitting off from the federation in an atmosphere of recrimination and resentment. The Philippines and Malaysia had a serious territorial dispute over Manila's claim to the Malaysian state of Sabah. Over the decades since then the slow development of a real sense of community among the ASEAN countries has been an important achievement. Without it, the economic and social transformations of recent years would have been impossible.

By 1991, the end of the Cold War had made it possible for the first time to contemplate the realistic prospect of a cooperative future for the entire region, including the communist states of Indochina. The first clear indication of this possibility came in Cambodia, whose killing fields were a by-word for violence. Cambodia was the place where Vietnamese and Thai strategic interests in South-East Asia traditionally intersected and collided. The barbarous Khmer Rouge regime had been forced out by Vietnamese troops in 1979. Hanoi continued to back the replacement government in Phnom Penh but a civil war broke out between that regime and a strained coalition involving the remnants of the Khmer Rouge and non-communist forces, including some which supported Cambodia's traditional ruler, Prince Sihanouk. Cambodia and the Cambodians were being fought over indirectly by Vietnam and the ASEAN countries, and, in proxy form, in a three-way conflict between China, the United States and the Soviet Union.

Such proxy conflicts now mattered less to the great powers. Thanks in critical measure to the conceptual work and tireless diplomacy of Gareth Evans, with great assistance from our diplomatic service, Australia showed that another future was possible. The result was the 1991 Paris peace accords which, with much help from Ali Alatas, the Indonesian Foreign Minister, among others, provided for the withdrawal of Vietnamese forces from Cambodia and a comprehensive peace settlement.

With the peace process underway in Cambodia it was possible to begin the integration of the Indochinese countries – Vietnam, Cambodia and Laos – into the broader South-East Asian community.

If the end of the Cold War had made the region's strategic outlook more reassuring in some ways, in others it had become more uncertain. In 1986, the Philippines 'people's power' revolution brought Cory Aquino to office and ended the Marcos dictatorship. By 1992, the Philippines Senate voted not to renew the US leases on the huge Clark airbase and Subic Bay naval base. The American forces began pulling out. Because one of the main strategic purposes of the bases had been the projection of military power globally against the now defunct Soviet Union, Washington found it easier to acquiesce than would have been the case a few years earlier. But the ASEAN countries had long relied, tacitly if not openly, on this offshore American presence as insurance against any potential problems inside or outside this region. US interests in South-East Asia had not disappeared with the Philippines bases, but they were certainly fading, however politely Washington demurred. The departure of the American forces therefore raised new uncertainties about regional security.

The story of Australia's relations with South-East Asia in the first half of the 1990s was about how these changes affected our neighbours and how their views of us altered.

The two ASEAN countries with the longest and closest relationships with Australia were Singapore and Malaysia. Like us, they were former British colonies. We had inherited British public institutions that were recognisably similar. Our defence relationship with each of them dated back to the defence of Singapore during the Second World War. It had stretched on through Australian participation in the anti-communist Malayan

Emergency in the 1950s, the defence of Malaysia and Singapore during the period of Sukarno's confrontation in the 1960s and the development of the Five Power Defence Arrangements set up in 1971 after Britain's decision to withdraw its own military forces east of Suez. These arrangements made us defence partners by committing Australia, New Zealand and Britain to consult Malaysia and Singapore in the event of an attack, or threat of an attack, on either country.

Our educational links were deep. Over 120,000 Malaysians had studied in Australia and many of them, and their Singaporean counterparts, had risen to senior positions in government and business. Four members of the Singapore Cabinet were alumni of Australian universities. More than 11,000 Malaysian and 3000 Singaporean students were studying in Australia at any one time.

Hundreds of thousands of tourists travelled each way every year, and trade and other economic links with both countries were healthy and growing. We were familiar with each other.

Despite this shared history, however, the government-to-government relationship with one of these two countries had developed much more smoothly than with the other.

SINGAPORE

Singapore is strategically, if precariously, located at the tip of the Malay peninsula at the entrance to the world's busiest shipping route. From its earliest days as an entrepot port, it has been conscious of where its strategic advantages lie, and what it needs to do to preserve them.

Singapore's small size – 633 square kilometres – and population – 3.3 million people – have given it a keen awareness of its own vulnerability. Malaysia lies just over a narrow causeway to the north, while only a few kilometres to the south, over the torpid, oil-slicked water of the Strait of Malacca, are the 210 million people of Indonesia. Singapore has a sensitive and often difficult balance to maintain with its neighbours. It is a multicultural city state with a strong Chinese core located in an essentially Malay environment. Like Australia, it has its own national debate about identity, about what being a Singaporean means.

Singaporeans know they cannot hide from change and therefore must try to shape it. This has given the country's leaders an outward-looking approach and an alertness to regional change that has made them valuable interlocutors for Australia. Singapore's views on free trade, on the importance of coalition-building and the need for workable regional institutions have been very similar to Australia's.

However, although Singapore and Australia had known one another for a long time, it was time to look at each other with fresh eyes. The first thing I wanted to do as prime minister in relations with Singapore and the rest of South-East Asia was to redefine the view of Australia, to explain how Australia's national act of reconstruction in the 1980s had changed us. Because even in Singapore, and at high political levels, I encountered a persistent view that Australia was a lazy, strike-ridden, racially prejudiced society; a second-rate outpost of Britain that survived on the bounty of its resource base and its lucky isolation.

I had to point out in many conversations that, contrary to Asian myths, Australian workers were actually more productive than their Asian neighbours. Research in Singapore had shown, for example, that Australian construction workers were four times more productive than their Singaporean counterparts. I had been as critical as anyone of the old Australian dispensation, but Australia had changed, and the message was too slow in getting through.

Our job of redefinition was harder at the beginning of this period than it later became because Australia was emerging from recession and the Asian countries were still in a buoyant growth phase that seemed as if it would go on forever.

I visited Singapore for the first time in September 1992. The Prime Minister since 1990 had been Goh Chok Tong, who had been given the formidable task of taking over from Lee Kuan Yew, the founder of modern Singapore and whose values had shaped it so firmly. Goh was an impressive leader and his own man. I came to value highly his friendship and his calm, sensible and balanced advice.

Goh accurately described the relationship between Singapore and Australia as an 'easy partnership'. With connections through APEC and the Commonwealth, as well as strong bilateral links, he and I met often during the period of my prime ministership. On APEC issues he and his colleagues were strong supporters of our efforts to drive the agenda forward. We were each committed to strengthening our bilateral ties and many of the ideas came from the top. This was one relationship which really did benefit from high-level engagement by political leaders.

We wanted to encourage Australian and Singaporean companies not only to build direct relationships but to explore ways of working together in third countries, especially in the region, through what we called strategic linkages. To help this process we instituted a Singapore–Australia Business Alliance Forum, which we backed with government seed money.

With no hinterland of its own, Singapore was keen to build closer bilateral defence relations with Australia. The loss of its training facilities at the former US bases in the Philippines made this need more urgent. Singapore established its own airforce flying school at RAAF base Pearce near Perth, in November 1994, which I visited, and it was using other facilities like Shoalwater Bay in central Queensland for army training.

After a short visit I made to Singapore in March 1995 we asked our senior officials to conduct a comprehensive review of the relationship to see where we were going. The result, ten months later, was a joint declaration called 'A New Partnership', which I signed on my final visit to Singapore as prime minister in early 1996 to deliver the government-sponsored Singapore Lecture. The declaration underlined the extent to which Australian and Singaporean interests coincided. It noted our common view of the global and regional strategic environment, our commitment to free and open international trade and investment, and our support for the US presence and strategic engagement in Asia.

The declaration pointed out that the significance of our partnership went beyond what we could do together bilaterally: 'For Australia, it is a very important element in its engagement with the South-East Asian region. For Singapore, it is recognition of the value it places on Australia's role in regional affairs.'

At the heart of it, that mutual recognition was what was missing in the relationship between Australia and Singapore's neighbour, Malaysia, which took an altogether less steady course over this period.

MALAYSIA

The Prime Minister of Malaysia since 1981 had been Dr Mahathir bin Mohamad. Born in 1925, Dr Mahathir's view of the world seemed to have been shaped by the anti-colonial struggle of his youth and by Malay nationalism. He was an economic moderniser who wanted to see Malaysia – and the Malays – become a leader of the third world.

Malaysia's politics are played out in communal terms against a complex racial and ethnic background. Just under half its people are ethnically Malays, 30 per cent are Chinese, 13 to 14 per cent indigenous groups from the east Malaysian states of Sabah and Sarawak and eight per cent are Indians. Since independence in

1957, Malay pre-eminence in the political system had been entrenched. The main Malay party, the United Malays National Organisation (UMNO) dominated politics at the head of coalition governments in which the other major communities were also represented by ethnic parties.

An economic policy specifically aimed at positive discrimination in favour of the Malays, who were generally poorer than the Chinese, together with rapid rates of economic growth, had kept racial tension at bay. Perhaps because of the need to strengthen national unity, Dr Mahathir had emphasised Malaysia's generic 'Asianness'.

His public ambition was to turn Malaysia into a developed country by 2020 and the economic growth rates were leading him there. But although Malaysia remained heavily dependent on western markets for its exports, Dr Mahathir's vision was of an East Asia that was finally standing up for itself and would create its own institutions separate from those of the 'West'. This approach lay behind his proposals for an East Asian Economic Group (later a caucus), and his subsequent opposition to Australian participation in Asia–Europe summit meetings.

Australia's relations with Malaysia had traditionally been close. In addition to the students who had studied here, our economic relationship was strong. Two-way trade by 1993 was nearly $2.3 billion and growing by more than 20 per cent a year. Around 100,000 Malaysian visitors came to Australia each year and the same number of Australians went to Malaysia. Seventy thousand Malaysian-born people lived in Australia. Under the umbrella of the Five Power Defence Arrangements, an Australian officer headed the Malaysia/Singapore Integrated Air Defence System and a RAAF Support Unit was maintained at Malaysia's Butterworth air base. Australia was Malaysia's major source of external military training.

So the people-to-people relationship could scarcely have been better. And yet when it came to the formal level of government we kept tripping over new obstacles. From our point of view, it sometimes seemed as if these obstacles had been erected deliberately.

In 1986, relations had been strained when Bob Hawke described the hanging of two Australian drug traffickers as a barbaric act. In late 1990, Malaysia froze high-level contacts and urged Malaysians to 'buy Australian last' because of perceived biases in the Australian media. Consular cases involving family law or drug trafficking generated more emotional heat in our relationship with Malaysia than did similar cases elsewhere.

In 1991, an ABC television series 'Embassy' became another cause for dispute. The Malaysian Government saw parallels between Malaysia and the fictional country of the television program. We tried to convince them that the Australian Government was not responsible for the programming decisions of the ABC. The disagreement, as with many others involving Malaysia, slopped over into the broader relationship. The Malaysian Government banned the Australian High Commissioner from official Malaysian Government functions. This was an extraordinary decision. Bob Hawke had finally restored some equilibrium to the relationship, but at the expense of promising Dr Mahathir at a Commonwealth meeting in Harare in October 1991 that the Australian Government would be prepared to dissociate itself from 'insulting and inaccurate' media reports about Malaysia.

In February 1992, soon after I became prime minister, new concerns were expressed by Dr Mahathir and others in Malaysia about an Australian film, *Turtle Beach*, which was based on Blanche D'Alpuget's novel involving Vietnamese boat people landing in Malaysia in 1979. The film portrayed Malaysian villagers in a critical light. The protests took Malaysian sensitivities to a new sort of peak. We were not talking here about a statement by the Australian Prime Minister, or even a program on the government-owned television channel. This was a commercial film based on a work of fiction.

I was privately sceptical about the Hawke agreement to dissociate the government from criticisms of Malaysia but, on its basis, Gareth Evans told Parliament before the film's release that it was manifestly a work of fiction and that its representations were not historically accurate. But this careful diplomacy had no obvious effect. Despite Gareth's public comments, Dr Mahathir told the Malaysian media that *Turtle Beach* would make it difficult for Malaysia to maintain good terms with Australia. He added: 'It's very difficult for Malaysia to be nice to the Australians as they are so inclined to telling lies and insulting those they claim as friends.' He added, however, that Malaysia would not be protesting to Australia and there was no freeze on bilateral relations. And despite some huffing and puffing from the youth wing of the ruling UMNO party, the issue (like the film itself) faded away.

In May 1993 I wrote Dr Mahathir a friendly and reasonably substantial letter telling him that I would like to make an official visit to Malaysia, partly with the aim of 'improving Australian public understanding of the achievements of the Malaysian economy and of the strength and potential of our bilateral relationship'. I suggested some specific dates in the following July, or mutually convenient dates later in the year.

We heard nothing back until 17 June when Dr Mahathir replied that the dates I had proposed were inconvenient. There was no reference to dates later in the year but a suggestion that the visit 'take place early next year at a mutually convenient date to be worked out through diplomatic channels'. The letter had a surprisingly abrupt tone about it, which made me feel no better about the relationship. It is always difficult to arrange overseas visits and, as it turned out, the specific dates I had proposed in July were genuinely hard for Malaysia. But it seemed to me that we were being sent a message about where Australia fitted into the Malaysian Government's view of the world, and that we were not located among that group of friendly countries for which you would always try to make room for a high-level visit, especially if the relationship had been as rocky as ours.

I then proposed that Dr Mahathir and I should meet at the Commonwealth heads-of-government meeting which we would both be attending in Cyprus in October 1993. Our meeting in Cyprus took place in Dr Mahathir's suite. It was the first time we had met and I found him polite but essentially a listener. He gave little back. It was already clear that Dr Mahathir was the main – indeed the only – opponent of the proposed APEC summit meeting scheduled for the following month. He had been sending strong hints that he would not accept Bill Clinton's invitation to go to Seattle. I had deliberately not raised this issue with him because he seemed by then to have made up his mind not to attend. So I was irritated to read of a Malaysian press briefing after the meeting suggesting that I had tried to 'woo' him over the meeting.

Nevertheless, I wrote to him again, just before the Seattle meeting, offering Australia's help with Malaysia's difficult Indochina refugee problem, which we had discussed. I sent this letter precisely to underline that, in my view, there was more to our bilateral relationship than simply the APEC issue.

I then went to Seattle and, thanks in large part to President Clinton's sensitive chairmanship, the meeting had gone as well as I had hoped. On 22 November 1993, the day following the Blake Island summit, I visited the huge Boeing factory outside Seattle. At an impromptu press conference under the wings of a half-built Boeing 777 I was questioned by Australian journalists not about what had happened at the APEC meeting but about Dr Mahathir's decision to stay away. In *The New York Times* that morning, Dr Mahathir had been quoted as saying he had no regrets about not being in Seattle. 'Sometimes you have to thumb your nose at people before they notice you,' he said. 'Perhaps that may be a strategy we will follow.' Reportedly laughing, he added: 'We should arrest a few foreign journalists. Then we will be noticed.'

I told the reporters: 'Everyone had a chance to come here. If he did not come, it is his business.' Asked again about him, I added: 'Please don't ask me any more questions about Dr Mahathir. I couldn't care less, frankly, whether he comes or not.' Asked a third question about whether I would see him next year, I said: 'Yes. I'll see him in his own right. Malaysia is a country which Australia has interests with and which is a neighbour and I'll see him on these terms. But APEC is bigger than all of us – Australia, the United States, Malaysia, Dr Mahathir, and any recalcitrants.' It was not, it must be acknowledged, one of the more searing insults of international diplomacy, or even of my own political career.

Recalcitrant is defined by the Macquarie Dictionary as 'resisting authority or control; not obedient or compliant; refractory'. One of the oddest suggestions made during the dispute was that Dr Mahathir, a man of high intelligence and a fluent English speaker, might have thought that the word recalcitrant meant something much more insulting in Malay. If I had been Dr Mahathir, that is the charge that would really have hurt.

The Australian media reported my comments the following day under headlines such as the *Age*'s 'P.M. lashes head of state', although Dr Mahathir was not a head of state, and my words were hardly a lashing.

Back in Malaysia, Dr Mahathir was asked about Malaysia's reaction. He said: 'We can't do anything if people have no manners. I mean children, we can smack them. But a whole nation, or the journalists of one nation who have no manners, it is very difficult.'

Orchestrated campaigns began, with the youth wing of the

governing UMNO party advocating a 'Buy Australia Last' campaign and bans on Malaysian Government-sponsored students studying in Australia. The Malaysian press took up the issue with enthusiasm. Our High Commission received bomb threats. Dr Mahathir said the government would 'study' these UMNO Youth proposals.

The Australian media, the business community and the Opposition (after a hasty political backflip from initially supportive comments from Andrew Peacock and Tim Fischer) largely took the view that the problems lay only in my words in Seattle, and that if I apologised it would all go away. I thought the Malaysian reactions had deeper roots.

On 27 November, Dr Mahathir said Malaysia would not be lodging an official protest over the remarks. Asked about an apology, he said: 'It is not for me to decide ... I don't know if it is serious or not. It depends on what follows.'

On the same day, the first formal action against Australia was taken by the Malaysian Information Minister, Mr Mohamad Rahmat, who announced that all cooperation with Australia in broadcasting and information was to be suspended until I 'and the Australian media' openly apologised to Dr Mahathir, the Malaysian people and country. The measures included a suspension of news cooperation with the ABC and a ban on news coverage of Australia except for bad news, such as the ill-treatment of Aborigines. This seemed an extraordinary act which Australia could do nothing about. The 'Australian media', for one thing, were hardly in a position to make such an apology.

On 29 November I told the ABC's 'Lateline' program on the subject of an apology that Dr Mahathir had said no apology was required. I confirmed that I wanted good relations with Malaysia. I said: 'There are a lot of hard things being said about Australia and Australians ... I don't go requiring statements to be made. I don't go expressing disappointment. That is part of ... the rough and tumble of national and international life, and I think that is fair enough. But the key thing is, is the core relationship here good and working well? I think it is.'

Our High Commissioner in Kuala Lumpur was asked to draw these remarks, and our decision not to retaliate for the media bans, to the attention of the Malaysian Government. He was to say that they represented a deliberate effort to rule a line under the dispute and to avoid a further deterioration of bilateral relations. Both governments, we said, needed to avoid any slide into 'tit for tat' retaliation.

The Malaysian response through diplomatic channels was that this was not enough. The High Commissioner was informed that, although apologies were not required, it might be useful if I were to drop a line to Dr Mahathir referring to what I had said and 'regretting the misunderstanding'.

We had advice on 1 December that the Malaysian Cabinet had discussed the relationship with Australia. It had decided that that government agencies and departments should 'do as they saw fit' in dealing with Australia. Only defence was to be quarantined, although even there, any potential defence sales by Australia were under threat. (Transfield Holdings were unsuccessfully trying to sell the Malaysians navy patrol boats worth $3 billion.)

I decided to write to Dr Mahathir. I asked for a draft, and a couple were prepared in the public service. I discarded them, however, and hand-drafted a different response. I wrote that I believed the issue was being blown out of proportion, and that it was not in the long-term interests of either country for it to continue. My remarks had not been intended to give offence to Dr Mahathir, unlike some subsequent remarks about me from the Malaysian side. I wrote that he and I did not agree about APEC, and that I had been annoyed about Dr Mahathir's criticisms of APEC being too large while he was encouraging even more countries to join. I said the relationship between our two countries was more important than the present issue and that I did not wish to keep the fracas going, but that this would only be useful if Dr Mahathir accepted its validity and encouraged his ministers to regard the matter as behind us.

My colleagues were shocked by the tone of the letter. Both Gareth Evans and Robert Ray thought it was too hard. It was certainly not an apology. But given the intractable way these problems kept cropping up in our relationship with Malaysia I no longer saw the point in sending off some diplomatic form letter. I thought I should at least lay out frankly what I felt, so Dr Mahathir could understand directly from me what the differences of substance were between us.

Dr Mahathir's response was to say that the letter was not conciliatory, but only an explanation of my concerns. By 4 December, the Malaysian Foreign Minister, Mr Badawi, was issuing a press statement saying that my letter 'does not appear to have come from a person who regrets the repercussions of his extreme comments... If this is the attitude of Keating ... how can we ... accept that Australia truly intends to foster better relations with Malaysia. From now on,' he said, 'relations with Australia will deteriorate further... (T)he decision made by the Cabinet last Wednesday will continue in effect; that is, all government agencies and departments from now onwards will be given the freedom to review their cooperation with Australian authorities.'

This was a remarkable document for the foreign minister of one country to issue about the head of a friendly government, and the description of the phrase I had used in Seattle as an 'extreme comment' suggested that the Malaysian Government was more interested in prolonging the dispute than resolving it.

I was determined, however, that Australia's relationship with Malaysia had to break out of this cycle of overreaction, and that it had to be clear to the Malaysian Government that we had a two-way relationship which needed commitment from both sides.

Throughout this period we were taking care to brief Malaysia's ASEAN partners and other Asian friends about what was happening. We did not ask them to take sides but we wanted to ensure that they knew what was going on in public and what was happening behind the scenes. This was useful, and we received a number of private messages of understanding from other Asian neighbours.

On the 'Sunday' television program on 5 December, I said that my remarks were not intended to offend Dr Mahathir, and that if he had taken offence I was sorry about that. Asked whether we would engage in tit-for-tat retaliation with Malaysia, I chose my words carefully: 'I don't think we would like to. That is the point. We would prefer a constructive relationship to continue.'

The issue of retaliation was certainly on my mind. At the request of my office, a 22-page paper had been prepared in the Department of Foreign Affairs and Trade setting out possible options for Australian responses if Malaysia implemented sanctions. The paper went through all the possibilities in trade, defence, education, aid, and civil aviation.

Australia's membership of the Five Power Defence Arrangements was one of the issues at play. The Defence department was arguing strongly that we should not permit this dispute to spill over into the defence area, which had long been one of the strengths of the relationship. (Defence officials argue routinely that the defence relationship should be isolated from the broader bilateral relationship, but they have a point when they complain that defence is usually the first choice of foreign affairs officials when they are looking for possible avenues for diplomatic retaliation.) I did not think we should quarantine defence. I did not see how Australia was advantaged by conceding that our economic links could be trodden on, but not defence, which the other side wished to preserve. I was conscious that we had another partner in the Five Power arrangements – Singapore whose interests needed to be protected, but I still believed we had to look at this relationship, like all others, as a whole.

I did not want to go down the route of retaliation, which would damage both Australia and Malaysia, but I was not prepared to sit back and do nothing if totally unfair sanctions were imposed on Australia by the Malaysian Government over a single phrase for which I had already expressed regret for any offence. I was angry that the Malaysian Government was ready to put at risk a relationship of depth with a country which had made a continuing contribution to Malaysia's development. Something had to be awry if we found ourselves going through this sort of turmoil every few years. It was not enough to say that Australia needed to understand Asian sensitivities: it was not Asian sensitivities that were at issue here, but Malaysian Government interests.

We were fortunate that both the Trade Minister, Peter Cook, and the Defence Minister, Robert Ray, were scheduled to visit Malaysia the following week. Both were experienced, calm and tough exponents of Australian interests, and each was responsible for an important part of the relationship. We knew by then that the next Malaysian Cabinet meeting, which was likely to decide whether to implement new measures against Australia, was to be held on Saturday, 11 December.

Peter had a call scheduled on Foreign Minister Badawi on 6 December, but the Malaysian side cancelled it, despite strong efforts by our High Commission and Peter himself to have it reinstated. He did, however, meet his direct counterpart, Trade Minister Rafidah. He left her in no doubt that the interests of both countries would be affected if threatened actions against Australian interests went ahead and that, although retaliatory measures were not on our agenda at this time, it should not be assumed that Australia would take no action at all in response to any Malaysian decisions against our interests.

Ray was due to arrive in Malaysia on 7 December for an arms exhibition at which more than thirty Australian defence industry firms were represented. In the lead-up to this visit, Malaysian Defence Minister Najib had been reported as saying that, while the Five Power Defence Arrangements would remain intact, Australia would be 'disfavoured' in any arms purchases if I remained unapologetic. But at their meeting, Robert Ray made it clear to Mr Najib in his inimitably implacable way that it would be very difficult to quarantine defence and trade if Malaysia went down the path of sanctions. Ray also told Najib we might be obliged to re-impose the now-dormant exchange controls on Malaysia, drying up Australian capital inflow to Malaysia if Malaysia took pre-emptive economic action. The clarity and force of the messages conveyed by Cook and Ray was very important in getting our message across.

I was due to give the inaugural 'Weary' Dunlop Asialink lecture in Melbourne on the evening of 8 December. The speech was to be beamed directly into Asia on Australia Television. These were the days when we had a government that thought it in our national interests to project an Australian voice into Asia. I wanted to underline again the points we had been consistently making over the preceding three weeks, but I wanted them to come directly from me rather than through the medium of the press. I repeated that my remarks had not been intended to cause offence and that I regretted it if any offence had been taken. I added:

> The Australian Government wants to preserve the interests we share and the friendship between our two countries and our two peoples. We want to work in harmony with the Malaysian Government. But any relationship of substance and value requires commitment from both sides. For our part, we are committed. We are willing to put in the effort necessary to keep the channels of communication open.

Gareth followed this up with a letter to Foreign Minister Badawi, with whom he had already had a lengthy conversation.

The Malaysians, I believe, also began to think about the impact of the dispute on their other commercial relations. Because if a quarrel ostensibly over one word could balloon out to threaten the whole bilateral trade relationship, investors from other countries would have to think carefully about the safety of investing in a place where commercial arrangements could be disrupted by government diktat.

On 11 December, the Malaysian Cabinet met as planned, and we got the news that it proposed to take no further action and regarded the matter as closed.

Looking back on this period, it is clear how important a role the press in both countries played in the development of the dispute (although with somewhat less government direction on the Australian side). The Malaysian newspapers appeared to have been doing work exchanges with the London tabloids. 'Keating ... more or less exemplifies the totalitarian countries leaders' style, be it the Russian leaders of the 1920s ... or the style of Nazi Germany in the 1930s,' declared one newspaper on 5 December. Another commented about me – and, more to the point, about Australians generally: 'His roots are those of a convict and hence the lack of manners is a characteristic that has been passed down the generations till today.'

This was a good story for the media because it personalised an otherwise dry foreign policy issue and had the sort of conflict–clash–crisis dimensions that add drama to the daily rounds. Australian television journalists could don their safari suits and head for the tropics. The Australian media, in Gareth Evans's telling phrase, seemed to have only two stories about our relations with South-East Asia: 'row or kowtow'.

The whole issue underlined the extent to which the media is a player, not just an observer, in Australia's relations with Asia.

Almost all the issues that had arisen in our relationship with Malaysia were media-related in some way, and numerous examples could be found in our relations with Indonesia and other ASEAN countries. These problems by no means lay entirely on the side of the Australian media, and this is not an issue that governments can do much about. We did what we could to support exchanges of journalists and editors, and to get Australian journalists back into countries like Indonesia on the grounds that the more journalists we had with direct involvement in Asia the better. But too many Australian journalists still go to Asia on a mission rather than as reporters, too many editors seek intermittent drama from their correspondents rather than a linked and coherent story of our region and, while there are exceptions, too few proprietors are prepared to invest in the training of their staff in Asian language and culture.

The media response to this will be that they weren't responsible for my comments in Seattle or the Malaysian response – and they weren't. But there can be no doubt that journalists did all they could not just to report responses, but to sharpen them. I don't say this to bash the press. But anyone who looks back over this issue and does not see the press as a major actor in the drama is naïve or deluding themselves.

It is usually the politicians who are accused of personalising international relations and not understanding the currents flowing underneath it. This dispute with Malaysia was always about a much bigger issue than the word 'recalcitrant'. What was at stake was a fundamentally different view of Australia's legitimate role in the region. This was a matter about which – certainly from Australia's side – we could not compromise, because compromise would mean accepting a permanent outsider status in the region that meant most to us. This was the fact that Australian journalists should have understood.

Dr Mahathir's agenda was seen in remarks he made on 20

November – that is, before I said anything at Seattle – questioning whether Australia's desire to 'be a part of Asia' should be accepted at face value. 'I question it,' he said, 'because Australia, for example, wants to be part of Asia when its culture is hardly Asian at all. It talks down to Asians. It tells Asians how to behave themselves when Australians are not very well behaved anyway.' (Such misunderstanding of Australian ambitions was one reason why I repeated in the 'Weary' Dunlop lecture on 8 December 1993 my belief that Australians were not, and could not be, Asian, or European, or American, or anything other than Australian.)

Dr Mahathir is a formidable leader who has transformed Malaysia, but we had quite different views of the region into the twenty-first century. His view of the region was one based on 'culture' as he told the Japanese writer and commentator, Dr Kenichae Omae. This was a group to which Australia clearly did not belong because Asians 'rarely criticise or assess other countries openly'. The driving force of his vision was a strong pan-Asian nationalism which asserted that after centuries of colonial rule it was time for Asia to take control of its future. Mine was shaped by the conviction I set out earlier – that the interests of Australia and the region are best served by making the Asia-Pacific the focus of our institution-building efforts because the economic, social, and strategic dangers of creating a divide between the two sides of the Pacific were overwhelmingly greater than the advantages of an East Asia-only approach.

The dispute I had with him was, in essence, a dispute over Australian interests. I believed in pan-Pacific arrangements between the United States and continental Asia in which Australia had a part; he believed in an Asia-only approach in which Australia, like the United States, had no part. We simply didn't agree. And I was not about to surrender Australia's long-term interests to him. Australia and Malaysia had had a close and familiar relationship but precisely because the relationship was so familiar it brought with it a lot of preconceptions which could impede a clear view of each other.

After the 'recalcitrant' incident we saw a slow improvement in the relationship. The Department of Foreign Affairs and Trade said that Australian business reported virtually no damage to existing commercial interests.

In June 1994, Gareth Evans and Bob McMullan (by now the Minister for Trade) completed a review paper on the Australia–Malaysia relationship. It concluded that we needed to adopt a more clear-eyed and unsentimental approach to Malaysia than in the past and that we should seek to make it clear to Malaysia that we regarded maintenance of a healthy relationship as a two-way street.

In September 1994, Dr Mahathir spoke positively about the state of the bilateral relationship at the launch of the Malaysia–Australia Foundation. I replied to him in writing and we met twice in Jakarta at the subsequent APEC meeting in November.

At the launch of the private sector-funded Australia–Malaysia Society in Canberra in December 1995, I announced that I would be visiting Malaysia officially on 15 and 16 January 1996, just before I was to deliver a public lecture in Singapore.

Our officials were particularly keen that our arrival should go smoothly. We had more or less given up using for overseas travel the aging and uncomfortable RAAF 'VIP' 707 aircraft, which were now banned, for noise reasons, from most overseas and Australian airports. Finding myself under attack from the Opposition for imperial aspirations whenever replacements for the aircraft were mentioned, I now travelled commercially whenever I could. For scheduling reasons commercial flights had not been possible on this occasion, so it seemed that a malevolent fate was involved when our small RAAF aircraft packed it in during a refuelling stop in Darwin. We had to hitch a ride from a Darwin businessman on his personal jet to arrive in Kuala Lumpur on time. It was not the way I would have preferred to land in Malaysia, but it was better than arriving late.

I was impressed by the obvious economic prosperity in Kuala Lumpur and by the Malaysian ministers I met, including the Finance Minister and Deputy Prime Minister, Anwar Ibrahim, who would later fall from grace, to be bashed and imprisoned. Most of all, however, I was moved by the real warmth towards Australia from so many Malaysians who had contacts in this country.

If the tensions in the relationship with Malaysia had been the result of personal factors they would have been resolved easily enough by my departure from office, especially as one of the first acts of the incoming Coalition Government was to invite Dr Mahathir to visit Australia on his way back from New Zealand. But that is not what happened. Malaysia's veto on Australia's participation in the Asia–Europe meeting was not lifted, its attitude to APEC and the proposed EAEC did not change. Dr Mahathir did not attend the APEC leaders' meeting in New Zealand in 1999.

North of Malaysia and Singapore, two large societies, Thailand and Vietnam, dominate South-East Asia's mainland mass. The region's other large country, Myanmar (Burma), has isolated itself from the world for the past half century. As prime minister I had no contact with its military regime.

THAILAND

With 60 million people, Thailand is the most culturally cohesive and confident of all the ASEAN countries. A large part of that cohesion derives from the symbolic and actual role played by the king and the royal family who are held in universal respect. The Thais have impressive diplomatic skills which kept them, alone of the region's states, independent of European control during the colonial period.

After Indonesia, Thailand was ASEAN's second-largest economy. In the early 1990s it was undergoing an economic transformation from an economy based on access to cheap unskilled labour, land and natural resources to one based on higher value-added goods and services. Its economic growth had been impressive.

Politically, however, Thai politics had been dominated for most of the post-war years by alternating weak civilian governments and military regimes. In May 1992, soon after I became prime minister, widespread civilian demonstrations against government corruption had led to the military suppression of demonstrations, leaving 52 people dead. Australia responded by imposing restrictions on our contacts with the Thai military.

New elections were held in September 1992. Thailand now had its first democratic government with a reasonable prospect of seeing out its term. It was headed by Chuan Leekpai, a man of great dignity and good sense. In another example of the usefulness of the APEC leaders' meetings, I was able to meet Prime Minister Chuan in Seattle before I visited Thailand in April 1994.

Our relations with Thailand were dominated by economic and APEC issues, including the suggestion the Deputy Prime Minister, Dr Supachai, had raised during a visit to Melbourne in November 1993 for the development of closer links between ASEAN's free trade proposals – the ASEAN Free Trade Agreement – and the Australia–New Zealand Closer Economic Relations. Dr Supachai was an active supporter of free trade and saw this as a way of keeping the pressure up on his ASEAN colleagues. We saw it as a way of developing our economic links with Asia.

Our most sensitive political issue with Thailand was Cambodia. We kept receiving reports that elements of the Thai military were continuing to give commercial and logistical support to the Khmer Rouge in Cambodia. Australia and others had invested enormous diplomatic effort into the Cambodia Peace settlement and we were deeply concerned that actions like this might damage it. During my visit to Thailand in 1994 I expressed my concerns directly to the Thai military commander General Wimon. I was convinced by Prime Minister Chuan that the government was doing all it could to end any contact there may have been with the Khmer Rouge, but during this period the relationship between the military and the civilian government was still a matter of considerable sensitivity.

The principal reason for the timing of my visit to Thailand was the hand-over of an Australian-built bridge, funded by Australian aid, that joined Thailand and Laos by road for the first time. This was a symbolically important moment, the first time the Mekong, South-East Asia's mightiest river and political dividing line, had been spanned. The Friendship Bridge, as it was named, was a fine example of the construction and engineering skills of the Australian companies involved, as well as the productivity of the Australian construction industry. Fewer than twenty Australians were employed on the project, while about five hundred Thai and Lao workers learned engineering and construction techniques. Japanese officials in the region told Australian diplomats that they suspected we must have secretly subsidised its construction cost to bring it in so cheaply.

The bridge was opened by the King of Thailand and the President of Laos in a short ceremony in the centre of the span. Tens of thousands of Thais and Lao lined the streets of the surrounding towns and the bridge in ferocious heat to be there, and to see King Bhumibol cross into Laos for his first visit outside his kingdom in 27 years.

In Thailand I also visited Hellfire Pass on the notorious Burma–Thailand railway, the construction of which resulted in such horrendous loss of life during the Second World War. Thirteen thousand Australian prisoners had been put to work on the railway and more than one in five of them had died while building it. They were among 16,000 casualties of the allied prisoners of war. Ninety thousand Asian workers had died. This was also the place where one of the truly great Australians, 'Weary' Dunlop, had done so much to save lives, ease suffering and inspire faith when it was most desperately needed.

At the nearby Kanchanaburi war cemetery, where more than 1300 of the Australians are buried, I said:

> It is worth remembering that Australia's first major engagement with Asia was in war. In Korea and Malaya and Vietnam it was again war. Today, it is a partnership with Thailand and other countries of the region. A partnership which will extend the domain of our common interest and reduce the ground for conflict.
>
> It seems to me that there could be no better way to honour those Australians who suffered and died here than to succeed in this enterprise. No better way to see that what they endured, and what their allies and hundreds of thousands from the countries of Asia endured, will not happen again . . .

VIETNAM

I travelled on from Thailand to Vietnam.

Australia's relationship with Vietnam was layered with memory and meaning. For many Australians 'Vietnam' still meant more than the geographical place. It meant the war, and its legacy of domestic division and personal pain. For the 140,000 Australians who were born in Vietnam, it meant the place from which many of them had fled, often in painful circumstances, leaving so much behind. I believed the time had come to bind wounds and move on. Domestically, we had to address those Australians who had served in Vietnam and came back feeling ignored and discarded. It was a war in which 504 Australians had died and 2369 had been wounded. In October 1992, the Australian Vietnam Forces National Memorial was dedicated on ANZAC Parade, the great processional avenue leading to the National War Memorial in Canberra. Speaking of all who served in Vietnam, I said:

> These Australians believed in their country as those earlier generations did. They believed in democracy and freedom, and by defending it in Vietnam, they believed they were defending it everywhere. They believed in duty. They were brave. Those whose names are entombed in this memorial paid the ultimate price for their belief in Australia.
>
> It is true that no war divided Australia like the Vietnam War. It is true that often we remember those years more for the protests at home than for the fighting abroad. The years of Vietnam corresponded with a great social and political upheaval in Australia. The war itself was one of the catalysts of change.
>
> There is no doubt that in all the turmoil we lost sight of the reality of Vietnam. We lost sight of those who did the fighting and the waiting. And by doing that we made their reality worse. For all the drama in the streets, and parliaments and public halls, the real war was, as always, on the battlefields where young men and women died. The real tragedy was in their suffering and death and, as ever, in the loss which lives on in the hearts and minds of those who loved them. We cannot make good this hurt any more than we can undo the war itself. But, by this memorial, we can make good the memory.

As well as facing up to the domestic legacy of the war, I felt we needed to take a fresh look at our national relationship with

Vietnam. With its 80 million people, Vietnam was emerging as an important element of change in South-East Asia.

Vietnam's long-time ally, Russia, had withdrawn militarily and economically, taking with it the aid which had propped up the Vietnamese economy and accounted 10 per cent of its GDP. The Vietnamese Government was accelerating an economic reform program begun in 1986, and the private sector now represented 70 per cent of all economic activity. By 1992, the country was growing at over eight per cent a year, although from a low base. It remained a poor country with a per capita income only one-third of Indonesia's. Vietnam needed friends in this new world.

The Australian Labor Party had a good basis on which to build the relationship. Labor had opposed the war and the lottery that had sent young Australians there. Gough Whitlam had withdrawn our forces. We had been one of the first western governments to recognise the Socialist Republic of Vietnam. And, now, after the Cambodia settlement, we had been the first to resume aid.

Australian trade and investment in Vietnam was growing very fast. Our two-way trade in 1982 was $2 million. By 1993, it was $366 million. Australia had become at that time Vietnam's third-largest foreign investor with nearly $800 million invested. It was not an easy commercial environment for many companies, but the size of the country and the skills and energy of its people gave it real potential.

In May 1993, the Vietnamese Prime Minister, Vo Van Kiet, visited Australia. It was his first visit to a western country. The visit was not easy to manage: the Vietnamese community in Australia was heavily anti-communist and deeply suspicious of the visit. We undertook extensive consultations in advance of the visit to explain what we were doing. The visit had almost come unstuck on the first night in Canberra when certain members of the party threatened to pull out after seeing television coverage of demonstrations. Australian officials spent a difficult evening explaining that, although Australian citizens had every right to protest, such demonstrations did not represent any policy statement on the part of the Australian Government.

A year later, in April 1994, after my visit to Thailand, I became the first Australian Prime Minister to visit Hanoi and a united Vietnam. I thought the most useful contribution I could make to my discussions with Vietnamese leaders was to draw on Australian experience to show how one Labor Government, drawing its political support from working people, had dealt with the changing social and economic environment.

I urged Prime Minister Kiet and other Vietnamese leaders to try to get the right economic structures in place. I said I had learned as Prime Minister that the best use of scarce government resources was in education, health and the security of the very young and old. Private resources should be used for the rest. It did not matter a great deal who owned infrastructure; the important thing was that the resources were there and properly regulated. This was still a radical thought for a communist government to accept. I said Vietnam had a chance to begin with the best infrastructure because it was beginning afresh and Australia could help with this. I announced a doubling of Australia's aid program to $200 million over four years.

Throughout this period, we were trying to develop a human rights dialogue with Vietnam and I raised certain issues, including some specific cases of interest to the Australian community, with the Prime Minister. We had also reached agreement on sending an Australian parliamentary consultative delegation to Vietnam, in part to look at these issues. It was not easy, and as with all such dialogues we did not go into them assuming that the other side would quickly come to see the world through our eyes. The value lay in the process itself, both the repetition of international interest in particular cases, and in the debate and dialogue about human rights which we hoped would open minds.

Like most first-time visitors, I was surprised by Hanoi's beauty. It had avoided the development blight of many other Asian cities. Ancient Vietnamese quarters and many beautiful French colonial buildings had been preserved. But how long would it be before greedy developers sank their teeth into it? In the twenty-first century, workable Asian cities like Hanoi will be in short supply. They will bestow an economic, and even a strategic, advantage on those who live in them. Hanoi may be the last chance Asia has to develop a really livable city like Paris or Prague. Other Australians, including the architect Philip Cox, had been involved in efforts to preserve the city before, but I was able to announce an aid contribution of $3 million to help fund a development plan for the conservation of the old sections of the city.

My visit was dogged by a media-induced flurry about why I wasn't demanding permission to hold a memorial service for Australians who died in Vietnam. The answer was in part that, unlike our other wars, our dead had been returned to Australia, so there was no war cemetery at which to hold such a ceremony. I thought, in any case, that it was not appropriate on this, the first visit by an Australian Prime Minister since the end of a war which had, after all, been fought against our hosts. But within five years of my visit, Australia would be holding ANZAC Day services on Australian naval ships in Ho Chi Minh City.

On the final day of my visit to Vietnam I was to meet the General Secretary of the Communist Party, the 78-year-old Do Muoi. I was tired and the visit was drawing to an end. We had to drag ourselves to the former Saigon presidential palace where, under a portrait of Ho Chi Minh, the two delegations were seated facing one another in the formal ranks of Asian protocol.

Do Muoi had been on a provincial tour in the south and had

come back specifically for this meeting. It turned out to be one of the most interesting I held as prime minister. The general secretary had been imprisoned by the French in the 1920s and had then fought the French, the Japanese, the French again and the Americans. (Vietnam's 4000 years of fighting off invaders was a regular theme of leadership conversations.) Do Muoi had taken over as head of the party in mid-1991 and in the period that followed he had presided over a transformation in Vietnam's leadership. After a lifetime of commitment to Marxism–Leninism, to revolution and to centrally planned economies he had, in his seventies, seen that change was essential and had moved with it I invited him on the spot to visit Australia and, on the spot, he accepted.

His visit to Australia in July–August 1995 was his first to a non-Asian democracy, and only his second outside Vietnam. I regarded this as an important signal to Australia and, indeed, in Canberra he described Australia as a focus for Vietnam's regional relations. He was accompanied on the visit by Phan Van Khai, who went on to become Prime Minister of Vietnam. We again put a lot of effort into talking to the Vietnamese community and I met with community leaders in advance of the visit.

I had promised Do Muoi that if he came to Australia I would travel with him. The Vietnamese leadership had little experience of the western world and feared the loss of face that might follow from demonstrations against them. I wanted him to know that he would not be left alone. As a result, despite suffering the worst case of flu during my time as prime minister, I took him up to the Gladstone aluminium refinery and to Port Douglas. Do Moui was enough a man of his communist generation to be impressed by the Queensland Alumina Ltd refinery, which is indeed a formidable facility. But I pointed out to him how few people it employed compared with the tourism industry.

My real purpose in adding Port Douglas to the itinerary had

been to show the Vietnamese party that it was possible to develop tourism infrastructure without destroying the environment with high-rise horrors. Do Muoi's security guards seemed nonplussed as I helped the General Secretary of the Communist Party of Vietnam into an electric golf cart on the morning of his departure and drove him at stately pace around what had once been Christopher Skase's glittering temple to 1980s capitalism.

The Australian Opposition's decision to snub Do Muoi in the course of this visit was one of the crassest and most short-sighted acts I encountered during this period. The Opposition Leader, John Howard, refused to meet him, to attend the official lunch, or to send a frontbench representative to support my speech of welcome at that lunch. This was the first time this had been done by any Australian political party and was a clear effort to try to make domestic political capital among the Vietnamese community. (Do Muoi's Chinese equivalent had been received by the Opposition, so it was not a matter of protocol as they tried to indicate at one point.) It was short-sighted in the fact that Vietnam had become ASEAN's seventh member only days before Do Muoi's arrival and relations with the United States had finally been normalised a few weeks earlier.

The same short-term political motivation led the Coalition to promise they would pull out of the construction of the giant My Thuan Bridge, the first bridge across the Mekong in Vietnam, which I had announced as Australia's largest-ever infrastructure aid project during my visit. Our studies found that the bridge would significantly improve the living standards of the 15 million people throughout the delta region of southern Vietnam. The cancellation, happily, was later rescinded.

I am sure that over time, as Vietnam develops economically, as it becomes more integrated politically with the rest of South-East Asia, we will develop a closer relationship. Australia's Vietnamese community will be a rich resource for us.

Vietnam has a long way to go before it catches up economically with its ASEAN neighbours, and the legal and political system will have to change as well. But the Vietnamese have lived through much and they are the hardest of hard thinkers. Over the longer term, Vietnam offers real prospects for growth and economic success. It has a large, young population – remarkably, half of its people are aged under 19. And in the streets of Ho Chi Minh City and Hanoi, you can see the consequences of even the current, limited and tentative unshackling of restraints on Vietnam's natural entrepreneurial instincts. Compared with its neighbours, Vietnam has a good education system – turning out excellent results in science and mathematics especially – and a literacy rate of 92 per cent. The Vietnamese have all the cultural attributes necessary over time to enter the ranks of the Asian tigers.

Well after I had left the prime minister's job, one Vietnamese minister put the country's dilemma succinctly to me: 'Everyone says time is money,' he told me. 'And the biggest thing we have lost is time.'

THE PHILIPPINES

Across the South China Sea from Vietnam, the Philippines is offshore South-East Asia, both geographically and politically. Its history of Spanish colonialism, followed by the American brand has left it with different institutions and approaches from its ASEAN neighbours. (Explaining their culture, Filipinos say they spent three hundred years in a Spanish convent and fifty years in Hollywood.)

I was disappointed not to be able to visit the Philippines as prime minister. I had promised the President, Fidel V. Ramos, that it would be my first visit after the 1996 elections. But I was pleased to be able to host the first-ever visit to Australia by a

President of the Philippines in August 1995 after nearly fifty years of diplomatic relations. I had met 'Eddie' Ramos at APEC meetings and liked him very much. With astonishing energy he had made the transition from military man to politician presiding over, and responding to, Asia's most assertive democracy, including a wilful senate and a famously free press. Like the Australian Government, President Ramos had been trying to introduce economic reforms to a calcified system and to refocus the Philippines' foreign policy on its own region.

Whatever the regional strategic complications caused by the departure of the Americans from their Philippines bases, it was an entirely good thing for the Filipinos, helping them to face up to their own future. We signed a Defence Cooperation Agreement during the Ramos visit. Australia is now the largest source of training for the Philippines military and a substantial aid donor. This is another relationship with great potential, but it also underlines how important it is to continue to develop familiarity with each other.

INDIA

The other great seedbed of South-East Asian culture, apart from China, is India. For a variety of reasons relating, in part, to the circumstances of its independence struggle, India had followed a path of autark since independence. It emphasised self-reliance rather than interaction, and the result had been slower economic growth than most of the rest of Asia.

India's external policies since 1947 had been shaped in its immediate region by the unresolved outcomes of independence – that is, the relationship with Pakistan – and globally by the East–West strategic dispute and the north–south economic debate. The East–West dispute caused India to develop its role in the non-aligned movement and helped fuel its suspicion of external involvement in the Indian Ocean. The north–south debate led it to position itself as a leader of the Third World in a global division between developed and developing countries. But the magnetic poles that formerly showed us what was East and West, what was North and South, were shifting.

Australia and India have tended to look past one another. New Delhi has thought of Australia principally as a junior member of the Western alliance rather than as part of our own region; Australia has failed to see all the richness and complexity of India. Our trade was low, reflecting, in part, India's essentially closed system, which offered relatively fewer opportunities than other parts of Asia.

I had planned a visit to India in 1994 but a parliamentary crisis over their budget forced my hosts to cancel it. We were, however, seeking new ways to engage with South Asia and the Indian Ocean region, underlining the fact that Australia faces two of the world's major oceans. Gareth Evans launched a new 'Look West' strategy in Perth in August 1994 and Bob McMullan worked deliberately to expand trading opportunities.

In South Asia and the Indian Ocean, regional approaches are both more recent and more tentative than in East or South-East Asia. We worked with India to try to develop a greater community of interest around the Indian Ocean rim, including by hosting an international seminar in Perth which we hoped would help stimulate the process.

In the wider Asian region, India's links are growing. It has become a dialogue partner of ASEAN and a member of the ASEAN Regional Forum, in which both India and Australia will be able to make a contribution to the emerging Asian security dialogue.

India remains one of several countries that has expressed an interest in joining APEC. It is no secret that I was an opponent of India's attempts to join APEC. I was equally an opponent of

Chile and Russia and other new applicants. This had nothing to do with any hostility to India or the other potential members, or to any doubts about India's global importance. It came rather from a conviction that if APEC's membership expanded too much or too soon, its agenda would become too diffuse and it would fall apart, or at least slump into the lethargy and immobility of too many international bodies.

I believe strongly, however, that the world needs India. Without its resilient democracy, its size, its effective legal structures and commercial law and, above all, its ambitious and practical people, the global debate is diminished. And the sooner the disconnection between India's size and its economic engagement with the world is resolved, the better it will be for all of India's neighbours and for the world at large. India can help transform the region and the globe, but a continuing effort to open up its economy is a prerequisite for this new role.

On the whole, I have always felt that the world is better off if the larger powers in it – of which India is indisputably one – are confident about their place in the international system and clear in their purpose, rather than victims of the uncertainty that comes from non-engagement or exclusion and the introspection that follows. India needs more of this sort of confidence.

CHAPTER 8

THE OTHER PACIFIC

For Australian foreign policy there is another Pacific, as far removed from the Asian megacities as it is possible to imagine. It consists of the small island states scattered through the vast Pacific Ocean. The largest of them – Papua New Guinea, Fiji, Solomon Islands and Vanuatu – have sizeable populations and potentially rich mineral and timber resources. But the smallest, like Tuvalu, Palau and tiny Niue, have populations in the thousands and economies based on little more than fish and coconuts. The coral atoll states like Kiribati rise at their highest point just a few metres above the relentless Pacific waves. The result, for most of the regional states, is a pervasive sense of isolation and vulnerability. The issues in this other Pacific may have been much smaller in scale than those facing Asia, but during my time as prime minister they sometimes seemed no less intractable.

By 1992 the Pacific Islands, like the countries of East Asia, were feeling the results of the end of the Cold War. Whatever leverage they might once have been able to extract from the global competition between East and West had now been lost. The hearts and minds of remote Pacific Islanders no longer attracted a premium in the capitals of the great powers. And as the powers departed, a rather scummy residue of greedy businessmen, carpetbaggers, crooks and confidence-tricksters was being left behind.

This disengagement by the international community was one of the reasons why all through the dispute over French nuclear testing at Mururoa in the mid-1990s we continued to support France's involvement in the South Pacific. We wanted it there for the long haul because it was important that the outside world did not entirely lose interest in the region.

For Australia, disengagement from the South Pacific wasn't an option. We were the region's major aid donor, its most important security partner and, with New Zealand, we provided its window to the world. Regional organisations like the South Pacific Forum, the South Pacific Commission and the Forum Fisheries Agency depended heavily on our financial support.

A large – and largely unreported – amount of my time involved in foreign policy as prime minister was spent dealing with the South Pacific. Short of coups, cyclones or tsunamis, the Australian media tends to ignore the region (although it has attracted some of our best foreign correspondents).

My direct introduction to the South Pacific came in July 1992 in Honiara, the dusty capital of Solomon Islands. I was there to attend the annual meeting of the South Pacific Forum, the principal regional organisation. Our host for the meeting was the Prime Minister of Solomon Islands, Solomon Mamaloni. Small and intense, chewing betel nut as he chaired the forum, Mamaloni was clever (or at least cunning), but he adopted policies and political approaches that I thought were disastrous for the people of the Solomons.

The meeting itself turned out to be a rather tedious affair. It was clear that the forum's proceedings were carefully prepared in advance by officials. Each year's meeting took the previous year's agenda as its starting point and many of the same comments were recycled. There was a good deal of routine business which did not require the attention of heads of government and, to my mind, too great a tendency to blame other people for the region's ills. (This sense of victimhood was encouraged by some of the international lobby groups that descended on the forum each year.)

Despite the aridness of much of the agenda, however, I found myself quite interested in the problems of the region and I felt sorry for neighbouring countries struggling to survive – let alone develop – with such limited resources and so many challenges. The town in which we were meeting, for example, had the tragic distinction of suffering the world's highest rate of malarial infection, a terrible human (and economic) burden for any country.

But I also felt that Australia needed a new approach to the Pacific. As in any relationship on which one side is heavily dependent on the other, we encountered frequent accusations in the Pacific of Australian arrogance. No doubt this was a problem from time to time. Yet it seemed to me that just as serious a problem was the alternative voice with which Australia often addressed the region, that of a patronising do-gooder, reluctant to talk about anything difficult in case we offended the Pacific Island peoples. In the interests of the Pacific Island countries as well as our own, I felt Australian policy needed to be more direct and honest. I also accepted that such an approach would require active engagement by Australia at the highest level.

I subsequently attended every forum meeting while I was prime minister. (It is a record which I would be happy to see equalled, but no challenge is yet in sight.) And, after the 1993 election, I recommended the appointment of Gordon Bilney to the new position of Minister for Pacific Island Affairs and Development Cooperation, an appointment designed to underline our commitment to the South Pacific.

The sort of problems the region was facing were illustrated starkly by Nauru, the country that was to host the forum in the following year. Papua New Guinea apart, Nauru had been Australia's only colony. A tiny island of 21 square kilometres, its revenues came from the phosphate rock of which it was largely composed. The areas of the island where mining had taken place – and that meant most of it – looked like a tortured moonscape, with hard pinnacles of limestone outcroppings rising out of the ravaged and abandoned land. The Nauruans themselves, fewer than 11,000 in number, huddled around the thin coastal fringe.

It was the phosphate that brought the colonial powers to Nauru. In 1920 Australia had replaced Germany as the island's governing power under a mandate of the League of Nations, but the real power in the territory lay with the British Phosphate Company, owned jointly by the Australian, British and New Zealand governments. Nauru had been occupied by Japan during the Second World War and more than 1000 Nauruans were taken off the island to work as forced labourers elsewhere in the Pacific. Many of them had died. Australia then resumed administration of Nauru as a trust territory of the United Nations until independence was granted in 1967. But in the years since independence, instead of rehabilitating the island and investing sensibly for the people's future, Nauruan governments had squandered the phosphate revenue in investments that included a failed West End musical and the financial black hole of Air Nauru.

Now, the phosphate was running out. Nauru had taken Australia to the International Court of Justice (ICJ), claiming that we had duped it out of money in the financial settlement we had made at independence. Australia was being asked to pay for the island's rehabilitation, although two thirds of the mining had taken place after independence. In June 1992 the ICJ had made a procedural decision that did not look promising for Australia. Although, at this stage, the court had not yet begun considering the matter on the merits, its ruling revealed it to be a much more political body than our lawyers had expected. We were increasingly uncertain about what it might finally decide, and who would benefit if the issue was dragged out. After a Cabinet discussion, we concluded that the best course was to settle the case out of court.

In this case, I believed the Nauruans had some natural justice on their side. Australia and the other administering powers had driven a relatively hard bargain at independence, requiring Nauru to pay for capital equipment while we maintained the supplies of relatively cheap superphosphate which had done so much to help Australian farmers.

Eventually, as a result of some excellent work by Gordon Bilney and Gareth Evans, we reached agreement on an out-of-court settlement. This provided for an initial payment of $57 million and an additional $2.5 million annually, indexed for inflation, for the following 20 years. We also agreed on a Joint Declaration of Principles similar to one we had with Papua New Guinea, governing our relationship as a whole. The whole package became the focus of my visit to Nauru for the forum meeting in August 1993, which was timed to commemorate the 25th anniversary of independence.

Anxious to see whether there wasn't some greater quid pro quo for Australia in this, I had asked Robert Ray and the Defence department to explore whether there might be defence benefits in terms of staging rights for RAAF flights we could try to bargain for as part of the deal. Defence's answer was that Nauru was of only marginal strategic use to Australia.

I was hopeful, though not confident, that the money we paid out would, in fact, be used to rehabilitate the island. But twelve months later, our cash payment under the Compact of Settlement appeared to have gone to short-term debt reduction. The annual payments, however, can only be used for jointly agreed rehabilitation and development projects.

Walking around the stark, treeless landscape of Nauru's mining areas, my view that the South Pacific Forum was not adequately addressing the practical problems of its members was reinforced. Although the environmental challenges facing the Pacific Islands included deforestation, coastal pollution, the depletion of in-shore fisheries and poor watershed management, much of the debate at forum meetings centred around global climate change and nuclear issues. These were important. The issue of global warming and rising sea levels was far from an academic concern for the coral atoll countries like Kiribati and Tuvalu. And within a couple of years nuclear issues would return with new force when the French resumed their testing at Mururoa. But the island states faced more direct and urgent environmental concerns which they could do more about. Towards the end of the forum meeting in Nauru, although it was not in my official brief or apparently in anyone else's, I intervened to put the issue of logging and sustainable forestry on the agenda for the following year.

Australia was scheduled to host the next meeting of the forum, and I did not want to waste the opportunity. I wanted the forum to be a place where leaders got inspiration and ideas. I thought we should spend less time ticking off issues on an agenda already canvassed heavily by officials and more time exchanging personal experiences about some of the genuine challenges facing the region.

The South Pacific was doing badly on a worryingly wide number of fronts. In 1993, the World Bank estimated that real gross national product in Pacific Island countries had grown by less than one per cent over the previous ten years, despite average aid flows ten times higher than for comparable countries. Aid accounted for nearly 40 per cent of the GDP of the Pacific Island countries, compared with around 17 per cent for the Indian Ocean countries and less than five per cent for the Caribbean (although the Caribbean had the huge advantage of proximity to the markets of North America).

The Australian National University's Pacific 2010 research project painted a nightmare vision in the South Pacific of mass unemployment, urban slums, growing lawlessness and a degraded environment if current population trends remained unchecked. And those resources the region had – fish and forests, in particular – were not being managed in ways that could sustain development.

The island countries may have been small in land area, but they had sovereignty over 20 million square kilometres of ocean. This rich fishery supplied around half the world's canning tuna, with a commercial value of around $1.5 billion a year. But of this amount, the island countries received just over $70 million. Vanuatu, for example, had a bilateral agreement with a Taiwanese company that enabled the company to cover its access fees and operating costs in just one week of fishing. Poaching and inaccurate catch reports, especially by Taiwanese trawlers, continued to rob the islanders of income. Negotiating individually, they were vulnerable to being picked off by the more powerful distant-water fishing states.

The situation in forestry was even worse. Most of the region's timber was being logged from tropical rainforests in Papua New Guinea, Solomon Islands and Vanuatu. Partly because logging concessions in Asian rainforests were being exhausted, partly because the issue had become politically hotter in their own countries, foreign interests, especially Malaysian and Indonesian timber companies, were moving fast into the Pacific. They were gaining access to the resource at very low cost as a result of bribery, greatly understating the value of the resource they were taking out, and logging at unsustainable levels. According to the World Bank, logging in Solomon Islands was taking place at four times the sustainable limit.

Australia estimated that Papua New Guinea lost $285 million by failing to tax logging profits properly, while in Solomon

Islands a spot check had shown that over one ten-day period alone, $250,000 in revenue had been lost through inaccurate reporting.

Poor forestry practices caused other problems. In tropical areas like these, with annual rainfall between 3000 and 5000 millimetres, once the vegetation was removed the topsoil was swept out into the rivers and seas. Fish stocks close to shore, on which villagers relied for food, were killed. Future eco-tourism prospects, and the employment opportunities that went with them, were being destroyed. For example, the clear waters of the Morovo Lagoon in Solomon Islands, one of the most beautiful areas of the Pacific, were being silted up as a result of rapacious logging in the catchment area.

Australia had practical as well as altruistic interests at stake. We gave hundreds of millions of dollars in aid to the region and did not want to see money that could have gone to development being wasted.

Papua New Guinea was failing to collect from forestry revenue an amount roughly equal to our annual aid. Over the preceding three years four regional airlines in Solomon Islands, Nauru, Western Samoa and Marshall Islands had accumulated losses equal to all the aid those countries had received in that period from Australia and New Zealand.

The core of any policy response by the Pacific Island countries to these problems had to centre around sustainable development. Over the twelve months prior to the 1994 Brisbane forum, Gordon Bilney did much of the groundwork to prepare this new approach. He set out our agenda in a June 1994 speech in which he stated the obvious truth: 'No amount of regional and international assistance will bring about sustainable development in the South Pacific unless the countries of the region themselves play the leading role through the adoption of ... national policies, including public sector reform and private sector development.'

This was not the message some Pacific Island countries wanted to hear, and our message caused discomfort around the region. But we had ourselves been through a tough period of reform in Australia and had done hard political work to get there. We knew there was no point in hiding from reality.

The forum had already shown that regional action could shape international behaviour. As a result of an initiative Bob Hawke had taken at an earlier South Pacific Forum, a ban had been placed on the devastating practice of drift-net fishing, and the forum countries had developed an equitable multilateral fisheries arrangement with the United States.

We proposed that the Brisbane forum, from 31 July to 2 August 1994, take as its theme (in itself an innovation) the idea of 'Managing our Resources'. With the agreement of the other members, we reordered the forum's arrangements. We set aside greater time for an extended leaders' retreat in advance of the formal meeting. This was held in the Gold Coast hinterland. As we flew from Brisbane by RAAF helicopter past the architectural high-rise blight of the Gold Coast I urged the other leaders to take this as an example of what should be avoided at all cost in their own tourist development. I'm not sure I persuaded anyone.

I spoke very frankly at the retreat, pointing out that Australia had increased its aid to the Pacific by six per cent in 1994–95, at a time when other countries were losing interest, but we could not justify our aid unless it was delivering better social outcomes to the people it was designed to help. I said it was true that some of the South Pacific's problems were the result of shameless exploitation by outsiders, but that it was up to the countries of the region to manage our individual affairs in ways that made this impossible, by introducing good legal and administrative regimes and then enforcing them.

At the end of the retreat and the formal meeting in Brisbane I was pleased with the progress that had been made and by the response of the other leaders. We gathered support for a more multilateral approach to fisheries and moves to strengthen the Forum Fisheries Agency. I agreed to take up with the Japanese Government the question of the behavior of the Japanese fishing companies in their negotiations with the island states. I subsequently did this directly, and at the highest levels.

On logging, Prime Minister Francis Billy Hilly of Solomon Islands, who had replaced Solomon Mamaloni in May 1993 and was trying to reform logging practices, told the forum his country was suffering from 'environmental piracy' and that logging companies were 'squandering his people's livelihood'. There was good support from other leaders for his views.

As chairman of the meeting, I got the prime ministers of Fiji, New Zealand, Papua New Guinea, Solomon Islands and Vanuatu to work with Australia towards a common code of conduct governing logging of indigenous forests, to which forestry companies would have to adhere, and to increase urgently the monitoring of logging and exports of timber. We put follow-up mechanisms in place. Members agreed to examine options to rationalise money-losing regional airlines (the South Pacific had eleven, serving six million people). We also agreed to regular meetings of forum finance ministers to ensure some cross-fertilisation among the people responsible for the difficult job of managing the finances of the island countries.

Outside the forum proper, I agreed with Prime Minister Hilly on a 'debt-for-nature' swap, under which Australia would reschedule interest payment on a loan for fishing trawlers in return for the cessation of unsustainable logging in the catchment areas of the Morovo Lagoon.

Meanwhile, however, back in Honiara, Solomon Mamaloni was reported in the Solomon Islands and Malaysian press as warning me not to interfere. Australia's offers to assist the Solomon Islands with the management of its natural resources were 'offensive and disrespectful,' he said. We concluded that Mr Mamaloni had altogether too kind a view of the Malaysian loggers.

In any event, within two months Mr Mamaloni was again Prime Minister of Solomon Islands after Hilly was sacked by the governor-general, one of Mamaloni's nominees, and lost a parliamentary vote. The trees continued to be cut down, leaving future generations of Solomon Islanders to suffer the consequences. In the end, at least some of the forests were saved by the unlikely intervention of the Asian economic crisis, which caused demand to decline, prices to fall and exploitation finally to be held in check. But this is a battle which will not be easily won. The Pacific environment is one of the world's great pools of biological diversity, and its preservation will require constant effort by the regional countries and those who wish them well.

PAPUA NEW GUINEA

As prime minister, I probably spent more time dealing with the complex, psychologically sensitive bilateral relationship with Papua New Guinea than with any other relationship, apart from Indonesia. Over four million people live in Papua New Guinea, making it by far the largest of the South Pacific states. It is astonishingly diverse. Within the one country 867 different languages are spoken. This linguistic and cultural variety, coupled with rugged geography and a political tradition that is robustly contestable makes governance a challenge under the best of circumstances. Papua New Guinea's great triumph is that it has sustained, despite the difficulties and dangers, a healthy democracy. But twenty years after independence, social indicators for education and health had stalled or were falling, law and order problems were growing and the economy was becoming harder to manage.

Some officials and commentators in Australia argued that the only way of solving Papua New Guinea's problems was for Australia to become much more involved again. Others believed we should distance ourselves from what they saw as a looming disaster, and that we should force the PNG Government to stand on its own feet.

In fact, neither option was possible. Australia was too closely involved in Papua New Guinea and our interests were too great to enable us to walk away. On the other hand, we had neither the resources, nor the right, to resume a more interventionist role. The difficult policy goal was to find the right balance. What was the best way of encouraging Papua New Guinea's self-reliance?

The burden of history and geography makes this a hard relationship for Australia and Papua New Guinea to manage. In few other parts of the world are the former colonial power and colony such near neighbours, and where they are (Japan and Korea, for example), the results have seldom been easy. As colonialists, Australians may have been generally benign but I'm not sure we were much good at the task. Not least, we had bequeathed Papua New Guinea a public sector and a military force, modelled on our own, that were expensive and quite unsuited to the needs of a developing country.

Apart from a relatively small but committed group of academics and others with personal links to Papua New Guinea and who knew and loved the country, Australian views of Papua New Guinea ranged between ignorance, irritation that things weren't going in the direction we prescribed, and a romantic approach – the 'fuzzy-wuzzy angels' syndrome – which, stripped of its sentimentality, saw Papua New Guineans as bearers for Australian interests.

The mix on the other side of the Torres Strait was even more complicated, because Australia loomed so much larger. Australia was viewed, often by the same individual, with various mixtures of suspicion, resentment, envy, gratitude and affection. Among the small group of policy-makers in Port Moresby, however, Papua New Guinea's economic dependence on Australia was a – no doubt frustrating – reality. In the twenty years since independence, we had provided over $10 billion in aid, with a further half a billion dollars in defence cooperation. Australian aid was around $300 million a year, with an additional $20 million or so in defence cooperation assistance. Australian companies, especially in the mining sector, had invested around $1.6 billion in Papua New Guinea, and in 1992 12,000 Australians still lived there.

I had first visited Papua New Guinea twenty years earlier as an Opposition backbencher with Gough Whitlam, just before independence. I deliberately made it, along with Indonesia, the destination of my first overseas trip as prime minister. A particular point of that visit was to commemorate the role Papua New Guinea and Papua New Guineans had played in saving Australia during the Second World War. I strongly felt that the deeds and courage of the Australians who had defended their country in Papua New Guinea during the battle for Australia had not been sufficiently acknowledged.

On ANZAC Day 1992 – as it happened, the 75th anniversary of the landing at Gallipoli – I took part in a moving dawn service at Bomana war cemetery, then a commemorative ceremony at Ela Beach in Port Moresby. I told those present that:

> ... the Australians who served here in Papua New Guinea fought and died not in defence of the old world, but the new world. Their world. They died in defence of Australia and the civilisation and values which had grown up there. That is why it might be said that, for Australians, the battles in Papua New Guinea were the most important ever fought.
>
> They were fought in the most terrible circumstances ...

[T]hey were fought by young men with no experience of jungle warfare, by the very young men of the militia with no experience of war at all. They were fought by airmen of outstanding courage, skill and dedication. They were fought against a seasoned, skilful and fanatical enemy. At Milne Bay, the Australians inflicted on the Japanese their first defeat on land.

I paid tribute too, as all Australians must, to the Papua New Guinean servicemen and carriers who were essential to the victory. The support they gave Australian soldiers, the terrible conditions and dangers they endured with our soldiers, and the illness, injury and death many of them suffered constitutes one of the great humane gestures of the war – perhaps the great humane gesture of Australian history.

The following day was one of the most moving of my public life. Our party flew by RAAF C130 aircraft to Popondetta and then by Caribou into Kokoda village, on the Kokoda Track. Gazing out across the valley at Kokoda, I felt with overwhelming emotional force how hallowed this ground had been by the young and inexperienced militia men of the 39th and 53rd Battalions and later the soldiers of the 7th Division, who fought gallantly and finally drove the enemy back to the sea. This was the place where such horror had been experienced, but where Australia had been saved.

In the town square at Kokoda, I saw the memorials to the first young men who had died there in defence of Australia. At a momument which noted the actions of Private Bruce Kingsbury who had been awarded the Victoria Cross posthumously for his heroism, I thought that placing a wreath was too formal and unfeeling a gesture. As the Australian Prime Minister who came there and who understood his sacrifice and those of so many others, I bent down and kissed the base of the memorial so all would know he was not forgotten. Not him nor his mates.

Speaking to the local people, I promised that Australia would provide facilities for the village to help make the history, and their peoples' role it in, better known.

Three men held the office of Prime Minister of Papua New Guinea between 1991 and 1996, each very different. Rabbie Namaliu, whose decency and commitment to his country were admirable, was prime minister during my first visit. He was well-known and highly respected in Australia.

Namaliu was replaced in August 1992 by Paias Wingti, who became prime minister for the second time. Wingti's political approach was more populist and nationalist, and he had all the toughness of a traditional highlands leader. He signalled his independence from Australia by emphasising Papua New Guinea's relationships with Asia. He made an obviously symbolic decision not to make an early visit to Australia, but instead to visit Indonesia, Malaysia and Singapore. We finally met at the South Pacific Forum in Nauru in August 1993, and he made his long-delayed visit to Australia in February 1994. Although his approach generated some irritation among Australian officials I was perfectly relaxed about it. Papua New Guinea had to make its own way in the world and it seemed entirely healthy to me that it should establish strong relations with its other neighbours.

Then in August 1994, following a Supreme Court decision that established that Wingti's most recent re-election had been unconstitutional, Sir Julius Chan became prime minister. Sir Julius was a perennial figure in Papua New Guinea politics. He had been prime minister before, as well as deputy prime minister, finance minister and foreign minister. He was a successful businessman, and less instinctively interventionist than Paias Wingti.

Yet throughout these changes of personnel at the top, the same issues that formed the agenda for my initial meeting with

Rabbie Namaliu in 1992 kept recurring. They were the forms of Australian assistance to Papua New Guinea, law and order, the rebellion on Bougainville and the environment.

Papua New Guinea's problems were mounting in the 1990s. Law and order was deteriorating throughout the country. Urban crime was increasing as people from rural areas drifted into towns where no jobs were available for them, and tribal fighting was out of control in parts of the highlands. Where once the weapons had been spears and arrows, guns were now appearing. This was having harmful economic as well as social effects, severely limiting the prospects for tourism, deterring minerals exploitation and turning mining facilities – on which the economy depended so heavily – into armed camps.

Security force capabilities continued to decline. It was clear that the police force was under-trained and ill-equipped to deal with the problems it faced. For the army, internal security issues such as the rebellion on Bougainville were a much larger problem than any likely external threat, but it was badly structured and trained for such purposes. Its administration was chaotic and its budget routinely overspent. Soldiers, including those on active service on Bougainville, were not getting paid. Relations between the police and the army were strained. It was a dangerous mix.

We had been trying for some time to see if we could do something to help restructure the PNG defence and security forces so they were more effective and responsive. Bob Hawke and Rabbie Namaliu had signed an agreement in September 1991 under which Australia would provide further security assistance (training, infrastructure and personnel exchanges), provided Papua New Guinea prepared a joint plan of action in which it set out priorities between the Papua New Guinea Defence Force (PNGDF) and the police. Inter-agency rivalries had always prevented such a coordinated approach in the past.

I raised these issues with Namaliu and his colleagues in 1992, but the politics were too difficult for his or subsequent PNG governments to confront. The leaders of the army and police, not to mention the security intelligence agencies, all appeared more concerned to protect their turf than to countenance reform.

Bougainville was a continuing political and economic drain on the country. About 1000 kilometres from Port Moresby, on the border between Papua New Guinea and Solomon Islands, the island is about 200 kilometres long. Its rugged interior is covered with dense jungle. Bougainvilleans had a long record of support for greater autonomy, although they were not united about what this meant. They took pride in the intense blackness of their skin and their tradition of good education and they saw these as marks of their distinctiveness from the rest of Papua New Guinea.

The current phase of the independence struggle was started in 1988 by landowners near the huge Bougainville copper mine, whose majority-owner was Conzinc Rio Tinto Australia (CRA). The mine, which had been so important to the economy of Papua New Guinea as a whole, had been closed since May 1989 as a result of local resistance by the Bougainville Revolutionary Army (BRA), which wanted independence for the island. The closure of the mine was a powerful economic blow to the Government. But it now had the additional costs of supporting the Defence Force in its difficult and messy campaign against the BRA.

Periodic efforts had been made to restore peace, but between the fundamentalism of the most extreme BRA leaders like Francis Ona, and mishandling by the PNG military, every hope had come to nothing.

Human rights abuses had been committed by both sides. But there was no doubt that the PNG soldiers, under-trained, frightened, resentful and often quite beyond civilian control, had been responsible for some serious abuses. Australia's conviction throughout – and the message we gave at every meeting with

Papua New Guinea leaders – was that no military solution to this problem existed. We regarded Bougainville as an integral part of Papua New Guinea, but in the end the dispute could only be resolved politically. We were willing to provide additional assistance, including for Bougainville's rehabilitation, but only if it was contributing to this goal.

In April 1994, an Australian parliamentary delegation, led by Senator Stephen Loosely, visited Bougainville. It delivered a particularly thoughtful report which argued that military victory was unachievable and the best way forward was a combination of confidence-building strategies, rehabilitation and reconstruction. It also argued that the time was right for the PNG Government to initiate open negotiations with the leaders of the secessionist movement. The report was discussed with PNG leaders and tabled in both the Australian and PNG parliaments.

In June, PNG officials and representatives from the rebel 'Bougainville Interim Government' met informally in Honiara, the capital of Solomon Islands. Sir Julius Chan, then the Foreign Minister, had been trying hard to reinvigorate the peace process. Things seemed to be going well until Paias Wingti authorised a PNGDF attack on the Panguna mine site, which was situated in the middle of the territory held by the most unbending of the resistance leaders. The victory did not last long, and the PNGDF was driven out again, but at the cost of a further loss of confidence on both sides.

In August, however, senior PNG officials met a delegation led by the Bougainville Revolutionary Army military commander, Sam Kauona, in Honiara and agreed on an agenda for a peace conference, including an immediate cease-fire, the introduction of a regional peace-keeping force, reconciliation and compensation, and the island's economic rehabilitation. No mention was made of the political status of Bougainville, which was the sticking point.

On 30 August, Sir Julius Chan became prime minister, and stated that his highest priority was returning peace to Bougainville. Within a week he had signed personally with Kauona the Honiara Commitments to Peace on Bougainville, providing for a peace conference to be held on Bougainville involving people from all over the island.

Australia agreed to supply advisers to, and largely pay for, a Pacific Island Peace Keeping Force drawn from other Pacific Island countries to monitor and provide security for the peace conference. But notwithstanding Chan's efforts, the hardliners in the BRA refused to participate and the peace conference fell apart.

Chan continued to improvise in search of some agreement. Although most Bougainvilleans wanted a special position for Bougainville, they also wanted peace and the restoration of services. Eventually, other, more moderate, Bougainvilleans agreed to establish a Bougainville Transitional Government in April 1995, although the hard-core rebels remained intransigent.

Later, in 1997, Chan's frustration with the lack of progress on Bougainville would lead to the disaster of the Sandline mercenary affair, which would bring down his government.

One of the reasons for Chan's concern about Bougainville was Papua New Guinea's increasingly precarious economic situation. PNG leaders had grown used to thinking that whatever happened, the country would be able to rely on its minerals sector to bail it out of any problems (a thought pattern familiar enough to Australians in the past).

The country's long-term challenges were low investment, low competitiveness (with wages four to five times higher than its competitors) and misdirected expenditure. One third of the education budget, for example, was going to the two per cent of students in tertiary institutions. GDP growth was high but the budget deficit was around seven per cent of GDP. Foreign reserves were estimated at less than two weeks' import cover.

These were the sort of short-term difficulties that were encouraging the government to succumb to the entreaties of foreign logging companies.

After the Chan Government took office, it had announced a 12 per cent devaluation, an expenditure and public sector wages freeze and efforts to restore the budget to balance by 1995. But the outcome would depend on how effectively the measures were implemented.

Chan was more interested than Wingti had been in keeping Australia engaged in developments in Papua New Guinea.

In September 1991 Australia and Papua New Guinea had agreed to phase out Australian budget support aid – our quarterly cheque to the PNG Government – in favour of program aid, that is, specific expenditure for particular purposes on which we would both agree.

This development was not popular with PNG officials who, for understandable reasons, preferred direct subvention from Australia. But although the change caused difficulties (by making the administration of the aid program more complicated and generating new opportunities for friction between us), I believed it was inevitable. It was a more appropriate form of relations for two sovereign governments. Australian taxpayers wanted, and deserved, more direct accountability for their aid. Chan sought to have it changed, but I resisted all efforts to persuade us to revisit this decision.

Through 1994 and 1995 Papua New Guinea faced several crises over short-term debt, for which it sought Australian help. One of our policy goals for several years had been to get the international financial institutions more directly engaged in Papua New Guinea. This was partly because we felt their expertise could help Papua New Guinea, but we also saw the participation of such neutral outsiders as a way of stripping out of the debate about economic reform some of the emotional overlay in our bilateral relationship.

So our aim was to balance a desire to help, which we did, against a wish to avoid pulling the rug out from under the feet of the IMF and the World Bank, which were trying to secure some important reforms of Papua New Guinea's financial and administrative arrangements, including those in the forestry sector.

In September 1995, I visited Papua New Guinea again to attend the South Pacific Forum and the celebrations of the 20th anniversary of Papua New Guinea's independence. I was also there to fulfil the promises I had made to the people of Kokoda in 1992, by opening the hospital we had built there, with great assistance from Australian Rotary. For the only time as prime minister, I took my three daughters with me on this trip. I wanted them, as young Australians, to see Papua New Guinea and to experience something of its rich culture.

When the news came through a couple of months earlier that the chief of the Oro people from the Kokoda region wanted to hold a ceremony making me a paramount chief, I was grateful for the honour. As the details of the arrangements came trickling in from our High Commission in Port Moresby, however, the advisers in my office became increasingly nervous. Headdresses are the bane of politicians' lives. It is very difficult to look dignified while wearing part of another culture on your head. And the news that the ceremony would take place at the top of a ricketty bamboo platform and would involve the feathers of the hornbill, an endangered species, did not reassure my staff.

The event itself was deeply moving, however. It was a symbolic reminder that this place and these people were linked forever to Australia because of what had taken place nearby fifty years earlier. It was a sign, too, that we continued to honour our fellow Australians who had died there and the local people who had helped them so selflessly.

The relationship between Australia and Papua New Guinea will always require effort and understanding. In my conversations with PNG leaders during these years I frequently made the point that, in the modern world, genuine friends were hard to come by. They were worth preserving. I meant these words not as polite rhetoric, but as the literal truth. It is a truth that needs to be understood on both sides of the Torres Strait.

NEW ZEALAND

In all our dealings with Papua New Guinea and the South Pacific, New Zealand was a close collaborator and sometimes a more-or-less friendly rival.

I made my first visit to New Zealand from 20 to 23 May 1993. For some reason, the recent personal relationships between Australian and New Zealand prime ministers had seldom been entirely happy. Although they had come from the same side of politics, Malcolm Fraser's relationship with Sir Robert Muldoon, and Bob Hawke's with David Lange, were often strained. Jim Bolger and I were from different parties and did not always agree on policy, but we struck up a productive relationship and worked well together on issues like APEC and international trade. I valued his friendship (and agreed with his unexpected republicanism). He showed both steel and flexibility in his chairmanship of the Commonwealth Heads-of-Government Meeting in Auckland in November 1995.

The Closer Economic Relationship between Australia and New Zealand had become one of the most comprehensive free-trade relationships in the world, bringing important benefits to both economies. Trans-Tasman trade and investment had greatly expanded under it. On 1 July 1990, five years ahead of schedule, merchandise trade between us had become completely free. By 1992 New Zealand was our third-largest trading partner, and we were New Zealand's biggest partner. We already enjoyed free movement of people across the Tasman.

In 1993, the question was what happened next. Moves towards more comprehensive economic integration (like a common currency) or to political union were on neither side's agenda. The next objectives on the economic front were worthy, but intrinsically less dramatic, steps like the harmonisation of customs and quarantine regulations, and the mutual recognition of standards and occupational qualifications. New Zealand had taxation objectives, including mutual recognition of dividend imputation credits, that we were reluctant to pursue for reasons of precedent.

I had been keen for many years on a common services market across the Tasman because I thought the extra scale would give Australasian companies a better chance to compete globally. I had been disappointed when the New Zealanders had earlier passed up the opportunity to establish an integrated trans-Tasman telecommunications market by selling their Telecom company to a North American bidder. I now believed there was more we could do to set up an integrated aviation market behind a common border. We proposed the common border in our February 1992 economic statement designed to kick-start Australian growth called 'One Nation' (before the name was purloined). We wanted to make it possible for people to travel between the two countries via domestic terminals. At our first meeting at the South Pacific Forum in Honiara, Jim Bolger had agreed to this in principle. But it had to mean a common approach to external entry controls and New Zealand did not want to give up its visa-free arrangements for tourists from certain countries. We were told about mysterious technical problems which hampered efforts to organise immigration pre-clearance. For reasons which were never entirely clear to us, we failed to make the progress we hoped for. In October 1994, to strong complaints from New Zealand, we cancelled a proposed air services agreement. Air New Zealand was looking for additional 'beyond rights', which would allow it to carry passengers from Australia to third countries, but it was clear that New Zealand was not prepared to permit a single aviation market.

Defence had been an important point of disagreement between Australia and New Zealand over the preceding decade. The disagreement reflected our different histories and different senses of threat. Its core had been the nuclear issue and New Zealand's decision to exclude US warships from its ports so long as the Americans would neither confirm nor deny the presence of nuclear weapons on board. This had caused a breach in the ANZUS relationship.

Like my colleagues in the Australian Government, I had disagreed strongly with New Zealand's position on ANZUS. I believed that the balance of nuclear forces between the two sides was an important element of stability during the Cold War. So long as we were part of an alliance, I did not believe we should abandon the alliance's global responsibilities. I thought our focus should be on mutual and verifiable arms-control agreements rather than on unilateral gestures. But with the Cold War over, I willingly conceded that the international environment had changed. I did not want to make life any more complicated for New Zealand or to discourage the restoration of United States–New Zealand relations. I made it clear to Jim Bolger that on the ANZUS issue I had no intention of putting a spoke in New Zealand's wheel.

I was more concerned about a different defence issue. The resources New Zealand committed to defence continued to shrink and, as a result, its defence capabilities were declining. It was spending less than half as much as Australia on defence as a percentage of GDP (1.1 per cent compared with 2.4 per cent). We were dangerously approaching the point at which the two forces would not be able to operate together effectively.

Largely at New Zealand's behest, our defence forces were talking about something called Closer Defence Relations (CDR), which was intended to mirror Closer Economic Relations. The agenda for CDR included more integrated defence planning, force structure planning, and logistical and training support. I was sceptical. I worried that New Zealand would see this as a way of getting defence on the cheap. And I did not want any situation to arise where we might leave gaps in our own defence capabilities to be filled by New Zealand. (Robert Ray had equally strong views on this.) I argued the case for a stronger defence performance as persuasively as I could to New Zealand ministers during my visit.

I also believed, however, that there was too much unhealthy navel-gazing in the Australia–New Zealand relationship. Because the relative importance of the relationship is so much greater for New Zealand than for Australia, we had a constant, if vague, sense that we were being outsmarted by the New Zealanders while we weren't paying attention. They often felt affronted that we seemed to ignore them or take them for granted. I thought the remedy was for us both to look outwards together at what was happening in the Asia-Pacific. I believed we could use the lessons we had drawn from CER to build closer links with Asia and to shape developments in the Asia-Pacific. And so it proved to be. New Zealand was a solid collaborator in all we tried to do in APEC, and our experiences with CER have been important in the development of the global trade agenda.

In some ways, Australia's relationship with New Zealand is so close that it hardly seems appropriate to think about it as foreign policy at all. With our historical and cultural ties, the free movement of people, and such deeply integrated economies, it is easy to slip into thinking about New Zealand as something like another Australian state. In my experience that is a mistake.

Australia needs to give New Zealand as much objective attention as our other major foreign policy interests. If China defines its relationship with Hong Kong as 'one country, two systems', ours with New Zealand is 'one system, two countries'. So, contrary to the usual rules, I'm all in favour of playing down the family metaphors and thinking about New Zealand as a foreign country. This is not because I don't understand the closeness of the history or the ties, or their importance, but because I think we will understand each other better and get more out of the relationship if we try to look as objectively as we can at our individual interests.

For my part in this, I was determined in my dealings with New Zealand to make no comment about sport, which has become the ultimate cliché and reinforcer of stereotypes in trans-Tasman discourse. I may be the only politician on either side of the Tasman to have achieved this.

Looking back at my experience with the other Pacific, what stays with me most is the vigour of its cultures. Almost without exception, and despite the creeping incursions of global pop culture, these are not static or artificial but a highly integrated part of everyday life. Whether it was the deep attachment of Nauruans to their island, or the ease and grace with which well-educated Papua New Guineans could shift from the suit-and-tie business of modern life to traditional dress, or the pride of Tongans and Western Samoans in their music and dance, Pacific culture is tenacious.

The South Pacific is a part of the global garden that is both precious and precarious. In the twenty-first century the environmental health of these islands and the seas around them will be as important to a growing Asia-Pacific region as their geo-strategic position was during the twentieth century's Pacific war. It is something to which we must turn much more attention.

CHAPTER 9

NUCLEAR CLOUDS

On 13 June 1995, the newly elected President of France, Jacques Chirac, announced that from the following September France would conduct a series of eight underground nuclear weapons tests at Mururoa Atoll in French Polynesia.

With this decision, Chirac abandoned a moratorium on nuclear testing that his predecessor, François Mitterrand, had instituted two-and-a-half years earlier, in January 1993. Mitterrand had been following a decision by the Americans and Russians to suspend their testing programs, and had promised to stick to it as long as they did.

Chirac's announcement was not much of a surprise. It had been widely foreshadowed during the presidential election campaign. But although the French put a limit of eight on the number of tests they would conduct and committed themselves to then sign the Comprehensive Test Ban Treaty, the impact on international opinion, especially in Australia, was shattering.

France had taken the unilateral track with nuclear weapons before. Its first nuclear test in 1960, conducted in French-controlled Algeria, broke a moratorium that the United States, Britain and the Soviet Union had observed since 1958. And it took place despite a two-thirds vote in the United Nations General Assembly calling on France to refrain.

Forced out of its African testing facilities in 1966, France had moved them to Mururoa and a cluster of other coral atolls lying about 1000 kilometres south-east of Tahiti and 6000 kilometres east of Australia. Until 1974, the devices were exploded in the atmosphere, and it was only after Australia and New Zealand took a case to the International Court of Justice (a case boycotted by France) that the tests were finally moved underground.

For the small island states of the South Pacific, French nuclear testing far from Europe had been a catalyst for closer regional cooperation. Indignation at the French decision had been one of the incentives for the establishment in 1971 of the South Pacific Forum, the regional association of independent states. Given earlier British and American nuclear testing in the region, the Pacific Island states could be forgiven for their persistent sense that the large external powers – who were also the former (and current) colonialists – still felt they could get away with activities in the South Pacific that their own voters would never permit them back home.

Between the time of Chirac's election and the announcement that the tests would begin, the Australian Cabinet had considered a submission from Gareth Evans and Gordon Bilney (the Minister for Pacific Island Affairs) that canvassed our decidedly limited options.

In line with the Cabinet decision, after the announcement, we protested officially to the French, condemned the decision publicly and froze defence contacts. I had written to President Chirac on 8 June urging him to continue the moratorium. An important operational question for us was how far we should go immediately. Once Chirac had announced that the tests would begin in three months, did we have any chance of dissuading him? How, and with what leverage? How could our response be reconciled with our reaction to an earlier Chinese test on 15 May (albeit conducted on its metropolitan territory) which was limited to an official protest? I also took seriously my responsibilities as Chair that year of the South Pacific Forum, and I wanted to ensure Australian actions were coordinated with the South Pacific countries rather than simply presented to them, which would add Australian insult to French injury.

We sent a forum delegation led by Gareth Evans to Paris to put the region's case directly to the French Government. But the response to that visit and our national protests convinced us that Chirac was not going to budge.

From the time of the French announcement, public reaction in Australia began to build. Spontaneous boycotts of French products began together with widespread anti-nuclear demonstrations. The atmosphere was darkened by an indefensible arson attack on the honorary French consulate in Perth on 17 June.

Cabinet met again on 22 June to consider the next stage of our responses. We now recalled the Australian Ambassador, Allan Brown, for consultations, further curtailed defence contacts and pulled out the senior Defence Force representative in Paris. We convened a special meeting of South Pacific environment ministers. We provided assistance to mobilise and support community campaigns in the region and developed a public information program designed to take the message directly to the heart of France and Europe. (As part of this, Gordon Bilney, who was an excellent French speaker, led a parliamentary delegation to put the case in Europe.)

Even this did not assuage the public thirst for a response. The government was being accused of doing too little. Why did we not break diplomatic relations with France? Cut off all trade? Dispatch Australian warships to stop the tests?

In retrospect, there is no doubt that we at first underestimated the level of public concern in Australia about the nuclear tests. In practice, our responses were firmer than those of New Zealand but what people wanted was a validation of their understandable emotional responses not just action. We did not provide it strongly enough or quickly enough. Gareth Evans's entirely defensible agreement with one journalist that the testing decision 'could have been worse' (which was actually true – the tests might not have been limited in number, for example, or France might not have agreed to sign the Comprehensive Test Ban Treaty) came across publicly as though we did not care enough about the tests. Then the Liberal Party made the fortuitous discovery of a previously (and, it has to be pointed out, subsequently) entirely latent commitment to anti-nuclear activism. As a result, our handling of the crisis in the early stages too often had the appearance of reaction.

The media, especially radio and television, were important in shaping the public mood. Every television report about the tests seemed to be accompanied by footage of a mushroom cloud, implying that the radioactive wind would be blowing past our neighbourhood any time soon. And sections of commercial radio were running a campaign that became more anti-French than anti-nuclear. It felt at times as if the dead and wounded of the Battle of Agincourt had only just been carried from the field.

At several points Gareth and I had to underline publicly that Australia's opposition was to the nuclear tests, not to the people of France. This was particularly important because back in France the majority of French people also opposed the resumption of testing.

The selfishness of the Chirac decision angered me, and I was deeply concerned by the provocation it offered to some of the states on the threshold of acquiring nuclear weapons. In order to secure the extension of the nuclear non-proliferation treaty (which banned non-nuclear weapons states from getting them), France and the other nuclear powers had agreed as recently as 1993 to exercise 'utmost restraint' in nuclear testing pending the entry into force of the Comprehensive Test Ban Treaty. How could eight tests constitute 'utmost restraint'?

The claim that France was entitled to test in Polynesia because this was part of France was farcical. 'Oh yes,' I told Parliament, 'there are Polynesians all the way down to Aix-en-Provence. They pop out of the woodwork. They are doing Polynesian dances in the back end of the Loire Valley, in the walled city of Carcassonne... There are Polynesians everywhere.' And it was all unnecessary: a symbolic gesture by an incoming president anxious to burnish his Gaullist credentials. As I said at the time, France could best protect its security by engagement with the world, not by some 1990s nuclear Maginot line.

I was not interested in the sort of theatrical and ultimately pointless gestures that were being urged upon the government. Trade sanctions, including a refusal to meet current uranium contracts, would have harmed Australia more than France. We were committed to refuse any new uranium contracts with France so long as it had not signed the Comprehensive Test Ban Treaty. But if we had breached existing contracts, we would have lain ourselves open to compensation claims of $80 million and freed the French to buy cheaper uranium elsewhere. In any case, the French had ceased production of fissionable material, so even if the three sets of safeguards in place to ensure that Australia made no contribution to the French weapons program had been irrelevant, the fear that Australian uranium might end up in French bombs was misplaced. And as for sending warships to the test sites, I was certainly not prepared to permit Australia's military forces to be used for symbolic purposes. Short of going to war with France, which was absurd, the only option for any Australian ships would have been to steam around in circles while the French exploded their bombs. This would have underlined not Australia's strength but our impotence.

Greater discussion took place within the government about how we should respond to proposals to send an unofficial protest flotilla to witness the tests and whether the government should hire a boat to take part. Some in the ALP were urging us to do this. After a good deal of internal debate we decided against doing so. It would have been a costly exercise and we doubted it would have any practical effect. It was a matter of deciding where our resources could be used most effectively. Instead, we offered consular and administrative help to private members of any international protest.

The whole issue of French nuclear testing was foreign policy-making at its most frustrating: reactive, essentially a matter of rhetoric and gestures and, unlikely, we all agreed, to succeed in deflecting the French Government from its course.

As I thought about the French tests over the months between Chirac's announcement and the first tests in September, I came to feel increasingly that this public outrage was directed at a symptom rather than a cause of the problem. That problem was something we had all wanted to forget: the unique, sickening sense of insecurity that comes from knowing that weapons exist in the arsenals of governments that have the capacity to destroy humankind.

With the end of the Cold War, we had all breathed more easily. We had allowed the thought of nuclear weapons and nuclear war to fade from our minds, to assume that the nightmare of two generations was over. We had succumbed to the familiar human tendency to avert our eyes from problems; to hope that if we do not look directly at them, they will disappear. Perhaps no image in the twentieth century had branded our collective consciousness like that of the mushroom cloud. Although nuclear weapons had originally been conceived for a different conflict, they had become symbolically fused in our minds with the idea of the Cold War. So we allowed ourselves to believe that the weapons that defined the preceding fifty years had miraculously disappeared along with the Berlin Wall.

What the French nuclear tests had done was awaken Australians to the fact that the reality had not changed. Tens of thousands of nuclear warheads remained in the armouries of the five declared nuclear powers – the United States, Russia, China, Great Britain and France. And others – not just the so-called threshold states of India, Pakistan and Israel, but regimes like Iraq and North Korea – waited and worked to acquire nuclear weapons.

As I reflected on this, I thought we had an unprecedented and possibly unrepeatable opportunity to begin to move to a new strategic environment in which we could eliminate nuclear weapons, not just reduce their numbers. Just a few years earlier, the Gulf War had shown that new, accurate, conventional weapons could accomplish the military purposes for which nuclear weapons had once been intended, but without their appalling and indiscriminate consequences. It seemed to me that the security interests of the United States and its allies would be much better served by a world free of nuclear weapons. Disproportionate strategic advantages accrue to states with even limited numbers of nuclear weapons. No other country, however, could match the United States with weapons of high technology and unprecedented accuracy.

The Cold War had ended, all the declared nuclear powers were at least on speaking terms, and the proliferation of nuclear weapons had, for the time being, been reasonably contained. There was no prospect, however, that this situation would continue indefinitely.

The goal of a nuclear weapons-free world was not new. It had been a long-term aim of Labor Party policy and had been articulated forcefully by many others. The Labor Government had created a position of Ambassador for Disarmament and had played an important role in the creation of the South Pacific Nuclear Free Zone. But as long as the Cold War smouldered, the hope of securing a nuclear weapons-free world was unachievable. Now, however, I felt we had an opportunity to develop a concrete program to get there.

Australia had already played a major part in the successful final negotiation of the Chemical Weapons Convention in 1992, which banned the development, production, acquisition, stockpiling, retention, direct or indirect transfer, and use of chemical weapons. This convention showed that contrary to the propaganda cries of some of the advocates of nuclear weapons, it *was* possible to put the genie back in the bottle and ban a whole class of weapons of mass destruction. And the Nuclear Non-Proliferation Treaty committed the existing declared nuclear weapons states – the five super-powers – to 'pursue negotiations in good faith on effective measures relating to cessation of the nuclear arms race at an early date and to nuclear disarmament.' They needed to be held to their pledges.

Of course, the task of ridding the world of nuclear weapons was not something Australia could accomplish alone. We had none of our own to eliminate and we were committed not to get them. We were well regarded internationally for the contribution we had made to arms control negotiations. We had an impressively competent body of officials working on arms control issues. In the United Nations we had worked hard on both the Nuclear Non-Proliferation Treaty, for which we tabled a draft text, and the Comprehensive Test Ban Treaty. But we were now entering a domain where the deepest national security interests of the United States, Russia, China, Britain and France were involved. Every country was directly affected by the nuclear threat, but nothing could happen without the five declared nuclear powers.

At the Commonwealth Heads of Government Meeting in Auckland in November 1995, I spoke in favour of including a strong condemnation of France's resumption of testing in the meeting's communiqué. The motion was strongly opposed by

John Major. The opening British bid before the meeting began was that the British 'could not accept' any criticism of France. We pressed on undeterred, and the criticism of France went into the communiqué. Major told the meeting that he woke up each day with the burden of responsibility for nuclear weapons and that the rest of us could not know what that was like. I replied that many more of us were going to know exactly what it was like because, as a result of behaviour like France's, many more would get their own nuclear weapons (as India and Pakistan subsequently did). Major did not appreciate rebukes from Australia, but I believed the issue of the non-proliferation and removal of nuclear weapons was the most obvious opportunity of the post-Cold War period. Major was playing that tired old European game of scratching one another's backs. The rest of us were to watch on as though it was some solemn European mating ritual, that it was not our role to understand or even decipher. I got along quite well with Major, but not at the price of digesting humbug of this variety from him.

Issues of how international law affected the use of nuclear weapons had been raised by a case that had been brought before the International Court of Justice (ICJ) by the World Health Organisation and the United Nations General Assembly earlier in the year. The ICJ had been asked to provide an advisory opinion on whether the use of nuclear weapons was legal under international law. Australia's intention at the start had been to argue that the court should make no decision on the matter on the grounds that if it found that they were legal it might encourage others to get them, while if it found they were illegal, thorny problems would be caused for the existing nuclear states and their allies like Australia. But as the date of the court hearing grew closer, and we began to focus on our legal advice, it became clear to Gareth and to me that we could not sustain such a position. So when Gareth appeared personally before the court on

30 October it was to argue the case that the use, threat, acquisition, testing, or possession of nuclear weapons were illegal by virtue of fundamental principles of humanity, that all states were under an obligation to take positive action to eliminate nuclear weapons, but that during the course of the elimination process the principle of stable deterrence had to be maintained for the sole purpose of ensuring that nuclear weapons were never used by others. (The joint facilities Australia operated with the United States at Pine Gap and Nurrungar would be important to the verification processes we would have to enter into to achieve a nuclear weapons-free world as well as for early warning.) This submission was a significant step for a US ally like Australia, which benefited from the US security guarantee.

Yet in some ways questions of legality or otherwise were beside the point. International law might be an extra point of moral pressure on the nuclear weapons states. But the fact was that the weapons existed and they would continue to exist until those who had them came to feel it was in their interests to give them up, or until they were convinced they had no alternative to doing so.

We decided, therefore, that the most useful thing Australia could do was to try to shape the international debate more actively. Anti-nuclear groups had written many reports about the problems of nuclear weapons but, until that time, no government of Australia's standing had ever put its name behind a report committed to their elimination. So on United Nations Day, 24 October, I announced the formation of a commission comprising a group of eminent scientists, disarmament experts, military strategists and statesmen who would be asked to develop 'concrete and realistic steps for achieving a nuclear weapons-free world'. The emphasis was to be on 'concrete and realistic'. I saw no point in another rhetorical statement that nuclear weapons were evil and should be abolished. Any report which was to have a chance of convincing the hard-headed defence establishments of North America and Europe to change their positions had to be grounded in a deep understanding of what elimination meant, both technically and strategically.

Eliminating nuclear weapons is no simple task. It throws up genuinely complex problems. How can you be sure that everyone abides by any agreement? How would you deal with a situation in which one country tried to snatch a strategic advantage by secretly breaking out of the agreement? What are the consequences of such a change in the international security environment? For example, do nuclear weapons help to deter conventional war? These are not easy questions, nor trivial ones.

We wanted a commission small enough to engage in genuine deliberations, but large enough to achieve balance in terms of background and geographic representation. We were very lucky to get together an outstanding group of commissioners. Gareth Evans's international reputation and energy were critical to our success in this. The members included Joseph Rotblat, who had won the Nobel Peace Prize for his work with the Pugwash Foundation; General Lee Butler, who had been responsible until 1994 for all US strategic nuclear forces; Field Marshal Lord Carver, the former chief of the British Defence Staff; Robert McNamara, the former US Secretary of Defence and President of the World Bank; and a number of internationally regarded disarmament experts. The distinguished Australian strategic thinker, Professor Robert O'Neill was a member. Richard Butler, then the Australian Ambassador to the United Nations and later the UN Chief Weapons Inspector, was the convener. I believed the group should also include someone with direct political experience, so I invited Michel Rocard, the former French Prime Minister, to participate.

These were not people who had come down in the last shower. They had very different backgrounds and brought different assumptions about nuclear weapons to their work. Some were long-time peace activists; some had had nuclear weapons directly in their control. If this diverse and distinguished group could agree on the road ahead, we hoped they would be able to persuade others.

Any such group needs effective secretarial support, and here again Australia showed that one of our international assets lay in the experienced and effective experts we had in the Foreign Affairs and Defence departments who could provide the high level of staff work necessary for an exercise like this. We also provided resources to permit the group to commission more detailed papers on specific dimensions of the move to a nuclear weapons-free world from expert advisers. This brought a range of international scholars into the project. Their work provided a rich resource lode for further debate about the issue.

The commissioners met for the first time in Sydney in January 1996. In the same week, the French Government announced that, after six tests, it was concluding its program. I hoped the Canberra Commission's work would enable us to salvage some positive and enduring legacy from that unnecessary manifestation of Gaullist pride.

The Labor Government was out of office by the time the Canberra Commission completed its work in the following August. The commission's recommendations were based on the fundamental assumption that 'the proposition that large numbers of nuclear weapons can be retained in perpetuity and never used – accidentally or by decision – defies credibility. The only complete defence is the elimination of nuclear weapons and the assurance that they will never be produced again.'

The report contained recommendations for immediate steps to reduce the dangers of nuclear war and longer-term moves to secure the elimination of nuclear weapons. The immediate steps proposed included removing warheads from delivery vehicles; ending the deployment of non-strategic nuclear weapons; ending nuclear testing; initiating another round of negotiations between the United States and Russia to reduce their arsenals; and a joint agreement by nuclear weapons states not to be the first to use nuclear weapons. The commissioners called for nuclear arsenals to be taken off alert. This would lengthen the nuclear fuse by extending the time needed to prepare for a launch, taking the missiles off their current hair-trigger alert status. It would involve removing vital parts of the systems. An agreement between Russia and the United States in 1994 to de-target missiles was essentially meaningless. Original targets can be fed back into the computer in seconds. But de-alerting – in other words, standing the missiles down – would require an effective and intrusive inspection system.

The commissioners argued that these measures should be reinforced by actions to prevent further 'horizontal' proliferation (that is, to stop new members, whether countries or terrorist groups, joining the nuclear club), the development of intrusive arrangements to verify that countries in a nuclear weapons-free world were abiding by their commitments, and the cessation of the production of fissile materials for nuclear explosive purposes.

As we hoped, the recommendations were realistic and practical. The commissioners did not ask for unilateral disarmament or suggest any measure that might threaten security during the process of moving to a world free of nuclear weapons. They did, however, make the fundamentally important point that, in the end, the decisions that need to be taken were not technical decisions but political ones.

The Canberra Commission made a good start. But many excellent reports lie languishing on dusty shelves in ministries around the world. The next step was the diplomatic one of trying to persuade others to embrace the ideas and adopt the policies. If we had won the 1996 election, I planned to take the report personally to the United Nations General Assembly to launch it myself. It would have been high on my agenda for discussions with President Clinton and the leaders of the other nuclear states. But beyond receiving the report in August and lodging it at the United Nations, the new Australian Coalition Government did not endorse its recommendations or try to sell them more widely. The Canberra Commission was associated with the government I led, and the incoming foreign minister had labelled it a 'stunt' in the political atmosphere of the time. So the political momentum – at least on Australia's part – was allowed to lapse.

I believe this is a great pity, and not just for Australia. I think the international policy agenda in 1996 could have been shaped in a productive way around the sensible conclusions of the Canberra Commission. But since then, the nuclear dangers have grown and the impetus for change has been allowed to stall.

The international environment has been getting steadily bleaker. Just three years after we convened the Canberra Commission two of the states on the nuclear threshold, India and Pakistan, had stepped over it. North Korea, another regime with a known nuclear program, had tested a medium-range ballistic missile. Meanwhile, Russia's capacity to control and store its existing nuclear arsenal was atrophying. It has not ratified START II. Russia and China have still not ratified the Comprehensive Test Ban Treaty, and the United States Senate, in an act of monumental irresponsibility, rejected it when it was submitted in 1999. It was sadly ironic to see President Chirac, who had resumed testing, telling reporters after the Senate decision that the rejection of the treaty threatened to 'set a bad example and start the arms proliferation race again'. He said that 'looking at India, Pakistan, Iran, we are afraid we are again entering a period of resumption of the arms race and proliferation.' By then, it was a bit too late for such fears.

After India openly tested nuclear weapons in May 1998, President Clinton said forcefully and accurately that 'to think that you have to manifest your greatness by behaviour that recalls the worst events of the twentieth century on the edge of the twenty-first, when everybody else is trying to leave the nuclear age behind, is just wrong.' But the problem, of course, is that no-one else was trying to leave the nuclear age behind, or at least not with any noticeable degree of urgency. The truth which the current nuclear states try to ignore is that the world can't have *non*-proliferation without *de*-proliferation, a point I had made to John Major at the Commonwealth Heads-of-Government Meeting.

It is not just states that we need to worry about as a source of new nuclear threats, but terrorists and other non-state groups as well. Nuclear weapons are not hard to make. You can get instructions for a workable device from the Internet. The only difficulty is access to fissile material. That is why the international community needs to address much more comprehensively the problems of 'nuclear overhang' – essentially, the security of stored nuclear weapons and excess fissile material in Russia. This is a second area that has become more dangerous since the Canberra Commission report.

At more than ninety sites across Russia, enough nuclear material is stored to fuel 40,000 weapons. Guarding this deadly treasure are military officers and soldiers of low morale and who have sometimes not been paid for months. In 1996 the then Director of Central Intelligence, John Deutch, told the US Congress that of the tonnes of weapons-useable nuclear material distributed to various centres around Russia over the past 40 years, *none* had what would be regarded in the United States as sufficient accountability. In July 1998, thousands of scientists at the nuclear city of Arzamas-16 went on strike after months without pay. The Russian Ministry of Atomic Energy, MINATOM, told its personnel that they could no longer rely on government funds to support them and that they needed to market their goods and services.

The dangers are real. In November 1993, a Russian naval officer walked out of a shipyard in Murmansk with about 10 pounds (four-and-a-half kilograms) of highly enriched uranium and went looking for a buyer while it was stored in his garage. In August 1994, almost a pound of weapons-useable plutonium was seized by German police in Munich. The dangers are not just in Russia: the reported theft of around 130 barrels of enriched uranium waste from storage in South Africa was reported in the press in August 1994.

Through the Soviet Threat Reduction program of 1991 – named the Nunn-Lugar program after the senators who co-sponsored the bill – the United States provides about $US400 million a year to help secure poorly guarded Russian nuclear facilities and to help dismantle weapons earmarked for destruction under current arms control negotiations. Nearly 5000 nuclear warheads have been deactivated. But the program so far has cost less than one per cent of the annual US defence budget. It is a solid investment, producing lasting security dividends, and could easily be doubled or tripled. If the build-down is to continue, it will have to be.

Some people willingly concede the dangers that nuclear material could be diverted to rogue states or terrorists. They say it just proves we need nuclear weapons: in order to protect ourselves against these very prospects. This is the circular argument that we need nuclear weapons because we have nuclear weapons. It is not an argument we think persuasive when applied to biological or chemical weapons.

The state of the Russian nuclear arsenal has other dangerous consequences. Thousands of Russian nuclear systems are on hair-trigger alert, ready to launch at the United States in a space of fifteen minutes. The deteriorating condition of Russian early warning systems and the erosion of military command and control heightens the danger of an accidental or unauthorised launch. It increases the incentive for the Russians to adopt a 'use them or lose them' strategy for their strategic arsenal. We reportedly came very close to such a situation in 1995 when a Norwegian research rocket was mistaken for a US missile attack and the whole Russian system went on alert. The economic collapse and the decline in conventional military capabilities tempts Russia to place extra weight on its nuclear forces to compensate. This is why Moscow has abandoned its long-standing declaratory policy of 'No First Use' of nuclear weapons.

Meanwhile, the strategic nuclear negotiations are stalled. The burst of activity from the conclusion of the Intermediate Nuclear Forces treaty of 1987, through START I in 1991, which halved long-range missiles, to START II in January 1993, which imposed a further 50 per cent cut in strategic nuclear forces, has run into the sand. And Russian hardliners are pointing to the expansion of NATO to the borders of the old Soviet Union as a reason for Russia to maintain its nuclear capabilities. The Russian Parliament has refused to ratify the START II treaty, which it believes advantages the United States. Russia cannot afford to modernise and replace ageing and decaying nuclear forces and it is slipping inexorably further behind United States numbers and capabilities. It wants much larger cuts.

In the United States, political pressure is growing for a National Missile Defence System to respond to a perceived evolving ballistic missile threat. This would certainly mean abrogating the 1972 Anti-Ballistic Missile Treaty and would cause the Russians to walk away from START I and II, fearing that the United States could quickly upgrade a missile defence system into a shield behind which it could launch a first strike. Even early discussion about extending a missile defence umbrella to Japan and Taiwan is heightening tension in North Asia between China, Japan and Taiwan.

In this depressing landscape – a period in arms-control negotiations that some have called 'the great frustration' – the agenda for action set out in the Canberra Commission report remains urgent. Other countries have since taken up the Canberra Commission's task. A 'New Agenda' coalition, drawing inspiration explicitly from the Canberra Commission, was formed in June 1998 by Brazil, Egypt, Ireland, Mexico, New Zealand, Slovenia, South Africa and Sweden to push for the elimination of nuclear weapons, and Japan has convened a group of experts from 16 countries called the Tokyo Forum to discuss nuclear disarmament and non-proliferation.

Much has to be done to reinvigorate the strategic arms-reduction talks in a way that will rectify the emerging numerical inequality in favour of the United States and get nuclear numbers down so low that the other nuclear weapons states can be brought into the negotiations. We also need to begin serious negotiations on a Fissionable Material Cut-Off Treaty, which will halt the production of fissile material (that is, weapons-grade plutonium and uranium) for nuclear weapons.

For my part, however, I don't believe that any objective short of zero nuclear weapons will be able to generate the political consensus necessary to stop an eventual breakout. Even if only a handful of weapons are held by Washington and Moscow and Beijing, even if they are held in 'strategic escrow' under some form of international supervision, I find it impossible to imagine why a future South American government, or some future African leader, convinced that Africa has been abused and marginalised, will not understand the disproportionate strategic advantages that accrue to states with even crude nuclear weapons and ask: Why not us? And there is no defensible answer to that question. Only a full commitment to the elimination of nuclear weapons will ever be sufficient to ensure our safety.

In some ways, I suppose, I am an unexpected campaigner for nuclear disarmament. I am a realist about international affairs and I don't have great faith in the inherent goodwill of the nation state. I have never seen much point to the politics of symbolism. During the Cold War I thought ideas of unilateral disarmament were naive and dangerous. And yet this issue of nuclear weapons worries me more than any other when I think about the sort of world young Australians will inherit. We face a long struggle to get rid of nuclear weapons and we might not succeed. But you can be absolutely sure that if the pressure is not kept on governments, if the issues and alternatives aren't debated, if the voice of public opinion is not raised, then the line of least resistance will be taken. And that line will always be to let things slide – to hope that in the next hundred years some new, more ruthless or more able Saddam Hussein won't emerge, that somehow the skills of Russian nuclear scientists now on the market will not be made available to terrorist groups, and that we will get through it all unscathed.

Three possibilities exist with regard to nuclear weapons, and three only. First, that they will be used, either deliberately or accidentally. Second, that they will not be used, but will be managed forever by wise, prudent and well-meaning governments and military forces, and will never fall into the hands of terrorists or the aggrieved. Or, third, that we agree to get rid of them. The first possibility offers catastrophe to the human race. The second requires us to make assumptions about the future that run completely counter to logic and experience. The third is the only possibility that can secure our safety.

Those who think the risks are manageable, who believe we are sure to glide safely past the rocks and shoals because we have done so before, should at least reflect on the history of the 1990s. Neither the collapse of the Soviet Union nor the Asian economic crisis seemed remotely possible to most professional observers before they were upon us.

The goal of eliminating nuclear weapons can't be accomplished by arms control alone. It is also – even essentially – a debate about global power and influence and it will only be resolved in that context. We have come to see nuclear weapons as the ultimate global status symbol, a point the new Russian President Vladimir Putin reminded the world of in 1999 when making very obvious his view of Russia's true status. Membership of the United Nations Security Council remains co-terminous with the possession of nuclear weapons. And UN reform, so high on everyone's agenda when the Cold War ended, has faltered. These broader questions of global institutions and the distribution of global power are ones I want to return to in chapter 11. But the task of addressing nuclear dangers is too urgent to be left until we have sorted out every other aspect of global geo-strategy.

In 1997, one of the members of the Canberra Commission, General Lee Butler, made a speech accepting the prestigious Henry L. Stimson award for distinguished public service. General Butler, the former head of United States Strategic Nuclear Command, said he was dismayed that

> even among more serious commentators, the lessons of fifty years at the nuclear brink can be so grievously misread, that the assertions and assumptions underpinning an era of desperate threats and risks prevail unchallenged, that a handful of nations cling to the impossible notion that the power of nuclear weapons is so immense their use can be threatened with impunity, yet their proliferation contained. Albert Einstein recognised this hazardous but very human tendency many years ago, when he warned that 'the power of the atom has changed everything save our modes of thinking, and thus we drift toward unparalleled catastrophe'.

I hope that is wrong. But 'drifting' is the right word to describe what all of us – nuclear and non-nuclear powers alike – have been doing over recent years.

CHAPTER 10

OUR PLACE IN THE WORLD

In an age like this, when money and goods flow freely around the world and knowledge is a more valuable commodity than anything found under the red surface of Australia's deserts, this country will always have international interests which extend far beyond the region immediately around us.

As we saw in the last chapter, arms-control issues like nuclear disarmament have to be tackled globally. Efforts to limit environmental damage by reducing greenhouse gas emissions or banning trade in endangered species must involve international cooperation. And a middle-sized country like Australia will always get a better deal out of international trading rules if we can build coalitions of interest within a multilateral framework.

In a globalised world you have to scout widely for markets and investments. The humanitarian instinct to do something to help, which Australians invariably show when confronted by famine or war, will always give us an interest in alleviating the causes of suffering wherever we see it. And in an immigrant society like ours, people will never abandon their connections with the places from which they or their families have come.

This means that Australia's foreign policy will always have a global dimension as well as an intense regional focus. During the years between 1992 and 1996, for example, we helped bring the Uruguay Round to a successful conclusion, completed the

Chemical Weapons Convention, committed Australian forces to the UN peace-keeping operations in Somalia, helped sustain the international sanctions-enforcing role in the Gulf by contributing an Australian naval ship, and developed our relations with the European Union (EU).

In this chapter I want to look at some parts of the world outside the Asia-Pacific, particularly Europe, and at the broader question of how the view Australians have of themselves affects our place in the world.

It is impossible to ignore Europe. The twentieth century may have been the American century, but it was Europe that set the tone. The strategic miscalculations that marked European statesmanship around the end of the nineteenth century did more than anything else to generate the carnage of totalitarianism and two world wars. But by the century's end Europe had shown a capacity to remake itself fundamentally and, in doing so, to generate new ways of thinking about the relationships between sovereign states.

The fifteen current members of the European Union, with their 370 million people, form the world's largest trading bloc. Europe's international economic influence will increase as its common currency, the Euro, forces structural change within Europe, and as it takes on a larger global role as a reserve currency. And, Asia notwithstanding, Europe remains vital to Australia's economic future. Our trade with the EU represents nearly a fifth of the total. Europe is Australia's largest source of foreign investment. In the other direction, Europe is the most important destination for Australian investment overseas. In fact, the value of sales generated by Australian direct investment in Europe is significantly greater than our annual exports there of both goods and services.

Economic issues that are critical to Australia's future well-being, like the future of agricultural protectionism, can only be settled with the involvement of the Europeans. Vigorous cultural and scientific contacts with Europe are part of our everyday lives. But much more fundamentally than any of these practical contacts, Australia's relationship with Europe is an ineradicable part of what makes us Australian. No matter how we shape our future in the Asia-Pacific, the legacy of our links with Europe is entrenched in the structure of our society, the forms of our institutions, and in the way we think about the world. However Australia changes in the future, that will remain.

More than 2.3 million Australians were born in Europe and a further 2.6 million had one or both parents born there. My own children are among them. For many Australians, as for me, Europe is important beyond the facts of our history and the vigour of our economic relationships. I love visiting Europe. I've always admired the architecture and human scale of the best European cities. I respond to the place from which the music I most enjoy has come. Few things moved me more on my overseas trips as prime minister than a civic reception in the village of Tynagh in Ireland from which my great-grandparents had set off for Australia all those years ago.

It is a pleasant (and unusual) experience for an Australian Prime Minister to be cheered at a sports match, as happened when we attended the 1993 Gaelic Football Grand Final at Croke Park in Dublin. When the Irish fans sang along to the words of 'Waltzing Matilda' no-one could doubt the depth of the cultural and emotional chords between us. But although I was very conscious that my family's roots were in Ireland, I had never felt, as an earlier generation of Australians might have done, that Europe was 'home', a word that was being used about Britain without irony by some Australians well into my adult life.

Australia has always had trouble getting our relationship with Europe right. On the one hand, we have seen it as a distant, too-easily romanticised place; on the other, as an overwhelming presence. We have often held those two views simultaneously.

Australia's modern origins involved us in no great act of differentiation from Europe. Unlike the United States, we had no puritan sense of moral separateness, no New Jerusalem to build, no shining city on a hill. We did not need to redefine ourselves in revolutionary ways against the place most of us had come from. We did not seize our independence but were set adrift, some of us still complaining about it. We were exiles long after this country should have been home to us. We looked to Europe for psychological as well as physical security in a world to which we did not feel we belonged.

When I became prime minister in 1991 the common accusation was that, because of my known personal interests in European arts and music, it must follow that I had no interest in Asia. It was a strange charge that you had to be a cultural orientalist to know where Australia's interests lay. The Liberals, so keen to scour the Hansard for my quotable quotes, seemed to pass over remarks by me about Asia dating back to my earliest period in Parliament. Later, the line from my political opponents changed to an assertion that I had an 'Asia only' policy – an 'obsession' with it – and was ignoring Europe.

Over the course of a long political career, you get accused of many unflattering things. But I have to say that the most spectacular of all the charges against me came from an American political scientist, Professor Samuel Huntington from Harvard University, who accused me of precipitating the fall of a civilisation.

The central idea in Professor Huntington's book, *The Clash of Civilizations and the Remaking of World Order*, which was published in 1996, is that the ideological divisions of the Cold War will be succeeded by a world divided along the fault-lines of civilisations. It is a much more elaborate and footnoted version of the words of that grand old imperialist Rudyard Kipling: 'East is East and West is West and never the twain shall meet.'

In a section about Australia and the changes my colleagues and I were trying to bring to Australia's relationship with the region, Professor Huntington writes: 'At the beginning of the twenty-second century historians might look back on the Keating–Evans choice [of engagement with Asia] as a major marker in the decline of the West.' In a way, it's a flattering accusation, I suppose. It's certainly a reminder that there is nothing much about hyperbole that a politician can teach an academic in full flight. But I can confidently reassure Professor Huntington that future historians will be doing no such thing.

The choice I was said to have made in the early 1990s was that Australia should 'defect from the West, redefine itself as an Asian society, and cultivate close ties with its geographical neighbours.' The last claim is right; the first two are rubbish.

Paul Keating 'liked to say', Professor Huntington asserts confidently, that I was going to change Australia from being 'the odd man out (in Asia) to the odd man in'. Despite Professor Huntington's authoritative quotation marks, I liked to say no such thing, and I never did. What I did say, and many times, was that Australia was not Asian or European or American or anything except Australian. This is what history and geography have delivered us. It is the only option we have and one we have every reason to celebrate.

Certainly I wanted to sharpen the focus of Australian foreign policy on the region around Australia. It was the area of foreign policy where an investment of time by Australian political leaders was most needed and could pay the largest dividends. And because the stakes for Australia in Asia were, and are, so high, and because there were powerful cultural and historical forces resisting this transition, I wanted to make our intention abundantly clear. The issues facing Europe – enlarging and deepening the EU, managing the transition from communism in Eastern Europe, constructing new security mechanisms, dealing with the crisis in the Balkans – were very important internationally, but they were areas in which Australia could do little more than express opinions. And declaratory foreign policy is a fundamentally empty enterprise. The obvious truth, I believed, was that the more Australia was integrated into the Asia-Pacific, the greater would be our relevance to Europe and our influence there on the things that matter to us.

In the first half of the 1990s the future of Europe was highly unsettled. The Cold War had ended unexpectedly and in a way no-one had predicted. The prospects for Russia and the former states of the Soviet Union seemed chaotic. The consequences of German reunification in 1990, not just for Germany itself but for the general balance of power in Europe needed to be worked out. Questions about whether to give priority to broadening the EU by adding new members, or deepening it through greater economic and political integration were becoming more pressing. These were all dimensions of one central issue facing Europe: growth. How to broaden the EU's membership, how to enlarge the definitions of European security, and how to expand the European economies.

In a political sense, the last of these was the most immediate problem. As Lester Thurow records in his book *The Future of Capitalism*, not one net new job was created in Western Europe from 1973 to 1994. Europe's unemployment rates, which had been about half those of the United States through the 1950s and '60s, had risen by the mid-1990s to be more than double the US rates. Unemployment in Germany, for example, was at its highest levels since the 1930s. Throughout the 1980s and early 1990s Australia's economic performance consistently outstripped Europe's. The cause of Europe's slow-down had been the deliberate constraint of growth and avoidance of structural change in favour of protecting existing jobs, maintaining low inflation and the status quo.

It was partly in response to this problem of growth that Chancellor Kohl of Germany and President Mitterrand of France – representing the two countries at the core of Europe – had given the mandate to Jacques Delors, the President of the Commission of the EU, to move Europe towards tighter economic integration. The chief instruments of integration were, first, the Single European Act of 1987. This turned Europe into a single market, with fewer barriers to trade than existed between even the states of Australia, and established the framework for a more integrated foreign policy. The second instrument was the 1993 Maastricht Treaty, which set out the arrangements for economic and monetary union. (I was able to point out with some pride to Helmut Kohl in 1995 that of all the developed western economies only Germany, Luxembourg and Australia would at that time have met the stringent economic performance conditions set out in the Maastricht Treaty for participation in monetary union.)

The economic objective of the single market and of economic and monetary union was to improve European economic performance in the new global environment. But there was also a political aim: to deepen European integration, and especially the nexus between France and Germany, the two largest countries of continental Western Europe, whose strategic rivalry had shaped and stained so much of modern European history.

With the unexpected end of the Cold War, most of the former communist countries in Central and Eastern Europe were now knocking insistently on the EU's door and demanding admission. The potential influx of new members raised questions about almost every aspect of Europe's organisation. What would happen to the EU's traditional consensus decision-making in a larger group? How would the priority for new members be determined? How would Europe accommodate a very different political and security agenda?

The addition of new members to the east would also have

security consequences. Since the end of the Second World War, Western Europe's security had been forged in an Atlantic Alliance with the United States. The clear purpose of the North Atlantic Treaty Organisation (NATO) was to contain Soviet power and defend the West against any aggression from Moscow.

NATO had served the cause of western security well. It helped ensure that the Cold War finally ended in ways that served open democratic interests. But with communism gone, and Russia in economic chaos, what was the purpose of the alliance? Who was the enemy?

In 1991, NATO had answered these questions admirably by declaring: 'We do not wish to isolate any country, nor to see a new division of the continent. Our objective is a Europe whole and free.' But within a few years, in 1997, Poland, the Czech Republic and Hungary were being invited to join the alliance. Just a decade after Mikhail Gorbachev had conceded that East Germany could remain in NATO as part of a united Germany, the alliance had climbed up to the western border of the Ukraine.

Russia could only read this message in one way: that although it had become a democracy, in the consciousness of Western Europe it remained the state to be watched, the potential enemy. Russian suspicion was fuelled, and the strains of nationalist thought in Russia opposed to full engagement with the West were strengthened. Arms control, and especially nuclear arms control, was made more difficult.

In the early 1990s, however, these developments lay well in the future. During that period the focus of Australia's relationship with Europe revolved around the fractious issue of Europe's refusal to countenance real reform of its agricultural export policies, an issue of deep importance to Australia, and one, as we have seen, which had brought the Uruguay Round to the brink of collapse. For Australia, one beneficial outcome of European enlargement was likely to be reform of the infamous Common

Agricultural Policy. Aid to farmers was already absorbing half the EU's budget, and the addition of new East European members would increase the EU's arable land by 55 per cent. The subsidies would become unaffordable.

The successful conclusion of the round at the end of 1993 disposed of this issue for the time being and we were able to look again at other aspects of the relationship with Europe. In June 1994, I visited Brussels to meet the EU Commission President, Jacques Delors. I liked and admired Delors, who was a great European, and in other political circumstances would have been a great President of France. It was clear both in a long private meeting I had with him, and in a broader discussion with other EU commissioners, that we had been trying to address many similar problems of public policy relating to unemployment, economic growth and competitiveness. I explained the work Australia had done with retraining programs for the long-term unemployed and he went through the Commission's own recent white paper on employment.

We agreed to set up meetings between our officials to share our experiences. This set the stage for a more active and wide-ranging policy agenda between Australia and the EU in the course of 1994 and 1995. We signed a science-and-technology agreement in February 1994, the first for the EU with a non-EU member. We began negotiating a mutual recognition agreement, and we expanded cultural exchanges.

In April 1995, I wrote to Delors's successor, Jacques Santer, suggesting that Australia and the EU negotiate a treaty-level agreement to provide a framework for our future relations. Negotiations about the treaty were still going on at the time of Labor's electoral defeat and it subsequently fell victim to the incoming Australian Government's refusal to agree to the inclusion of a strong human rights clause. We ended up, regrettably, with nothing more than a joint declaration.

Notwithstanding the growing authority and scope of the European Union during this period, however, Europe's future was still being played out, as it had been for a century, in the complex, historically deep relationship between Britain, France and Germany. This triangular relationship had been deeply affected by the end of the Cold War and the reunification of Germany. From a position of rough parity with France and Britain before reunification, Germany had become easily the dominant economy in Europe. Its centre of gravity had, as before, shifted towards the East.

GERMANY

Helmut Kohl was one of the most impressive statesmen of the late twentieth century, and the reunification of Germany, in which he played such a key role, was one of its critical events. Kohl had made the decision to press ahead with reunification in the face of a barrage of domestic and international advice to slow down. The Bundesbank warned of the economic costs; Margaret Thatcher of the political consequences. But despite the economic and political complications, I have no doubt that Kohl's decisive actions were not only best for Germany, but best for the world as well.

In March 1995, I became the first Australian Prime Minister to visit the reunited Germany. My meeting with Chancellor Kohl on 7 March was surprising and enjoyable. Kohl was physically dominating, consistently underestimated politically, and had a confident underlying determination which I admired. I'm not sure what either of us had in our official briefing notes to talk about, but we ended up spending two and a half hours discussing everything from monetary union to how Australia and Germany could work more closely together in Asia to the future of Berlin. As he often had, Kohl spoke of German unification and European unification being two faces of the same coin. Germany had to make sure it never made the same mistakes again, and the corollary of German reunification had to be European unification.

He talked movingly about growing up in post-war Germany and the symbolic importance of the slowly strengthening Deutschmark as a sign of national renewal. 'I believe it is important, but we have to give it up,' he said, referring to monetary union and the creation of the Euro. He discussed the decisions he had to make when the East German leader, Erich Honecker, had come to him pleading for money. We ended our private meeting with a discussion about the styles of various German conductors and listened to a CD of Mozart's D Minor piano concerto.

I travelled on from safe, sleepy Bonn – the village that had become the capital of the Federal Republic as Germans went through the post-war challenges of rebuilding their country and redefining themselves – to Berlin, with its dark, glorious and savage history. Berlin was soon to become the capital of the reunited Germany.

The feeling of the weight of this history was reinforced by a visit to the famous East Berlin opera house, the Staatsoper, to see a talented young Australian, Simone Young, conducting *Tristan and Isolde* by Wagner, whose person and music exemplifies so much German ambiguity.

That weekend I went privately back to Potsdam, 30 kilometres outside Berlin. It is a place that haunts me. It is the site of so much that is good and so much that is evil about Europe, and about human nature generally.

At Potsdam, in the 1760s, Frederick the Great built with his architect, Knobelsdorff, Sans Souci and the Neues Palace, with its ready-made ruins placed in the forest to give expression to the Romantic notion that nature could be improved by architecture. I visited again the Prussian neoclassical architect Karl

Friedrich Schinkel's castellated house at Babelsberg and his wonderful 1826 villa at Charlottenhof with its asymmetrical garden and baths built in the 'à la Grec' style. These buildings are among some of the greatest of the early nineteenth century, an apogee of the neoclassical and Romantic imagination.

But nearby, on the same stretch of water at Wannsee, just over a century later, the most scarifying decision of modern history was taken on a Saturday afternoon, near the romantic vistas these great people had created. There, in a few hours' conversation in 1942, Reinhard Heydrich, Adolf Eichmann and thirteen other Nazi leaders took the decision to industrially exterminate the Jewish race. Afterwards, they strolled out to take in the view.

In 1945, against this landscape of light and darkness, the victors of the European war decided to hold the conference on the division of Europe at the Cecilianhof in Potsdam. They clinically cut Europe into a political map that would determine its history for half a century. Stalin, whose countrymen and women did more than any others to win the Second World War, demanded his cordon sanitaire and got it. And while Truman grappled with the new order for his conference in San Francisco which would give birth to the United Nations, Churchill watched the old order pass, recording the event as the disgruntled representative of a marginalised power.

Six years earlier, on a trip to the IMF/Word Bank meetings in Berlin, I had arrived at the Glienicke Bridge nearby, accompanied by a friend who was the grand-daughter of Count von Moltke, the famous First World War General. Making our way from West Germany to the East, our car carefully threaded its way through the bollards set up on the bridge to prevent a hasty reversal. The booms came down just before and just behind the car, while the East German officer at the checkpoint looked sternly at our passports and made numerous telephone calls. Sitting there in the middle of the bridge on which so many Cold

War spies had been exchanged, I was struck by the juxtaposition of the romantic park on the Havel, peppered with Schinkel's icons at Babelsberg and Glienicke, and the dark transactions that had taken place beneath them – Kaiser Wilhelm's sojourns during the First World War, in such careless indifference to the shocking magnitude of his miscalculations, the Nazi infamy at Wannsee and front-line to the Cold War.

Potsdam, in its idealised setting, had to lie on the fault-line of Europe's humanity.

Now the Cold War was over and there was hope for better outcomes. As Kohl had made clear so many times, the relationship between Germany and France was central to the future of Europe.

FRANCE

France has been present in the Australian consciousness ever since our modern foundation. In 1788, as the British raised the Union Jack on the shores of Sydney Harbour, La Perouse was anchored just offshore. And the coast of Australia from Perth to Hobart is dotted with the names left behind by La Perouse, Boudin and D'Entrecasteaux.

I believed our modern relationship with France offered great potential. As an example, the French Socialist Party leader Michel Rocard and I had worked together closely and successfully in the 1980s to begin a process that banned mining in Antarctica and had the entire continent declared a wilderness park. But the potential for the Australia–France relationship seemed constantly under assault. French agricultural protectionism, differences over the future of the French Pacific colony of New Caledonia, nuclear testing, and a pervasive sense on the conservative side of French politics that Australia was a branch office of the worldwide Anglo-Saxon conspiracy all hobbled the prospects.

It was the history of our military relationship which brought me twice to France as prime minister. In two world wars, Australians had fought and died in France and for France. In September 1993, after visiting Britain and Ireland, I paid a one-day visit to Villers-Bretonneux, where in the middle of undulating farmland stands the memorial to the 45,000 Australians who died in France and Belgium during the First World War. Twelve hundred Australians had died during the second battle of Villers-Bretonneux in April 1918. The sight of the memorial moved me, as it does all Australians, and when at a subsequent civic reception the local French member of the National Assembly made some insensitive remarks about Australia's responsibility to take account of the special interests of French farmers, I became deeply irritated and held an impromptu press conference in which I made some direct criticisms of the selfishness of French farm policy. We then boarded our RAAF plane for Monte Carlo and the announcement of Sydney's selection for the 2000 Olympic Games. It was probably a good thing that we left quickly. My comments (as any criticisms of France tend to do) led to another bout of irritation with us on the part of the French. In 1994, however, after President Mitterrand's decision to impose a moratorium on French nuclear tests, and after the conclusion of the Uruguay Round, the relationship was in much better shape.

I returned to France in June 1994 for the commemorations of the D-Day landings in Europe. After attending similar celebrations in Britain, I arrived with my wife as a guest of Queen Elizabeth, aboard the Royal Yacht *Britannia* – an irony which, I suspect, did not escape my hostess.

After the official commemoration ceremony on 6 June at Omaha Beach, I attended a much smaller, but no less emotional, event in the village of Noyers Bocage, which has a memorial to the pilots of the Typhoon ground attack aircraft, including eight Australians, who lost their lives in the Battle of Normandy. The role of the Royal Australian Air Force in the European theatre is one of the insufficiently recognised stories of the Second World

War. Over 20,000 RAAF aircrew served in Bomber Command, and 3486 of them were killed. This was as high a proportion of deaths as those of the Australians on the Western Front during the First World War.

As I had said at the Air Forces memorial at Runnymede in Britain two days earlier, of all those who served in Europe:

> Never were men braver or more selfless. They gave their lives so that we might enjoy freedom.
>
> We honour in particular our countrymen: those Australians who left their homes and all they loved to cross the world and fight in a war against evil.
>
> Their deeds bestowed great honour on Australia, indelible honour on themselves.
>
> We should tell our children what this war concerned. Why Australians came to fight alongside the British, the Americans and the Canadians. Why a generation of Australians believed freedom was worth fighting for. Their spirit can nourish the life of a nation.

I went from Normandy to Paris for my first meeting with President François Mitterrand. The President was already ill but he still had a forceful presence and a complex, engaging mind. He had spoken powerfully in Normandy on the previous day about the war. My main aim was to leave him with the sense that Australia was a different country from the one he might have had in his imagination – a diverse community finding its future in the Asia-Pacific. We talked about the way the Asia-Pacific region was developing and about the opportunities for Australia and France to work together. I congratulated him on his decision to suspend France's nuclear testing program. He explained the reasons for his decision and said he would maintain the moratorium so long as would the other nuclear powers.

At the end of our meeting, after some discussion of my interest in French decorative arts, he took the unusual and unscheduled step of giving me a personal tour of the private apartments of the Elysee Palace, including the Silver Room where Napoleon had signed his abdication statement. He had the statement on its stand brought out. As we were saying goodbye he suggested I make an official visit to France later in the year. I would have liked to do this but time and other priorities, and Mitterrand's own deteriorating health, made it too difficult.

By the following year another president was in the Elysee, and he had reversed Mitterrand's nuclear moratorium. Australia was once again embroiled in a dispute with France.

GREAT BRITAIN

Of the three countries whose interaction was shaping Europe, Britain was the one that loomed largest for Australia, and where the policies I was pursuing on both foreign relations and constitutional reform seemed to confront long-standing interests most directly.

From the beginning of my time as prime minister I had been a subject of fascination to the British tabloids. A gentle effort to guide the Queen through a large physical throng at the opening of the new Parliamentary session in 1992 had become characterised as a physical assault on the royal person. (I was in fact trying to lead her towards Dame Pattie Menzies, whom I knew she would like to meet again.) 'Hands orf, Cobber!' screamed the tabloids, unwittingly making my point for me. Although she was, in fact, Australia's Queen in constitutional terms when she was in Australia, not even the British could understand this subtle constitutional point. My wife's decision when greeting the Queen to bow her head rather than curtsey (although completely acceptable in protocol terms) was portrayed as a republican attack on the monarchy. And some strong, but historically incontrovertible, criticism of Churchill and the British Government for placing British national interests before Australia's during the Second World War was transformed into a Fenian assault on British courage and an affront to the whole British legacy to Australia. (Churchill himself had said that the Japanese menace 'lay in a sinister twilight compared to our other needs', and that for the campaign in the Middle East, he was 'resigned to pay whatever forfeits were exacted in Malaysia'.) In fact, as I said in the first speech I gave on foreign policy as prime minister, and in different ways on many later occasions, it was thanks largely to our British heritage that Australia was a stable and mature liberal democracy of long standing.

In September 1993 I made my first visit to London as prime minister. We were met on the tarmac at Heathrow by a wild melee of tabloid journalists and photographers more appropriate to a visit by a pop star than a Commonwealth prime minister. The 'Lizard of Oz' had arrived.

The problem with the relationship between Australia and Britain was that accretions of meaning had clamped to it like barnacles, and it could no longer move smoothly through the water. It needed to be scraped clean – 'modernised' in the words of the British Prime Minister, John Major. In Australia, the relationship had been commandeered by the conservatives after the First World War, and was still clutched closely to the commodious bosom of the 'Land of Hope and Glory' brigade, who saw our relationship with Britain and our constitutional link with the Crown as one and the same thing. This difference was drawn much more clearly by John Major, for whose clear-eyed insistence on the distinction between them throughout this period I was very grateful.

Australia had much to gain from a strong, independent relationship with Britain. We thought about the world in very similar ways, and long connections between our institutions and our people gave us an ease of communication through innumerable strands of contact. Almost alone among the Europeans, Britain had stood strongly in favour of free trade during Australia's struggle to get agriculture included in the Uruguay Round negotiations and in opposing French efforts to reopen the issue. Britain was by far our largest trading partner outside the Asia-Pacific, and Australia was a larger investor in Britain than was Japan. In the new Europe, Britain was going to remain a very important partner for Australia.

I was sure that constitutional change would strengthen, not weaken, Australia's relationship with Britain. I said in a speech at Australia House during my visit in 1993:

> It is not because our affections for Great Britain are reduced, or the friendship between us frailer, or our respect and admiration for the culture and institutions Britain has bequeathed us in any way diminished, that now, in this last decade of our first century as a nation, we are considering the option of becoming a republic.

The event that will demonstrate the truth of my belief about the relationship between Britain and Australia will be the first state visit to the United Kingdom by the President of the Commonwealth of Australia.

Before the 1996 election, and afterwards, the Liberal-National Party coalition criticised the Labor Government's foreign policy by claiming that Australia 'does not have to choose between its geography and its history'. That was a coded but clear message that we did not have to choose between Europe and Asia. That we could continue doing the sort of things we had always done, thinking about ourselves in the same sort of way, and that, somehow or other, a close relationship with our neighbours would just turn up.

It is a deeply mistaken message. No choice we can make as a nation lies between our history and our geography. We can hardly change either of these immutable facts. The only choice we can make is the choice about our future. Australia does not have to deny its past. We *must* not deny our past. But we do have choices to make as a people. Our national path is not a one-way track to a sun-lit mountain summit. It has forks that lead to different destinations. And the burden of choice over which direction to take is not a weight that can be lifted from our national shoulders.

When I became prime minister I thought that choice needed to encompass not just the economic reforms on which my colleagues and I had spent so much of the 1980s working, but broader issues of what it meant to be an Australian a century after federation.

Australia is an extraordinary accident of history. Europeans came to live on this continent only the equivalent of four of my own lifetimes ago. From the earliest years of European settlement, Australia has been redefining itself, shifting its image of what it means to be Australian in response to the changing world. I thought in the 1990s this required us to look at our place in the Asia-Pacific region, at the changing pattern of immigration to Australia and how that affected our ideas about what it was to be an Australian, at the sorry history of our relationship with Aborigines and Torres Strait Islanders, and at the anomalous fact that a century after Australia became a nation, not one of its people could hope to be our head of state. 'No!' the conservatives shrilled in chorus. It was not legitimate to look at these issues. They were 'distractions'. Of course they were not. They were issues which were central to Australia's aspirations, as the Coalition itself was to discover to its chagrin in the years that followed.

After the 1996 elections, the rise of the One Nation party and its mishandling by the new Australian Government brought immigration and multiculturalism to public prominence with unpleasant force. Pauline Hanson and her supporters played on the politics of envy and resentment.

I am an unabashed believer in immigration. I believe Australia will be better able to survive and prosper in the world if we have a young and growing population. I regard our post-war immigration policy as one of the greatest strategic decisions this country has made. The 42 per cent of our people born outside Australia or with one parent who was born overseas have transformed this country and strengthened our economy. The immigration program has made Australia a culturally richer, more varied and much more interesting place to live. It has given us weight.

Some sensible people worry on environmental grounds about whether Australia can sustain a much larger population. The environmental problems facing Australia, especially the quality of our soils and water, are serious. But the way to address them is not to slam down the shutters and put up a 'house full' sign at our borders.

You can find substantial discontent with immigration policy anywhere and any time in Australia. For half a century, when asked whether they supported the immigration program, most Australians would tell the pollsters, no. But these responses – and we still see them – reflect in my view a shallow dissatisfaction, a feeling of apprehension about future competition for jobs, rather than a commentary on what has already been done.

The reasons we favour or oppose migration have more to do with the sort of country we want this to be rather than any empirical evidence about migration's impact on unemployment, or any expectation that it will provide an immediate boost to economic growth. Had a referendum been held to consider changing the White Australia Policy in, say, 1970, I don't think there's much doubt it would not have been changed. And had it not been changed, Australia would today be – deservedly – an international pariah, and in every way a much poorer country. It is one of the responsibilities of governments to protect the national interest against the tide of prejudice.

For twenty-six years I represented in the Australian parliament the working-class electorate of Blaxland, centred around the western Sydney suburb of Bankstown, where I had grown up. By the time I left office in 1996, around 20,000 of my 70,000 electors were of Lebanese background, both Moslem and Christian, 18,000 had come from Vietnam and the rest from a huge variety of European and Asian backgrounds. This was the society Australia was becoming, and compared with the Anglo-Celtic monoculture of the same area during my own childhood there, it was a change I welcomed. What is more, it had been achieved with remarkably little tension or unrest.

Related to the size of the immigration program is the question of what we expect migrants to become after they arrive here. What does Australian citizenship mean? The policy approach successive Australian governments since Malcolm Fraser had adopted was multiculturalism. Multiculturalism is an inelegant word which has almost as many meanings as it has users. I would be as happy as anyone to drop it from my vocabulary as soon as something better turns up. But I wholeheartedly support its purpose. In his book *The Culture of Complaint*, Robert Hughes describes it like this:

> Multiculturalism asserts that people with different roots can co-exist, that they can learn to read the image-banks of others, that they can and should look across the frontiers of race, language, gender and age without prejudice or illusion.

Like everything else in our society, multicultural policy reflects a balance of rights and responsibilities. It proclaims the right to express and share our individual cultural heritage, and the right of every Australian to equality of treatment and opportunity. But as I said in office (as opposed to what I am said to have said), it imposes responsibilities, too. These are that all Australians must accept the basic principles of Australian society. Such principles include the Constitution and the rule of law, parliamentary democracy, freedom of speech and religion, English as the national language, equality of the sexes, and tolerance.

In a speech I made to the Multicultural Advisory Council in June 1995, I said:

> The Australian Government continues to assert the right of all Australians to express their individual cultural heritage and their right to equality of treatment and opportunity. But it also asserts that the first loyalty of all who make Australia home must be *to* Australia – and that the tolerance on which multiculturalism is built must be recognised as a universal principle of Australian democracy, and practised universally.

These descriptions of multicultural policy are part and parcel of what multiculturalism in Australia has always been about, and few Australians would disagree with them.

The fundamental problem those who oppose cultural diversity must address is that at the beginning of the twenty-first century it is almost impossible to imagine a monocultural Australia, let alone contemplate how you could possibly enforce such a thing. How could there be one model of Australianness with which we could all identify? Who would decide it? Would it ever change? How? Would it be an urban, suburban or rural Australianness? Male or female?

The world has moved well beyond the traditional nineteenth-century United States view that an immigrant society is a melting pot in which settlers become the ingredients of a homogenising soup. If we need a culinary metaphor anymore, I think Australia should be like a wok, lightly stir-frying the ingredients of our population into a harmonious Australian whole, but preserving the freshness and integrity of the individual components.

If Samuel Huntington (of *The Clash of Civilizations* theses) was right the implications for Australia's immigration policy would be sobering. We would have to acknowledge that we were forever perched precariously on the edge of a cultural San Andreas Fault. We would be impelled towards an immigration policy of preference for our 'own' types. In a distorted and perverted form, this sort of approach lies behind the views of the followers of One Nation in Australia, by the radical nationalist groups in Japan, and by the pan-Asianists.

I believe Australia's history stands against this view of the world and the future. I certainly would not deny that culture is important in international as well as human relations. But cultures change, and it is in the merging of the culture pools that the most interesting ways forward emerge.

Just as I wanted to defend a multicultural society in Australia, so I thought that the way we dealt with our own Indigenous inhabitants, members of the oldest continuous civilisation on earth, was central to any hope we had of taking our place in the Asia-Pacific. We could hardly go around to our neighbours saying that we wanted to forge our future in this region while at the same time treating some of our own people as second-class citizens.

But much more importantly, as I said in December 1992 in a speech to a group of people gathered in the suburb of Redfern, long a centre of urban Aboriginal life in Sydney, the way Australia managed to extend opportunity, care, dignity and hope to the Indigenous people of Australia would be 'a fundamental test of our social goals and our national will: our ability to say to ourselves and the rest of the world that Australia is a first-rate social democracy, that we are what we should be – truly the land of the fair go and the better chance.'

Our policy in government revolved around one central premise: that this should be the moment in our history when we made a concerted effort to break the cycle of despair and disillusion that had engulfed successive generations of Aborigines. We believed that such a process would represent a sound national investment. That a real and mutual sense of reconciliation would bring immense national dividends.

Reconciliation would not solve the material problems, such as health, housing, and education, but it was an essential part of the process. Whatever the bean-counters or the paternalists might say, the challenge is psychological and spiritual as much as it is material.

I said in the Redfern speech that the process of reconciliation between Indigenous and non-indigenous Australians had to start with an act of recognition by those of us who were not Aboriginal.

> Recognition that it was we who did the dispossessing.
>
> We took the traditional lands and smashed the traditional way of life. We brought the diseases. The alcohol. We committed the murders. We took the children from their mothers. We practised discrimination and exclusion.
>
> It was our ignorance and our prejudice. And our failure to imagine these things being done to us.

When I said these things, it was not my intention to impress guilt upon present generations of Australians for the actions of the past, but rather to acknowledge that we now share a responsibility to put an end to the suffering. I said explicitly:

> Down the years, there has been no shortage of guilt, but it has not produced the responses we need. Guilt is not a very constructive emotion. I think what we need to do is open our hearts a bit.

There are plenty of people in this country who call the study of injustices done to Aboriginal Australians in our own past a 'black armband' version of history, or a 'guilt industry'. But such sloganeering cannot disguise the truth. And unless we acknowledge the truth about what happened, how can we go forward?

Six months before I spoke at Redfern, on 3 June 1992, the High Court of Australia made its own historic decision about the truth, which it brought down in a case that had been fought for ten years by Eddie Mabo and four others seeking a legal declaration of their traditional land rights in the Murray Islands of the Torres Strait.

The court recognised that European settlement of this continent had been based on a lie. The lie was that this continent had ever been '*terra nullius*' – a land of no-one. The judges now said that before the Europeans arrived the land had indeed belonged to someone, the Aborigines and Torres Strait Islanders and that in some places their legal right to it had survived the two hundred years of European settlement. The court recognised in this way that native title – and therefore Aboriginal custom and tradition – were a source of Australian common law, just as European custom and tradition were the source of British common law.

The Court accepted that native title existed only if two fundamental conditions were met: that the connection with the land had been maintained unbroken down through the years, and that the title had not been overturned by any action of a government to use the land or to give it to somebody else. It was a great and just decision, but it introduced a new uncertainty into land tenure. The government either had to leave the decisions on individual cases to the courts, which would have been economically and socially chaotic, or to try to hammer out legislation that would give practical effect to the court's decision, as well as dealing with other issues it threw up like how we should respond to the needs of those Indigenous people who had been forced from their continuous association with the land and therefore would not benefit from the High Court's decision. We decided that we had to face the issue and to develop what became the Native Title legislation.

This book is not that story. But I believe that through the Native Title legislation, the Indigenous Land Fund, the work of the Council for Aboriginal Reconciliation, the $400 million over five years put into our response to the Royal Commission into Aboriginal Deaths in Custody, and the National Inquiry established in 1995 into the Stolen Generation – those Indigenous children who had been so cruelly removed from their parents in the name of a policy of assimilation – Labor, working with outstanding Indigenous leaders, made some progress and could look back with pride on what it had done.

It seemed to me from the beginning of my period as prime minister that we would be able to debate and resolve issues like these as a community much more successfully when the structures of our government and the symbols of our nation reflected modern Australia better.

That was one reason why I believed an Australian republic had to come. I thought an Australian head of state could embody and represent our values and traditions, our experience and contemporary aspirations, our cultural diversity and social complexity in a way that a British monarch, who was also head of state of fifteen other member countries of the United Nations, could no longer adequately hope to do.

It was a measure of how much the debate about Australia's place in the world had shifted that in the five years between the time President Bush proposed the toast to 'The Queen of Australia' in the Great Hall of Parliament House in January 1992 and President Clinton's toast five years later, the words should seem so much more incongruous to the listening Australians.

The importance of the republic lies in what it says to Australians about ourselves rather than what it says to others. But the claim that the identity of our head of state has no effect on the way others perceive Australia – and through this on some very hard-headed economic and political interests – is defensive nonsense. The first question I was asked by an Asian journalist after my first public speech on my first overseas visit as prime minister was about the republic. And that question was repeated countless times in public and private.

The republic offers practical as well as symbolic advantages to Australian foreign policy. The Queen only travels to foreign countries as Queen of the United Kingdom. When she is in Tokyo on a state visit, how many Japanese pause to think, 'There goes the Queen of Australia'? Nothing is wrong with the royal family being used this way, but Australia was missing out on a useful implement in the diplomatic tool-chest. The few efforts we had made to send the Australian Governor-General abroad had generally been met with indifference. Because however hard the Australian monarchists wriggled, you could not escape the simple and incontrovertible constitutional fact that the Australian Head of State was the Queen of Australia, and the governor-general was her representative.

I put the republic on the political agenda by proposing the constitutional change in the policy speech for the 1993 election. For a party seeking so fundamental a change, this was the only and proper thing to do. It allowed the community to consider the subject before casting its vote.

Labor won the election. In the policy speech, I had promised to set up a bipartisan committee to examine the complex constitutional issues involved and for it to report to the government. We did so. On 28 April 1993, the Labor Government established a nine-member Republic Advisory Committee to prepare an options paper which would describe the constitutional changes necessary to create a federal Republic of Australia. The committee consulted widely around Australia. True to the word of the

Government, it was a bipartisan committee. It was chaired by Malcolm Turnbull. It included Nick Greiner and Naomi Dougal, who were prominent members of the Liberal Party, as well as constitutional experts such as Professor George Winterton and Dr John Hirst. The committee produced a coherent and valuable report.

I met the Queen at Balmoral on 18 September 1993 to relate the government's policy to her personally. It was dismal weather, and my task was difficult. I wanted to explain to her in the clearest but most respectful way (because I greatly respected the way she had undertaken her responsibilities) that, notwithstanding the high regard and affection in which she was held by the overwhelming majority of Australians, I believed most Australians now also thought the time had come for us to establish more clearly our own identity as a society, and that this was the course the Australian Government wished to follow.

I said to her that Australia was a country whose members came from many parts of the world and which had to work out its own destiny in the Asia-Pacific region. This did not mean turning our backs on the rich history of our association with Britain and the monarchy. I assured her that she would be treated with the utmost dignity and respect during any transitional period and would always be warmly welcomed to Australia as Head of State of Great Britain and Head of the Commonwealth.

For eighteen months after the committee's report was delivered and published, apart from occasional reference to the desirability and inevitability of a republic, I went out of my way to avoid any definitive references to the subject because I was not interested in enlarging the debate while I was unsure of the model the government would finally propose.

The matter underwent extensive Cabinet and Cabinet Sub-committee consideration, with substantial inputs from the Department of the Prime Minister and Cabinet.

When the Cabinet deliberation had been completed and all the elements of a proposed model had been decided, I made a speech on 7 June 1995 comprehensively outlining the government's preferred model to the Parliament. Not to a party conference or a legal gathering or a media event, but to the Parliament.

I repeated that we were attached to Great Britain by long threads of kinship and affection which, to a considerable extent, were embodied in the warmth of our regard for Queen Elizabeth. But I also went on to say:

> ... the creation of an Australian republic is not an act of rejection, it is one of recognition: in making the change we will recognise that our deepest respect is for our *Australian* heritage, our deepest affection is for *Australia* and our deepest responsibility is to *Australia's* future.
>
> Australia occupies a unique place in the world and makes a unique contribution to it. Our destiny is in no-one's hands but our own: we alone bear the responsibility for deciding what the nature of our government and society will be, what advantage we will take of our human and material resources, what kind of place our children will inherit ...
>
> Each and every Australian should be able to aspire to be our head of state. Every Australian should know that the office will always be filled by a citizen of high standing who has made an outstanding contribution to Australia and who, in making it, has enlarged our view of what it is to be Australian.

I then laid out the government's preferred position on the changes needed to our Constitution. We wanted to retain the name 'Commonwealth of Australia' and all the other governmental arrangements – the roles of the House of Representatives and the Senate, the role of the prime minister and Cabinet, the role and powers of the states. The change would be to appoint an Australian as our head of state and to describe him or her as the President of the Commonwealth of Australia.

The president would assume the governor-general's constitutional duties, most of which, by convention, are performed in accordance with the advice of the government of the day, and would take over the governor-general's role as titular Commander in Chief of the Armed Forces. The president would also retain the so-called 'reserve powers' which, in the most exceptional circumstances may be exercised without, or possibly contrary to, ministerial advice. These include the power to appoint the prime minister; the power to dismiss the prime minister and therefore the government; and the power to refuse a request by the prime minister to dissolve one or both houses of the Parliament.

We argued against writing down, or codifying, these reserve powers because we believed it would be impossible to do it in a way that would find general community acceptance and cover every possible contingency. As the system evolved, it needed to have some capacity to respond to circumstances we could not foresee. In any case, tightly defined rules could themselves have unforeseen consequences.

We also came out in favour of an appointed rather than - elected head of state. Although the election option was superficially attractive, I could see no way in the end of resolving the dilemma that the popular election of a president would fundamentally alter the political system in Australia because all other Commonwealth office-holders, including the prime minister and members of Cabinet were elected indirectly. This meant that the president would uniquely be vested both with the symbolic embodiment of the nation and great powers.

In any case, an elected president could never be 'above' politics in the ways almost all Australians wanted, and a symbol of the nation's unity. A distinguished former Governor-General, Sir

Zelman Cowen, made the telling point that popular election would ensure that people like himself or Sir Ninian Stephen (or Sir William Deane) were not candidates. If you subject candidates to popular election you will have endorsement by political parties and, with it, political campaigns. And a representative of one party will be elected. In short, a politician, the very species many, for a variety of reasons, seem to abhor.

We proposed, therefore, that the head of state be elected by a two-thirds majority vote in a joint sitting of both houses of the Commonwealth Parliament on the nomination of the prime minister and Cabinet. Obviously, before such a vote was taken the Opposition parties would have to be consulted to ensure that the candidate had their support. No government could dictate the outcome of such a process.

I telephoned John Howard, then Opposition Leader, in advance of my speech, telling him that I intended to make a statement to the House. He interrupted, asking what I was recommending. I told him and he expressed relief that I was not recommending a presidency elected by popular vote. I told him I was proposing to leave the reserve powers with the head of state, but that the head of state would be chosen by election of at least two-thirds of the House of Representatives and the Senate; in effect chosen by a bipartisan majority of which the Opposition would be a part.

I told Howard I had thought as much about the Liberal Party and conservative Australia in arriving at the model we were proposing as I had the Labor Party and that I hoped it would enjoy his support. I made it clear to him that he could reply to my speech whenever he chose; either on the night, the following week, or some time later. I said if he needed time to deliberate and consult before replying I would say nothing in the public debate that would hinder his deliberations or put pressure on him.

He knew I wanted him and his party to support it. He knew the model was thoughtful and impartial.

As it turned out, Howard took time. Eventually, pursued by the media as to his party's reponse, he decided on a proposal for a constitutional convention with elected and appointed representatives.

Howard was not for the republic, preferring the monarchy. He decided the convention route would give him an option to shape the outcome if he were to come to government.

Following the government's announcement, I spoke of the proposal in the public debate, but made certain I never closed off the option of the Liberal Party joining with us on the issue in the following Parliament.

It remains a source of mystery to me how the opponents of the republic managed to suggest that this utterly sensible approach to constitutional change was somehow 'Keating's republic' – a wilful attempt at personal aggrandisement. In fact, of course, the sort of republic I supported was the very sort that would prevent someone like me, a political person, becoming president. But for some monarchists at bay, honesty was never a strong point.

The Coalition sought to discredit the republic, saying I was seeking to distract attention from the economy. However, throughout this period (1997–1998 and 1995–1996) the economy was growing annually by 4.5 per cent.

Again, at another election policy speech, this time in February 1996, I took Labor's model for a republic to the people saying that, if elected, we would propose a plebiscite on the question 'Do you consider Australia should become a republic?' If the answer was in the affirmative, as I expected, I would then have sought Liberal Party support for the model proposed to Parliament in June 1995.

Had John Howard lost the 1996 election, there is every likelihood he would not have offered himself for re-election as Opposition Leader or would have been replaced. Either way, a new Liberal leader would have been more likely to support a move to a republic. This was another reason why I sought not to politicise the republic. I always wanted to keep open the option of the Coalition joining Labor for the change.

Unlike Howard, I wanted Australia to become a republic but I do not believe any more direct, proper or non-political approach to the republic was available to me than the one I chose. My proposal for a republic was put to the people before an election in a policy speech, deliberated upon by a bipartisan committee, responded to by the government after eighteen months of careful consideration, announced to Parliament with notice to the Opposition inviting it to join the government in the change, and the plan of implementation was put in another policy speech at a subsequent election.

In the years after the 1996 election Howard went about a series of very political manoeuvres designed to do everything he could to put a spoke in the wheel of the republic. This was the very politicisation of which he complained.

Following the defeat of the republic referendum Howard was reported in the *Australian* on 19 November 1999 to have told a group of monarchist supporters at a celebration at his Sydney residence, Kirribilli House, that 'he had helped as much as he could during the campaign' (that is, to defeat the referendum) 'in a very respectful and dignified way'. They all understood, even cheered.

I ended my June 1995 speech to Parliament by saying:

> The detail of the changes we propose may, at first glance, obscure the meaning of them. The meaning is simple and, we believe, irresistible – as simple and irresistible as the idea of a Commonwealth of Australia was to the Australians of a century ago.
>
> The meaning then was a nation united in common cause for the common good. A nation which gave expression to the

lives we lead together on this continent, the experience and hopes we share as Australians.

The meaning now is still a product of that founding sentiment – it is that we are all Australians. We share a continent. We share a past, a present and a future. And our head of state should be one of us.

The republic will come. The battle to retain the monarchy was lost in my view when its defenders started arguing, contrary to every fact and commonsense that we didn't really need to change because the governor-general was in fact our head of state (that is, if you ignored the Constitution and international practice and the way Australians themselves understood their head of state). When not even her last loyal defenders could bring themselves to argue that Australia would be well served in the twenty-first century by having as our head of state the hereditary monarch of Great Britain, the game was over.

However and whenever the republic falls into place, it will expand our view of ourselves and enhance our capacity to go confidently to the world around us. To go as ourselves, as we must.

CHAPTER 11
INTO THE NEW MILLENNIUM

The last years of the twentieth century echoed to the dull clang of doors to new opportunities slamming shut, one by one. We walked down a familiar corridor, furnished with the memorabilia of a world more than fifty years old, not quite brave enough to change our steps, or too engrossed in immediate conversation to notice the prospects that opened to our side. We did not turn.

No grand villainy was responsible for these missed opportunities, simply a collective failure of nerve – and imagination when it was needed. We found it too difficult to remake our international institutions so they would reflect the contemporary world, rather than the world at the end of the Second World War. We chose not to take risks by trying to get rid of nuclear weapons. We found comfort in the familiar existence of enemies. We made countless speeches about globalisation, but we didn't understand that globalisation required new institutions and new ways of utilising global power.

NATO extended its reach to the borders of the old Soviet Union, thereby defining Russia out of Europe. Despite its current irrelevance to the Asia-Pacific economy, Russia was given membership of APEC to compensate. In this way we ended up weakening institutional frameworks on both sides of the Eurasian landmass. The Americans and their European allies bombed

Serbia unilaterally, because they knew they could not get the green light for what they wanted out of the United Nations. China and India continued to be marginalised. We heard a lot of talk about reform of the international trade and financial organisations but in the end it was all too complicated and the developing countries were not given roles that reflected their growing importance.

As a result of this failed decade, the world we are entering will be darker and more dangerous than it could otherwise have been. It will not be as well equipped to deal with the challenges ahead. But it will also be more familiar. I'm not suggesting that with the end of the Cold War we were about to skip our way into Arcadia. Elements of competition and danger will be with us internationally until human nature itself is transformed. But we did have an opportunity to lessen the risks. Instead, we ended up increasing them and slipping back into the ruts of old ways. In doing this we made the dangerous assumption that violence in the world will continue to be managed as it was during the Cold War, at the centre at any rate, with careful strategic planners and reliable command and control systems, and on the Soviet side a wary and conservative leadership confident of its own power at home and of its ability to wreak havoc if it wished.

However, this era has now passed. With the spread of technology, especially nuclear technology, other states will get the weapons but they will not have the political and command and control systems to manage them. And that is without including tribal warlords of the Saddam Hussein or Slobodan Milosevic kind, who may at the first opportunity invest in weapons of terror. People's faith that violent conflict will continue to be managed as it was in the Cold War is tragically misplaced. That is why it is in the West's best interests to try to invest in better political structures to deal with these problems at source, and, as I argued earlier, to try to remove nuclear weapons while we still can.

In this final chapter, I want to look at the world in the twenty-first century and how it will affect Australia and the Asia-Pacific.

If the test of the validity of any scientific or social science theory is how well it predicts the events of the future, then current economic and international relations theories seem seriously flawed. The future is always cloudy, of course, and history is made up of discontinuities, but one of the main lessons of the 1990s – from the collapse of the Soviet Union to the Asian economic crisis – seemed to be that those discontinuities are becoming more frequent. Change is spreading faster. It is less subject to filtering and less easy to control. And in all its forms, change is being magnified by the speed, cheapness and variety of the transmission mechanisms of the information revolution through which it spreads.

As a result of this profound technological shift, the fundamental building blocks of our international system are beginning to carry different weightings, to have different impacts, and to act in ways different from anything we have known in the past. Geography, large populations, robust economies and strong military forces haven't become irrelevant. The near-monopoly of power which the nation-state possesses will keep it going for a good while yet. But more and more power lies outside its bounds. Large corporations, media interests, advocacy groups, and regional and global organisations elbow their way into the increasingly noisy international debate.

Non-government participants can enter the policy process more easily than ever before, and they can do so across national boundaries. From right-wing conspiracy theorists and militia groups to human rights and anti-government groups on the left, the people who have seized most enthusiastically on the new technologies and have used it most imaginatively are the powerless, not the powerful. Anyone who doubts the influence of their advocacy has only to look at the environment movement or the campaign against landmines to see how the agenda can be reset by forces outside government. As we have seen in every recent Asian political crisis, from Tiananmen to Timor, it is becoming easier for opposition groups to organise, coordinate and spread their messages. The heroes of the final battle against twentieth-century totalitarianism are the fax machine, the mobile telephone and the Internet.

In the past, information was a commodity in short supply, and where it was available it was often a government monopoly and rationed by remote authorities. But we are now in an era that is information-rich. There is an old saying that information is power. That is no longer true. Thanks to the Internet and mobile communications, information swirls around us in thick clouds. Digital technology does two things: it disseminates information more widely than ever before and speeds its distribution by orders of magnitude. In other words, information is more accessible and it arrives faster. And as the demands for transparency – for openness – from governments and corporations continue to grow, the amount of information in the public domain will increase exponentially.

Information is no longer a scarce commodity. In this sort of environment, power is not the information itself but the ability to collate, analyse and assess it. That is just as true for businesses looking for markets, for soldiers looking for battlefield advantage and for governments wanting to maximise their national interests. Power relativities among nations are changing in the direction of those societies that can handle all the dimensions of information.

Still, a great unanswered question hangs over us at the beginning of the twenty-first century. Will globalisation and the information revolution result in a fundamental diffusion of power within individual societies and between countries? Are they liberating technologies which, by connecting us at the edges, will help us to form new communities in cyberspace? Or will they, instead, deliver the sort of concentration of power that accompanied the last phase of the industrial revolution a century ago in the form of robber baron capitalism? Will the small and the unique be smothered by the large at the precise moment when choice has never been more possible for more of us?

That is one of the fears driving public hostility towards globalisation. Wherever we come from, we are seeing, day by day, as a result of the information revolution, the remaking of almost all markets – goods, services, finance, even labour markets. New sorts of skills are needed for the new economy and different groups of people are being rewarded as a result. The coming distribution of wealth will be one of our greatest challenges.

In the face of an increasingly homogeneous global marketplace, people are experiencing an alienating sense of being cut away from what defines and sustains them. Europeans wonder what will happen to their countryside of their memory if their farmers leave the land. Chinese worry about the flood of foreign advertising in their cities. Australians are concerned about how a small population like ours can maintain cultural identity in the face of the onslaught of Hollywood.

At the core of this concern is a loss of identity and spiritual frameworks, the feeling many of us have that our lives are increasingly beyond our individual control; that our cultural signposts are changing without our consent; that old definitions and boundaries are blurring; that the world is becoming an alarmingly small place, but also, paradoxically, moving beyond any individual control. The fear is not surprising, nor is the response, which often takes the form of a desire to turn back the clock. We have seen political manifestations of this in Australia, in support for the One Nation party and in a general mainstream political apprehension about change. Nostalgia secretes such a soothing balm over the troubles of the past that we are easily seduced into believing the myth of a golden age.

I have no belief in the mystical power or wisdom of markets. Human suffering is not ended by economic growth and human happiness is not the natural consequence of a market economy. In a flawed world, markets are useful in delivering efficient outcomes, but they do not have the answers to all the world's problems.

I do not in any sense think, however, that we should or can back away from the consequences of globalisation. For as far ahead as any of us can realistically pretend to look, I can't see anything short of nuclear war (although given our failure to seize the opportunities we were offered with the end of the Cold War, this certainly can't be ruled out) which will make the world any less globalised. The technologies driving globalisation will not develop any less rapidly. The intensity of global economic competition will only increase as electronic commerce expands and the world becomes in reality a single market.

There is no point in beating around the bush on this. We must understand – and political leaders should acknowledge – that lying in wait for us around every corner is change and then more change. The information revolution ensures that whatever happens in human history from now on, rapid change will be its permanent feature.

And of direct relevance to Australia, the global terms of trade will not suddenly flow back in the direction of commodity producers. So even if we wanted to, we can never again rely on export wealth generated by Australian farmers and miners to pay for the preservation of tariff walls to protect our manufacturing and services sectors from competition.

Any country can resist globalising forces. It can opt out, in whole or in part, by erecting barriers to openness. But it can only do this at the expense of a more impoverished and restricted future for its people.

The Labor Government in the 1980s and '90s was not forced

to prise open the protectionist carapace around the Australian economy. We could have set it out and quietly governed. But if we hadn't, Australians would have become steadily worse off. Instead of the nine per cent increase in average household income that Australia experienced between 1982 and 1994, we would have experienced a very sharp decline. Without deregulation and openness, without preparation, the country certainly would not have come through the Asian economic crisis so effortlessly.

In any case, the developing countries, whose entry into the global economy has been another essential element in globalisation, will not retire from the game. We are used to hearing people talk about the 'good old days'. But the days to which some look back so fondly were good for a relatively few privileged people in relatively few countries. They were not so good for Chinese peasants or Brazilian day-labourers. In the past twenty years, 150 million people in East Asia have been lifted out of absolute poverty. That is the equivalent of more than half the people of the United States having their lives transformed from a daily struggle for human survival to one in which it is possible to begin thinking about the other things that make life worth living. The people of the developing countries have enjoyed the experience of growth and they will want more of it.

Asian governments have already had a sharp foretaste of globalisation's swingeing impact, however. The collapse of the Asian economies in 1997 was a crisis unpredicted in its size and cadence by any commentator I know. On 2 July 1997, after months of pressure from speculators and after draining the entire reserves of its central bank in a futile effort to defend its currency, the Thai Government floated the baht. This marked the beginning of the Asian economic crisis. Then, like a virus, the contagion passed from one country to another. Within months the developing countries of Asia had turned from miracles into mendicants. Between 1996 and 1997 the economies of the five Asian countries most affected – Korea, Thailand, Indonesia, Malaysia and the Philippines – shrank by 18 per cent. More than $US600 billion simply evaporated from their economies. The responses of Asian governments to the experience will shape the next phase of growth in the region.

You can identify plenty of causes for the crisis. They range from the global and geopolitical – the information revolution and economic globalisation, the end of the Cold War and the decline in the strategic importance to the United States of the emerging economies in South-East Asia – to the local and particular – the absence of adequate prudential arrangements in the finance sectors of regional economies, reckless lending by foreign banks, and corruption and cronyism. But many of these factors were also present during the time of high growth. The immediate causes of the collapse were fixed currency exchange rates (which Australia had abandoned in the early 1980s when we floated our dollar) and the subsequent rapid movements of formerly tied currencies which the information revolution made possible. (This movement is just part of the $US1.5 trillion of currencies traded each day around the world – less than five per cent of this amount is needed to cover trade in goods and services.)

As we have seen in the case of Indonesia, most of the Asian countries had established formal or de facto links between their currencies and the US dollar. As an economic strategy it served them well for a long time. By making production costs cheap, it facilitated the long boom in foreign direct investment into the region, with all the technology transfer that came with it. Asian businesses borrowed US dollars cheaply at low rates of interest, assuming that the fixed tie to their own currencies would give them a natural hedge.

Then the game changed. The US dollar rose 60 per cent against the Japanese yen, dragging the pegged Asian currencies up with it. As a result, their economies became less competitive, and their current accounts were exposed to much closer examination, especially as regional exports began to fall after 1996. The artificiality of the dollar pegs became more obvious, and devaluation became inevitable.

When the crunch came, it showed that the pressures of growth had become too great for the institutional structures of the Asian countries to cope with. Their economic systems lacked transparency, banks were often seriously under-regulated, lending was politically directed and legal structures were inadequate. Their debt to equity ratios were also by and large too high.

The catastrophic combination of all these factors produced the worst slow-down in developing countries for thirty years. Millions of people were plunged back into poverty. Tens of thousands of children lost their chance for education. Health care was eroded. By late 1998, the total market capitalisation of the Thai stock exchange was worth less than 15 per cent of its dollar value three years earlier. For Indonesia, the same effective drop took less than a year.

Alan Greenspan, the Chairman of the US Federal Reserve Board, pointed to the way new technology appeared to have facilitated the transmission of financial disturbances far more effectively than ever before. Vicious cycles of ever-rising and reinforcing fears had become contagious and were emerging more often. Greenspan saw the root of the sharp exchange rate changes in Asia as 'a process which is neither measured nor rational, one based on a visceral, engulfing fear'. And once such cycles are triggered, he said, 'damage control is difficult. Once the web of confidence which supports the financial system is breached, it is difficult to restore quickly'.

When the emergency paramedics from the IMF and World Bank first arrived on the scene they nearly bludgeoned the Asian patients insensible. With the enthusiastic backroom support of the US Treasury, they insisted on the strenuous application of austerity medicine, involving budget cuts and high interest rates – in other words, current account solutions to a capital account problem – that forced viable businesses to the wall and, in Indonesia's case, engineered a banking panic.

Over the longer term, however, much of the prescribed medicine will be a tonic for these economies. As growth returns they will have the benefit of stronger banks, tighter prudential supervision and better corporate governance. Investors will be able to litigate their interests more effectively. The result will be more productive investment decisions.

The Asian countries will resume their growth path because their fundamentals lead them back to it. They have young populations, high savings rates, sensible macroeconomic policies (broadly, and commendably, adhered to by regional governments during the crisis despite the huge pressures on them), entrepreneurial cultures, and they place high value on education. These will be even more competitive economies. But a fundamental question they now have to ask themselves is: competitive at what?

Warning in 1996 and 1997 that we could not assume Asian growth would continue unchecked, I said Asia's future depended on what I called the 'three opens' – open economies, open societies and an open region. Openness is the key to Asia's future, as it is to Australia's. Open economies underpinned Asia's economic boom. East Asia was so good at harnessing flows of foreign capital that by 1995 nearly 60 per cent of all private investment in developing countries was coming to the region.

The crisis brought that to a sudden stop. Between 1996 and 1997, Korea and the ASEAN countries experienced a $US100 billion reversal in capital inflows. But Asia has to get the investment flowing again because, in many ways, the real Asian crisis still lies in wait for the region. This is the crisis of funding and building the roads, power stations, communications infrastructure, schools and hospitals required to support, feed and educate more than two billion people, and of dealing with the profound environmental consequences of growth. It is a crisis that will only be surmounted with open economies.

Giving up on growth is not an option. Even when the Asian miracle was in full swing in 1993, nearly 400 million East Asians were still struggling to survive on incomes of less than $US1 per day. China has to grow at seven per cent a year simply to accommodate the number of young people entering its labour force, let alone raise the living standards of its people. And as the size of the economic base gets larger, it will be tougher to get the increments to growth. Many Asian economies have passed the point at which the economic cake will rise each time if you throw into the recipe more labour and capital. From now on, what will matter most is productivity and innovation. That is a harder job, and it requires a better-educated work force. By 2020, according to the World Bank, 30 per cent of the work force in developing East Asian countries will have moved from the informal to the formal sectors (in other words, from farming and casual work to paid employment). Much higher levels of skills will be needed.

The most pressing need for all the developing Asian economies will be to add value to what they produce and keep moving up the manufacturing chain towards high technology.

One of the many causes of the Asian economic crisis was the over-capacity generated by the global capital spending boom of the mid-1990s. From the 1980s, Japan built as many factories in South-East Asia as exist in France. As more and more factories sprouted, capacity utilisation rates, unsurprisingly, began to fall. And because Asia produced what have become the world's low-tech products, things like steel, ships, cars and commodities – in other words, that part of the world's economy most sensitive to economic cycles – the fall, when it came, was sharpest in Asia.

The export of these manufactured goods had powered the Asian miracle, and they will continue to be vital for the region's economies. But with the world's production capacity exceeding its expected consumption by more than a third, there seems no easy relief to the continued downward pressure on prices. What is more, East Asia now has new competitors from Latin America, Eastern Europe, and India. And the United States will be unable to act indefinitely as a sinkhole for the world's exports.

It won't be possible for Asia to rely for the next-stage of its growth on the unimpeded export of manufactured goods. It needs to embed itself in the new technology, as well as the old. And that will require agile and flexible economies which depend for success on their ability to understand foreign markets and to learn rapidly from them. Economies which can easily plug into the global community. Because in future, very few countries will have all the components 'in house' necessary for a technologically advanced society. Asia's need for open economies will again be reinforced.

The traditional sources of investment capital for governments – export credit organisations, multilateral lending institutions or foreign aid agencies – can't cope with capital amounts like those Asia needs over the next couple of decades. All the foreign aid to China, for example, represents less than half of one per cent of the country's GNP. An increasing amount of the urgently needed infrastructure will have to be provided by the private sector. Access to venture capital will be critical. In the United States, which has moved further into the new economy than the rest of the world, you can fill up your business with venture capital, almost like driving your car into a gas station. Asia (and Australia) need to match this, if we are to take full advantage of the new oppporunities of the information age.

So one of the most important challenges for the governments of developing Asian countries over the next few years will be to develop and implement the public policy changes needed to ensure that they can secure this private sector involvement in infrastructure on the best possible terms, political as well as economic. This again requires a continuing openness to international markets.

The second form of openness Asia needs is open societies. By this I mean communities in which information flows freely and effectively between members and from outside, and in which the transmission lines conveying the views and feelings of the society's members to their leadership – whether political, economic or cultural – are rapid and effective.

Quite apart from the moral imperatives which operate in favour of open societies, I don't think it will be possible to operate effectively far into the twenty-first century without them. In part, this is because the only effective way for any country to deal with the transforming impact of the information revolution is to embrace it.

Open societies will emphasise a questioning and involving education system, the easy movement of people, and the rapid transmission of ideas. And you can't do that half-heartedly or only in part. Despite the hopes of some in Asia, it is not possible to take the economically advantageous bits of the information revolution and expect to suppress the rest of it.

The information age and its abacus, the computer, has spawned a new way of thinking. What will underpin growth in the future is the capacity of countries to develop a milieu which sustains creativity. Provided the creativity is there, new industries will emerge from this flux, many of them having little to do with information itself. In this new environment, knowledge-workers will be in shorter supply than capital.

Education must be at the core of any government's response to the challenge of the new age. But a new sort of education and literacy is required. We may need a different kind of education system to cope with it, one which not only makes better use of the new technology but which understands that children, who have been brought up with computers and the Internet, learn in quite different ways.

The old dichotomy we know so well between youth and experience doesn't apply any more because the people with the most experience of the new world are the young. I'm not just talking about their familiarity with the technology, but the fact that they are culturally at home with new ways of thinking. They have internalised the social changes the information age brings with it in a way their elders seem unable to do.

One of the keys to American economic success has been its openness to others. It's like a magnet for talented knowledge-workers the world over. The Indian and Chinese influence in Silicon Valley is an example. But the force of America's attractiveness is not simply the financial rewards it offers or the size of its market alone; it is its cultural openness to all comers. The most successful countries in the information age will be those at one with diversity.

In the information age, it is going to be a struggle for countries to be truly innovative and clever. Those societies which keep a clamp on expression and communication will also, to their detriment, clamp creativity.

Open societies can be very different in form. No single model exists, any more than one model of an open economy does. Australia, Japan, the United States, the Philippines, Hong Kong and Singapore are all open societies, but their cultures and institutions, shaped by national experiences, are very different. Some Asian societies will find openness easier to deal with than others, but I don't believe it will be possible to reach the highest levels of economic success without it.

Asia's final requirement will be for open regionalism. By that, I mean forms of cooperation which are inclusive in their approach within the region, and which do not cut themselves off from the rest of the world but are compatible with the global trading system. The emergence of inward-looking and competitive bloc mentalities – an Asia-only approach – would have harmful consequences for Asia's economic prospects and its security, as I argued throughout the 1990s.

Southern China and the various South-East Asian growth areas have shown that economic development can no longer be easily or productively constrained behind existing national fences. Regional cooperation can help governments respond to some of the worries about globalisation in their communities by building a sense of a broader community with which their people can identify. This has happened already to a large degree in Europe. It is important that it also happens in the Asia-Pacific.

As we discussed in earlier chapters, regional organisations can sometimes achieve practical outcomes to immediate problems more quickly and more effectively than the sometimes cumbersome processes of large multilateral bodies like the United Nations permit.

Nowhere will open regionalism be more important than in helping Asia deal with the environmental challenges ahead. Because even if we assume that the power, water, roads and the rest of the infrastructure developments Asia needs can be funded, the results will generate new social and environmental problems, including air pollution, deteriorating soil quality, water shortages and urbanisation.

Asian governments are beginning to recognise that the protection of the environment is not an alternative to economic growth, but the only thing that will ensure its continuation. In the early 1990s, around 500 million East Asians lived in towns. By 2020 this figure will have trebled to 1.5 billion. By 2015, Tokyo, Shanghai, Jakarta and Beijing will all have populations of over 19 million. This shift to the cities will put huge strains on basic services such as water, sanitation and shelter. Even under present circumstances only half Asia's city-dwellers have access to water supplies and less than half to sanitation. The developing East Asian countries need to invest an estimated $US150 billion a year in water and sanitation facilities, transportation, power, and telecommunications.

China adds 300,000 new cars to its stock each year. One million new cars are bought annually in the ASEAN countries, pumping exhausts into air that is already dangerously unhealthy. If China's growth targets are to be met, it will probably have to double coal consumption by 2020. Yet the one billion tonnes of high sulphur coal it currently burns each year spout 10 million tonnes of sulphur into the Asian skies.

Asia faces significant problems in securing future food supplies, too. The region is already experiencing, as we have in Australia, the consequences of unconstrained, heavy use of fertilisers, irrigation and pesticides. Agricultural productivity may rise, but will it be at the expense of soil erosion, salinity and pollution.

The irritated reaction of many Asians to hearing lectures on environmental responsibility from developed western countries which have already passed through their own phase of industrialisation, is understandable. But no-one can avoid the fact that the environmental challenge facing Asia is real and pressing, and that if it is not addressed the people who suffer will be mainly Asians.

These environmental problems argue in favour of openness, too, because their resolution often requires cooperation with neighbours, and technology that must come from outside the region.

The environmental picture is not all bleak. Asia will be able to leapfrog whole generations of technology. In telecommunications, for example, countries like China can move straight into fibre optics and wireless communications. Congestion in the region's cities will be relieved by more efficient distribution systems and supply chains. Better communications systems, especially broadband technology, will also help address the region's education and health needs.

Just as important as the economic imperatives in favour of an open region are the strategic considerations. Many things might make Asia's future economic growth more difficult, but none would be more dangerous than the re-emergence of political divisions and conflicts. There are plenty of ways this could happen. The environment is one of them. Smoke from forest fires in Indonesia has already generated friction with Malaysia and Singapore. Control of water resources on Asia's great river systems like the Mekong is another potential problem area. (China's history vividly illustrates the link between security and the environment. When the mean annual temperature on the Mongolian steppe dropped in the late twelfth century, the Mongols could no longer find enough grass to feed their grazing animals. This drove Ghengis Khan and his successors to begin their conquests of agricultural lands including in Northern China. One of the main factors in the fall of the Song dynasty was climate change.)

Wherever you look in Asia the most obvious candidates for potential conflict come from within the region. The strategic consequences of nuclear competition between India and Pakistan threaten the subcontinent and will reach far beyond it. Overlapping patterns of territorial claims in the South China Sea, with its rich oil and gas potential, may become a greater source of tension as Asia's energy needs grow. The communist regime in North Korea could still unravel in very messy ways, and the question of Taiwan's place in the region could give rise to conflict. Active and imaginative regional responses can play a part in moderating all of these problems.

APEC has a role to play here, despite the difficult sovereignty issues the questions throw up. Over time, the APEC leaders' meeting needs to take on more of an umbrella role, however informal or off-line this may initially be, to deal with regional security. It is the only regional organisation with the structure, standing and membership to address such issues effectively. It has the participation of key leaders.

It is possible to imagine a structure in which the ASEAN Regional Forum, for example, reports not to the APEC Ministerial Meeting but to those of its own leaders who attend the leaders' meeting. Russian membership is an advantage here, at least. In the margins of the APEC meetings we can already see such a process beginning. It is another reason why it is important that APEC be given a stronger secretarial structure.

For nearly a decade after the mid-1980s, the major international issues in Asia were, in one form or another, manifestations of the broad, lumbering adjustment the world had been making to the end of the Cold War. With the old East–West security concerns no longer sufficient to hold in check the tensions arising from economic competition, Japan and the United States tested and redefined their alliance relationship. Washington withdrew from its forward bases in the Philippines and the Soviet Union disappeared from the map. These developments made possible the Cambodia settlement and the expansion of ASEAN and the development of APEC. But that period of adjustment has ended.

The region Australia will have to deal with now will be more fragmented, more democratic and less predictable than we have been used to. In the three largest Asian countries, China, India and Indonesia, traditionally centralist forms of government will have to cope with more assertive and active regional centres of power inside their own countries. And as we have seen in Indonesia, economic modernisation will generate new pressures for democracy from more affluent and better-educated citizens who want a greater say in the decisions that affect them.

The new Asian leadership will be less brash and triumphalist than we sometimes saw in the 1980s and '90s, but more democratic societies are quite likely to be more nationalist and populist, and sometimes more difficult for Australia to deal with. Just as the experience of the Depression affected a generation of Europeans and Americans, the views of new Asian leaders will be shaped not by the anti-colonial struggle of half a century ago but by the economic boom and bust of the 1990s.

One of the strange but consistent flaws in human behaviour is our tendency to draw moral lessons from the performance of our economies. We like to think that if we are doing well economically, the reason must be superior virtue rather than greater efficiency. It's a modern version of the old belief that if the crops succeeded it must be because we had pleased the gods.

We saw some of this from the proponents of Asian values in the early 1990s. Now the boot is on the other foot and we are seeing from the United States, and unfortunately from some in Australia, a similar form of triumphalism.

Reflecting from his great age and long experience, George Kennan, the American diplomat and scholar, author of America's Cold War policy of containment, told an interviewer in 1999:

> ... this whole tendency to see ourselves as the centre of political enlightenment and as teachers to a great part of the rest of the world strikes me as unthought-through vainglorious and undesirable. If you think that our life here at home has meritorious aspects worthy of emulation by peoples elsewhere, the best way to recommend them is ... not by preaching at others but by force of example.

I couldn't agree more. And the same goes for all of us.

The Asian economic crisis and its aftermath will generate a new perspective on the world from a particularly Asian angle. This is a process Australia needs to be involved in and contribute to.

Just as I believe the United States should be engaged economically and strategically across the Pacific, so I also think we need an Asia-Pacific market in ideas, in which this side of the Pacific plays a more forthright and dynamic part. I'm not suggesting that there will be, or could be, a single Asian world view. But I think it is very important that there are world views from Asia. These will differ sometimes from the dominant western view. Their development depends on frequent exchanges between governments, an active dialogue between universities and other private and public institutions, including the media, and better and more frequent educational exchanges.

We used to hear talk of the twenty-first century being the century of Asia or the century of the Pacific. But I don't think the world will be like that anymore. While I am sure Asia will have more influence on international developments, no one area will be able to dominate the global agenda in the way Europe and North America did in the twentieth century.

The planet can no longer be run from one country or one region. America is the greatest republic. That is without doubt. But it is not so great that it can manage the world alone and single-handedly impose its sense of democracy and ideology upon it. Certainly the United States Congress doesn't have the power, wisdom or internationalism to do it. The United States can and does give admirable leadership, but it cannot impose its will on great states like China. We can encourage China to be more open and more democratic, but managing a nation of one-and-a-quarter billion – the vast majority of whom are farmers – without the levers of power of a developed economy, is beyond the experience of any US administration or congress. The management of the world has to be a cooperative process.

These changes underway in Asia will also change the forms of Australia's engagement with the region in some quite specific ways. For example, Australia's economic relationship with Asia has been built for half a century on a happy complementarity between our mineral and agricultural wealth and the industrialisation and development needs of our neighbours. But this will not sustain us indefinitely. Our traditional excellence in agriculture, mining and manufacturing will continue to be important to us and our customers. But as Asia's economic structures change, Australia has to become more of a service and technology provider for our neighbours' increasingly sophisticated economies.

This new sort of complementarity, growing out of services and information, will be a harder relationship for us to sustain. Decisions on whether to educate your children in Australia rather than Britain, to holiday on the Gold Coast rather than Hawaii, to put your regional headquarters in Sydney rather than Singapore, to have your heart problem treated in Brisbane rather than Dallas, or to seek creative support for a website from Melbourne rather than Vancouver involve a much more complex range of reasons and emotions than the cost and assurance of supply questions that dominate the commodities trade.

That is why the way we present ourselves in the world and the image others have of us matter. That's the reason why the handling of the Hanson debate in 1996 and 1997 was so damaging to Australia. It harmed us not because immigration or multicultural issues are an impermissible subject for debate; nor because it showed that in Australia, as everywhere else, the fearful, the ignorant or the economically threatened tend to blame their present troubles on outsiders – Jews or immigrants or blacks or Irish or Moslems or Bosnians or Tutsis. It was damaging mostly because it seemed to be officially sanctioned, part of a supposed new atmosphere of 'free speech'. But, in fact, the only freedom involved was the freedom to shirk responsibility for the rising tide of prejudice. The debate was mishandled in a way which suggested to many Asians and other observers of Australia that at some level it had official sanction. It was interpreted by many as a sign that the 'real' Australia, which had been cunningly disguised in the twenty-five years or so since Gough Whitlam's Government abolished all forms of racial discrimination in our immigration policy, was throwing off its cloak of tolerance and revealing its true personality again.

If you were asked to identify the requirements any country needs for success in the information age, you could hardly go past what we have in Australia – a diverse, technologically mature, scientifically and culturally creative society, with strong legal and administrative structures, and open to the world. Is it possible for us to squander these advantages? Easily. Our course won't be set by predestination or Manifest Destiny or a Marxist dialectic. And our passage along it is entirely in our own hands.

It sometimes seems as if the world we get is the world we must have: that international events are propelled by forces outside human control which deliver the same outcomes regardless of the particular ministers, officials and community leaders who walk across the stage for a short time. I believe it is a profoundly wrong assessment. In the twentieth century, the lows – the bumbling into the European civil war in its first half – as well as the highs – the great reconstruction of the world as a result of American generosity during the second – were shaped by the men and women who held onto the levers of power for a short period of time and made judgements that were farsighted or foolish, generous or narrow-minded, rash or tardy or timely.

Nothing has changed. The world we get in the twenty-first century will still be one that we make ourselves, shaped by active and engaged public policy.

A significant shift took place during the first half of the 1990s in the way Australians saw themselves in the world. Many forces, including global economic developments and the opening up of the Australian economy in the 1980s, helped propel that change, and many people inside and outside government were involved. But its form, speed and impact were shaped by the conscious and active decisions of the government. By conscientious ministers.

Through the development of the APEC leaders' meetings

we helped to create a regional architecture able to provide the foundations for a more integrated Asia-Pacific community. In the Bogor and Osaka declarations we developed an ambitious free-trade agenda which, if it is adhered to, will help ensure that the growth in Asia, which has been so important to Australia and the region, continues. Our bilateral relationship with Indonesia, our largest neighbour; Japan, our biggest trading partner; and other regional countries like Singapore reached new levels of maturity and complexity.

We still need to take the message of what Australia is and deliver it confidently to the world; to help shape the international environment, because it will be impossible to disentangle that environment from our domestic ambitions. Whatever hopes Australia has for its children, whatever sort of society we want to create, we can get there only by engaging the world. And for Australia this means a comprehensive engagement with the region around us.

The simple questions we must ask ourselves are these: Is our country's future in Asia? Will hundreds of thousands of jobs continue to depend on Asian markets? Will our security still be shaped there? Do we want to play a role in Asia's political institutions? Will more Australians have family links with Asia? Is Asia really where our vital interests lie? If the answer is yes, we have no alternative to engagement with it.

This continent of ours is not a drop-in centre; it is not some passing fancy. There is no 'home' across the seas to which we can return if the going gets tough. We live in an unsentimental part of the world. Regional governments know their own interests and pursue them vigorously and sometimes ruthlessly. We need to have clear eyes and a clear head. But it is not necessary to romanticise Asia to see our engagement with it as one of the most exciting enterprises in which Australia can be involved.

In October 1994, I said in a speech to the University of New

South Wales's Asia Australia Institute that I hoped Australia would become a country in which:

- more and more Australians speak the language of our neighbours;
- our businesspeople are a familiar and valued part of the commercial landscape of the Asia-Pacific;
- we are making full use of the great resource of the growing number of Australians of Asian background;
- our defence and strategic links with the countries around us are deeper than ever;
- our national identity is clearer to us and our neighbours through the appointment of an Australian as our head of state;
- our national culture is shaped by, and helps to shape, the cultures around us.

It still seems to me to be a useful, modest and easily attainable checklist.

Australia's relationship with the region is not a one-way affair. Over time, Australia will be increasingly important to our neighbours. Australia provides Asia with the resources of a continent and the skills of our people. We draw on a rich Anglo-Saxon tradition of pure research in our universities, if we are sensible enough to maintain it, and the creative resilience which comes from our whole heritage of immigration and cultural diversity, if we are wise enough to see it.

Stability is important in the centre of change. Australia's political stability within a sharply contested democracy is a strategic benefit to our neighbours and a signal to those in Asia who believe that democracy always brings with it chaos.

We also provide Asia with a more intangible thing – space. Space not only in a physical sense but also in a psychological sense.

For an Asia of two billion people, the experience of wilderness will be increasingly important. We would be wise to share it.

The twentieth century has taught us many important lessons, but none has been more important than that of ecology. However slowly and incompletely, an understanding of the profound interdependence of complex systems has become part of the framework of our thinking over the past fifty years. And it may be the single most important idea we take with us into the twenty-first century.

It leads me to the belief that in a globalised world, the central responsibility of government will be the preservation of diversity in all its forms. This task will be the essential response to the centralising and homogenising pressures of globalisation. Whether governments are dealing with political, environmental, strategic, economic, social or cultural issues, they will increasingly have to see themselves as custodians of the system's diversity, tending the interconnections between its elements and preserving its variety.

Australia's engagement with the region around us is not settled. A clearly different view was emerging – or rather reemerging – as the twentieth century ended. The Australian people didn't want to go down the path of engagement, we were told, and governments should not be pushing them. The aims of the early 1990s had been too ambitious. Full Australian engagement with Asia was impossible because our neighbours were too 'different' – too racially different for one group, too culturally different for others, too politically different (in other words, not democratic enough) for another group. The differences were underlined as though they were immutable. But leaving aside the fact that differences are a reason for engagement, not an argument against it, I believe the facts of Australian history and the experiences of our people stand in contrast to those who argue such views.

In the first foreign policy speech I made as prime minister in April 1992 to the Asia Australia Institute I said about Australia and its relationship with Asia:

> We don't go to Asia, cap in hand, any more than we go, like Menzies went to London, pleading family ties. We go as we are. Not with the ghost of Empire about us, not as a vicar of Europe or a US deputy, but unambivalently. Sure of who we are and what we stand for. If we are to be taken seriously, believed, trusted, that is the only way to go.

It is still the only way to go. Ideas that Australia is a western outpost which drifted by mistake to the wrong part of the globe; that our role is to be part of a western civilising mission to Asia, or an assistant sheriff imposing our will on our neighbours, are certainly futile. But more than futile, they are wrong. Any Australian efforts to seek our security *from* Asia rather than *in* Asia must fail. Engagement is the most powerful idea in Australian politics.

Here we sit, nineteen million of us, drawn from more than 120 different countries, on the edge of Asia, and with all the resources of a continent to draw on. What an astonishing bequest that is. We cannot turn away and we cannot turn back. It is the most exhilarating and promising prospect.

The twenty-first century – the second century of Australia's nationhood, the third of European settlement, perhaps the 60th millennium of continuous human occupation of this continent – offers this great opportunity to Australia: to redefine ourselves and our place in the world. Each generation finds its own challenges. The challenge of engagement is ours.

INDEX

Agreement on Maintaining Security 144, 156
agriculture
   and Bogor commitments 120
   and European export policy 248–9
   Japanese market 63
   and Uruguay Round 35, 36–9, 80
aid 52
   to PNG 207, 211–12, 214
   to South Pacific 196, 200, 202, 203
Alatas, Ali 127, 132, 139, 140, 156, 160–1
ALP (Australian Labor Party)
   achievements for Indigenous Australians 266
   and defence relationship with US 39
   and development of foreign policy 7, 8
   recognition of China 55
   support for Indonesian revolution 8, 18
   and White Australia Policy 18
Amnesty International 54
ANZUS Treaty 38–9, 42–3
   and NZ 139, 218
APEC (Asia-Pacific Economic Cooperation forum) 60
   challenge of the future 291–2
   and EAEG 87, 89

Eminent Persons Group 92–3, 105
   formation 10, 76–77
   and free trade 33, 99–108, 297
   and globalisation 77–9, 80–1, 296–7
   members 58, 63–4, 75, 76–7, 93–4, 122, 219
APEC (heads of government) (leaders) group 94
   Bogor meeting 91, 120, 99–116
   formation 30, 81–91
   future challenge 291–2
   Osaka meeting 117–22
   Seattle meeting 37, 44, 93, 94–7, 102
Aquino, Cory 161
Arndt, Heinz 8
ASEAN (Association of South-East Asian Nations) 18, 76, 86, 193, 292
   membership 77, 79, 132, 159–60, 190
   and US 32, 161
Asia
   challenge of the future 284–92
   economic crisis 41, 122, 148–52, 281–4
   engagement with 5, 8, 17–18, 20–2, 32, 41, 293, 294–5, 297–300
   and globalisation 5

historically a threat 18–19, 146
trade with 19–20, 21
see also specific countries
Asia–Pacific Economic Cooperation forum (APEC) *see* APEC
Association of South-East Asian Nations (ASEAN) *see* ASEAN
Australia–Indonesia Merdeka Fellowships 135
Australia–Japan Ministerial Forum 135
Australia–New Zealand Closer Economic Relations (CER) agreement *see* CER
Australian Aborigines *see* Indigenous Australians
Australian Labor Party (ALP) *see* ALP
Australian Secret Intelligence Service 13
Australian–Japanese Treaty on Commerce 61

Badawi, Foreign Minister 177
Baker, General John 138
banana republic 15–16
Beaumont, Admiral Alan 138
Beazley, Kim 39, 148
Beazley, Kim Sr 7
Bergsten, Fred 92, 105
Bilney, Gordon 11, 197, 199, 202, 222, 223
Bintoro, Tjokroamidjojo 101
Blewett, Neil 36
Bogor meeting of APEC leaders
Declaration of Common Resolve 114–16
lead-up 98–108
leaders' statement 91, 106, 107, 112–13
meeting 108–16, 120
Bolger, Jim 111, 216, 217

Bougainville 53, 210, 211–13
Bowan, John 77
Brass, Philip 97
Brunei 77, 112
Bush, George 3
and APEC leaders' group 30, 82, 83, 86
and US place in Asia 33
visit 24, 28–32, 81–2, 266–7
Butler, Richard 231

Cabinet role in foreign policy 11–12
Cairns Group (GATT) 36
Calvert, Ashton 12, 29, 132
Cambodia 52, 160, 161, 292
Canada 77, 95
Canberra Commission on the Elimination of Nuclear Weapons 231–4, 235, 238
Casey, R.G. 6
CER (Closer Economic Relationship) agreement 86, 216, 219
Chan, Sir Julius 209, 212, 213, 214
Chemical Weapons Convention 52, 228, 242
China 46, 160
and APEC leaders' group 83–4, 87
APEC membership 56, 76, 79, 106
and free trade in APEC 105–6, 107, 110–111
human rights issues 54–5, 57–8
investment in Australia 55–7
nuclear weapons 222–3, 234
place in international community 47–8, 50, 56, 59–60
recognition of 10, 55
and Taiwan 58–9
Tiananmen Square 55
and Tibet 58
trade with 55–7
visit to 57

INDEX

Chirac, Jacques 221, 222, 223, 224, 225
Chrétien, Jean 95, 108
Christopher, Warren 94
Chuan Leekpai 108, 182, 183
Clinton, Bill
  and APEC leaders' group 86, 88, 89, 90
  and free trade in APEC 104, 105, 106–7, 108, 109, 112
  meeting with 43–4
  nuclear testing 234–5
  Osaka meeting 120
  Seattle meeting 44, 93, 94–5
Closer Economic Relationship (CER) *see* CER
Cold War end 2–4, 71, 160
  and ANZUS 218
  defence considerations 39–40, 41
  and European security 246, 247, 248
  and nuclear weapons 226–9
  and regional cooperation 77–9
  US disengagement from Pacific 40, 161, 195–6
Colombo Plan 18
Common Agricultural Policy 36, 248–9
Commonwealth Heads of Government Meeting (CHOGM) 81, 90
Comprehensive Test Ban Treaty 221, 224, 225, 228, 234
Cook, Peter 11, 36, 175, 176
Costello, Michael 101
Council for Aboriginal Reconciliation 266
Critchley, Tom 8
Curtin, John 7–8, 9, 38

Dalai Lama 58
Dawkins, John 36

de Clerc, Willy 35
defence *see* security
Defence Signals Directorate 13
Defence Strategic Review 139
'Defending Australia' (white paper) 39, 59
Delors, Jacques 247, 249
Deng Xiaoping 49, 55, 58–9
Department of Defence 13, 232
Department of Foreign Affairs and Trade 13, 16, 36–7, 232
Dili massacre 129, 130
Do Muoi 188–90
Dougal, Naomi 268
Duffy, Michael 36

East Asia in world economy 78
East Asian Economic Group (EAEG) 87–8, 89
East Asian Miracle 5
East Timor 53, 128–31, 133, 156
Economic and Social Commission for Asia and the Pacific (ESCAP) 76
economic crisis in Asia 41, 122, 148–52, 281–4
economics and foreign policy 15–17
Eminent Persons Group (APEC) 92–3, 105
engagement with Asia 5, 8, 17–18, 20–2, 32, 41, 293, 294–5, 297–300
ESCAP (Economic and Social Commission for Asia and the Pacific) 76
European Economic Community (EEC) 79
European Union 242–3, 245, 246, 249–50
  new members 247–8, 249
Evans, Gareth 177, 193, 199
  and APEC leaders' group 83–4, 100

and ASEAN 32
and Cambodia 160–1
on disarmament 31
as foreign minister 11–12, 160, 231
and human rights 51, 52
and Indonesia 127, 130, 139, 140, 180
and Malaysia 168, 173
and nuclear testing 222, 223, 224, 229–30, 231
and security agreement 140
Export Enhancement Program 31–2

Field, Peter 37
Fiji 195, 204
First World War 6, 7
fisheries (South Pacific) 201, 202, 203
Five Power Defence Arrangements 139, 162, 174
foreign policy
under ALP 7, 8
Asia 245–6, 259
Cabinet's role 11–12
development of 6–7
and economics 15–17
Europe 242–3, 246
global dimension 241
and human rights 49–54
prime minister and foreign policy 8–14, 22–3, 81–2, 196, 197, 207
see also Evans, Gareth
Forum Fisheries Agency 196, 204
France 247, 253–6
nuclear testing 196, 200, 221, 222–6, 254, 255–6
visits to 254–6
Fraser, Malcolm 10, 216
free trade in APEC 33, 99–108, 297
Fretilin 128
Friendship Bridge 183

G7 (Group of Seven industrialised countries) 35
GATT General Agreement on Tariffs and Trade (GATT) 35, 85
Cairns Group 36
see also Uruguay Round
Germany 247, 250–3
reunification 246, 250–51
visits to 250–3
globalisation 5, 299
and APEC 77–9, 80–1, 296–7
in the future 278–9, 280–1
Goh Chok Tong 84, 90–1, 97, 100, 164
Gorbachev, Mikhail 3, 248
Gration, General Peter 138, 142, 143–4, 145
Great Britain 6–8, 256–58
and republic issue 266–7, 268, 269, 274
Greenspan, Alan 283
Greiner, Nick 268
Grey, Peter 101
Gulf War 2, 28, 30, 242
Gyngell, Allan 12, 109, 140, 142, 143–4

Habibie, B.J. 153, 156
Hanson, Pauline 260
Hartato, Minister 102
Hashimoto, Ryutaro 105, 121
Hastings, Peter 8
Hata, Tsutomu 65–6
Hawke, Bob 167, 203, 216
foreign policy 10, 39, 210
role in APEC 10, 75, 76
Hayden, Bill 39
heads of government (leaders) group
see APEC (heads of government) group
Hilly, Francis Billy 204, 205

INDEX

Hirst, Dr John 268
Holt, Harold 10
Honecker, Erich 251
Hong Kong 76–8, 87
Hosokawa, Morihiro 65
Howard, John 157, 190, 271–2, 273
Hughes, Billy 6
human rights
   China 54–5, 57–8
   and foreign policy 49–54
   Indonesia 130
Huntington, Professor Samuel 244–5, 263

immigration 260–3
India 192–4
   APEC membership 193–4
   and ASEAN 193
   nuclear weapons 229, 234–5, 291
Indigenous Australians 263–4
   native title 265–6
   reconciliation 264–5
Indigenous Land Fund 266
Indonesia
   and APEC leaders' group 82, 84, 88, 96, 97, 99, 101–3
   APEC membership 77, 102, 106
   ASEAN membership 132, 159
   and Asian economic crisis 148–52, 282, 283, 284
   confrontation with Malaysia 125, 159–60
   early relations with 8, 18, 123–7
   and East Timor 128–31, 133, 136, 156
   and free trade in APEC 104, 106, 109, 110, 113–14
   importance to Australia 146
   logging in Pacific 201
   media's view of 128, 135, 136, 145–6, 156
   Ministerial Forums 135
   perception of military threat 125, 127, 133, 142–4
   post Suharto 155–6
   relations with United States 88–9
   security agreement 138–48, 156–7
   Suharto's New Order 125–6, 133, 134, 154
   trade with 136
   visits to 131–5
Indonesian Human Rights Commission 52
information revolution 5, 277–9, 280
intelligence gathering 13–14
International Commission of Jurists 54
International Division, of the Department of the Prime Minister and Cabinet, 12

Japan
   and APEC leaders' group 82, 87
   APEC membership 63–4, 76
   defence 72
   and free trade in APEC 104, 105, 107–8
   importance to Australia 60, 61, 63–4, 68–9, 135
   internal problems 61–6
   links with 60–70
   Pacific fisheries 204
   relations with United States 29, 33, 39, 44, 46, 62, 63, 99, 119
   security considerations 38
   trade with 33–4, 63–5
   understanding of Pacific War 66–8
   visits to 64–5, 66
Japan-United States Security Treaty 46, 63
Jiang Zemin 57, 95, 108, 110–11

Joint Declaration of Principles with Nauru 199
Joint Declaration of Principles with PNG 139
Joint Declaration on the Australia–Japan Partnership 68–9
Joint Defence Facilities 31, 230

Kauona, Sam 212, 213
Kerin, John 11, 36
Kim Il Sung 71
Kim Jong Il 71
Kim Young Sam 71, 73–4
    and APEC leaders' group 87, 97, 100
    and free trade in APEC 109, 111, 113
Kiribati 195, 200
Kohl, Helmut 3, 247, 250, 253
Korea 46, 70–5
    APEC membership 76
    and Asian economic collapse 282, 284
    unification 73
    see also North Korea; South Korea
Korean Peninsula Energy Development Organisation (KEDO) 73
Korean War 18
Kristoff, Sandra 91–2

Lange, David 216
Laos 161
leaders' statement, Bogor 91, 106, 107, 112–13
Lee Kuan Yew 84, 164
Li Peng 57–9, 87
logging (South Pacific) 201–2, 204
Loosely, Stephen 212

Maastricht Treaty 247
Mabo, Eddie 265
Macmahon Ball, W. 8
Mahathir bin Mohamad 108, 165
    and APEC leaders' group 87–8, 91
    on Australia as part of Asia 20, 179
    and free trade in APEC 106, 107, 108, 111, 113–14
    'recalcitrant' 169–80
Major, John 228–9, 235, 257
Malayan Emergency 161–2
Malaysia
    APEC membership 77, 94, 105–6, 168–70
    ASEAN membership 159
    and Asian economic collapse 282
    defence relationship with 139, 161
    ethnic backgrounds 165
    and free trade in APEC 105–6, 107, 111, 113–14
    logging in Pacific 201
    relations with Australia 139, 161–2, 166–9
    relations with Indonesia 125, 159–60
    visits to 168–9, 180–1
Malaysia–Australia Society 180
Mamaloni, Solomon 196, 204, 205
Mantiri, General Herman 137–8
Marshall Islands 202
McEwan, John 15
McMahon, Billy 10
McMullan, Bob 11, 100, 101, 118, 180, 193
media
    and Australia in Asia 8, 177
    and interest in South Pacific 196
    and nuclear testing 224
    and relations with Indonesia 128, 135, 136, 145–6, 156

and relations with Malaysia 168, 172, 177–8
Menzies, Sir Robert 7, 10, 18–19, 125
Mitterand, François 221, 247, 254, 255
Miyazawa, Kiichi 64–6, 82, 87
Moerdiono, State Secretary 142, 143
Muldoon, Sir Robert 216
multiculturalism 261–3
Murayama, Tomiichi 65–6, 67, 105, 119, 121
Mururoa tests 196, 200, 222

NAFTA (North America Free Trade Agreement) 77, 93, 99
Namaliu, Rabbie 209, 210–11
Native Title legislation 265–6
NATO (North Atlantic Treaty Organisation) 248
Nauru 197–9, 202
New World Order 2
New Zealand
    and ANZUS 139, 218
    APEC membership 77, 219
    CER agreement 86, 216, 219
    Closer Defence Relations 218–19
    and free trade in APEC 111
    logging policy 204
    relations with Australia 218–20
    trade with 86, 216–17, 219
    visits to 216
Niue 195
Non-Aligned Movement 77
North America Free Trade Agreement (NAFTA) 77, 93, 99
North Atlantic Treaty Organisation (NATO) 248
North Korea 46, 71, 291
    nuclear weapons 72–3, 234
    relations with South Korea 71
Northern Ireland 52

Nuclear Non-Proliferation Treaty (NPT) 72, 228
nuclear weapons
    Canberra Commission 231–4, 235, 238
    China 222–3, 234
    Comprehensive Test Ban Treaty 221, 224, 225, 228, 234
    French tests 196, 200, 221, 222–6, 254, 255–6
    India 229, 234–5, 291
    media 224
    'New Agenda' coalition 238
    North Korea 72–3, 234
    Pakistan 229, 234, 291
    public concern 223–4, 226–7
    Russia 233, 234, 235–7
    Tokyo Forum 238
Nurrungar 43, 230

OECD (Organisation for Economic Cooperation and Development) 35, 71
Office of National Assessments (ONA) 13
Ona, Francis 211
One Nation 260, 263, 279, 295
O'Neill, Professor Robert 231
Organisation for Economic Cooperation and Development (OECD) 35, 71
Osaka meeting of APEC leaders 117–22

Pacific Business Forum 97, 106
Pakistan 229, 234, 291
Palau 195
Papua New Guinea 195
    aid to 207, 211–12, 214
    APEC membership 93
    Bougainville rebellion 53, 210, 211–13

defence cooperation assistance 207
economic problems 213–14
internal problems 210
logging 201, 202, 204, 214
relations with Asia 209
relations with Australia 139, 205–7, 215–16
role in Second World War 207–9
visits to 207–9, 215–16
Parsons, Alf 8
peace-keeping force Somalia 242
Perkins, Ed 107, 145
Phan Van Khai 189
Philippines 160, 191–2
  APEC membership 77
  ASEAN membership 159
  and Asian economic collapse 282
  United States bases 40, 161
Pine Gap 43, 230
Portugal 128, 129
prime minister
  role in foreign policy 8–14, 22–3, 81–2, 196, 197, 207
  supporting bodies 12–13

Qian Qichen 87

Ramos, Fidel V. 108, 191–2
Ray, Robert 11, 40, 41, 141, 142, 173, 175, 176, 199, 219
Reagan, Ronald 3
regional cooperation
  and Cold War 77–9
  regional organisations 79–80, 289
republic
  advantages 267
  constitutional issues 267–8, 269–70
  head of state 270–1, 274
  model 268–72, 273
  reserve powers 270, 271

Ritchie, David 101
Rocard, Michel 253
Roche, Imelda 97
Roosevelt, Franklin Delano 25, 27
Royal Commission into Aboriginal Deaths in Custody 266
Russell, Don 45, 92
Russia 46, 160, 248
  nuclear weapons 233, 234, 235–7

Sabah 160
Santer, Jacques 249
Scowcroft, General Brent 29, 82
Scullin, James 9
SEATO (South-East Asia Treaty Organisation) 38
Seattle meeting of APEC leaders 37, 44, 93, 94–7, 102
Second World War 7–8, 66–8, 207–9
security
  in Asia, not from Asia 41, 43
  defence spending 41–2
  intelligence cooperation 43
  non-paper with Indonesia 142–3
  self-reliance 39
  relations with US 38–45
  white paper 1994 40, 41
Siagian, Sabam 137
Siew, Vincent 103–4
Singapore 160
  'A New Partnership' 164–5
  and APEC leaders' group 84
  APEC membership 77
  ASEAN membership 159
  defence relationship with 139, 161, 164
  view of Australia 163–4
Singapore-Australia Business Alliance Forum 164
Single European Act 247

INDEX

Solomon Islands 195, 196, 201–2, 204–205
Somalia peace-keeping force 242
South Africa 52
South Korea
  and APEC leaders' group 87
  APEC membership 75
  and free trade in APEC 109, 111, 113
  OECD membership 71
  relations with North 71
  trade with 73–5
  US military support 72, 75
  visit to 73–5
South Pacific Commission 196
South Pacific Forum 196–7, 199–200, 222, 223
South Pacific
  active engagement policy 197
  aid to 196, 200, 202, 203
  economic problems 200–1
  and end of Cold War 195–6
  environmental problems 200
  fisheries 201, 202, 203
  logging 201–2, 204
  nuclear testing in 116, 200, 221, 222–5, 254, 255–6
  resentment of Australian help 204–5
  taking responsibility 203
  see also specific countries
South-East Asia Treaty Organisation (SEATO) 38
Statute of Westminster 6, 7
Stephen, Sir Ninian 52–3
Stolen Generation 266
Suharto, President 91, 125, 156
  and APEC leaders' group 82, 84, 88, 96, 97, 99, 101–3
  on ASEAN 132
  and free trade in APEC 104, 106, 107, 108–9, 110, 113–14
  relations with 132–5
  and security agreement 146–8
  stepping down 132, 150–1, 153–5
Sukarno, President 124, 125, 132, 159–60
Supachai, Dr 103, 104, 182
Taiwan 46–7, 291
  and APEC leaders' group 83–4, 87
  APEC membership 58, 77
  and China 58–9
  fishing rights 201
  and free trade in APEC 103–4
Taylor, Allan 142, 144
Thailand 160
  APEC membership 77
  ASEAN membership 159
  and Asian economic crisis 149, 281, 282, 283, 284
  and Cambodia 182–3
  and free trade in APEC 103, 104, 112
  Friendship Bridge 183
  internal politics 182
  visit to 183–4
Thawley, Michael 140
Tiananmen Square 55
Tibet 58
Tokyo Forum 238
trade 15–16
  with Asia 19–20, 21
  with China 55–7
  with EU 242
  'GATT-plus arrangement' 85–6
  with Indonesia 136
  with Japan 33–4, 63–5
  with New Zealand 86, 216–17, 219
  problem of size 34
  problem of structure 35
  subsidisation 35–6
  with South Korea 73–5

with US 31–2
with Vietnam 186
trade liberalisation in APEC 33, 99–108, 297
Turnbull, Malcolm 268
Tuvalu 195, 200

United States
  APEC membership 32, 33, 77
  and ASEAN 32, 161
  Bush and APEC leaders' group 30, 82, 83, 86
  Bush visit 24, 28–32, 81–2, 266–7
  Clinton and APEC leaders' group 44, 86, 88, 90, 91, 93, 94–5, 120
  and free trade in APEC 104–8, 109, 112
  importance to Australia 7–8, 25, 26–8, 30
  Joint Defence Facilities 31, 230
  nuclear weapons 233, 234, 236, 237, 238
  Philippine bases 40, 161
  relations with China 106, 108, 160
  relations with Indonesia 88–9
  relations with Japan 29, 33, 39, 44, 46, 62, 63, 99, 119
  relations with South Korea 72, 75
  role in Pacific 26–8, 30–3, 40, 44, 161, 195–6, 293–4
  security relationship 38–9
Uruguay Round 4–5, 32, 35, 36–8, 80, 85, 98, 241, 248

Vanuatu 195, 201, 204
Vietnam 160, 161
  ASEAN membership 79, 190
  Do Muoi's visit 188–90
  Russian aid 186
  trade with 186
  visit to 187–9
  war 159, 185, 186, 187
Vo Van Kiet 186

Wallis, W. Allen 35
Warner, Denis 8
Western Samoa 202
White Australia Policy 6, 7, 18–19, 127, 260–1
Whitlam, Gough 10, 55, 76, 186
Widodo, Mr 132
Wingti, Paias 209, 212, 214
Winterton, Professor George 268
Woolcott, Richard 8, 77
World Trade Organisation 37–8
Wran, Neville 92

Yeltsin, Boris 3

Zhu Rongji 47, 87